STRENGTHENING SPIRIT
—RELEASING POTENTIAL

"Linking cutting edge organizational thinking with Ignatian spiritual direction, which assumes the implicated order of a divine creation, she shows how leaders can open institutional paths which release untapped potential to transform their organizations in making real differences in the world, particularly when gripped by crises."

—JOHN BAZALGETTE, founding member of The Grubb Institute

"It is rare indeed to find a book in which in-depth scholarship, skilfully integrated across multiple disciplines, is charged with the sparks of stardust that illuminate whole new horizons. Dr. Miles has achieved this in remarkable measure. Her book is an essential companion, inspirer, and empowerer of all who engage in roles of authentic and holistic leadership in humanity's quest to become the best we can possibly be in whatever field we serve."

—MARGARET SILF, author and retreat facilitator, Scotland

"Skillfully and masterfully interweaves the dynamics of spiritual direction with spiritual leadership. It emphasizes in various creative ways how important a leader's inner life and prayerful presence is for the spiritual well-being of an organization and its members."

—MAUREEN CONROY, RSM, author of *Looking into the Well: Supervision of Spiritual Directors*

"In this book, Dr. Bernadette Miles shows how, through Ignatian spiritual direction, organizations can find deeper meaning and purpose by way of attending to their members' inner lives. Using knowledge from psychology, organizational dynamics, ethics, spirituality, and her own research, she points to how organizations might develop their creative potentials and fulfill meaningful roles beyond their transactional habits."

—SUSAN LONG, Director of Research and Scholarship, National Institute of Organisational Dynamics Australia

"The approach draws not only on the expertise of a seasoned spiritual director in the Ignatian tradition, and on a background of business administration, but is presented, refreshingly enough, from the perspective of a committed lay woman who has combined raising a family with co-establishing a dynamic spirituality center in Melbourne."

—GEOFFREY WILLIAMS, SJ, Sessional Professor of Ignatian Spirituality, Regis College, University of Toronto

Strengthening Spirit —Releasing Potential

SPIRITUAL DIRECTION FOR LEADERSHIP AND
ORGANIZATIONAL DEVELOPMENT

Bernadette Miles

Foreword by Wilkie Au

☙PICKWICK *Publications* • Eugene, Oregon

STRENGTHENING SPIRIT—RELEASING POTENTIAL
Spiritual Direction for Leadership and Organizational Development

Copyright © 2021 Bernadette Miles. All rights reserved. Except for brief quotations in critical publications or reviews, no part of this book may be reproduced in any manner without prior written permission from the publisher. Write: Permissions, Wipf and Stock Publishers, 199 W. 8th Ave., Suite 3, Eugene, OR 97401.

Pickwick Publications
An Imprint of Wipf and Stock Publishers
199 W. 8th Ave., Suite 3
Eugene, OR 97401

www.wipfandstock.com

PAPERBACK ISBN: 978-1-7252-7074-9
HARDCOVER ISBN: 978-1-7252-7075-6
EBOOK ISBN: 978-1-7252-7076-3

Cataloguing-in-Publication data:

Names: Miles, Bernadette, author. | Au, Wilkie, foreword.

Title: Strengthening spirit—releasing potential : spiritual direction for leadership and organizational development / by Bernadette Miles; foreword by Wilkie Au.

Description: Eugene, OR: Pickwick Publications, 2021 | Includes bibliographical references and index.

Identifiers: ISBN 978-1-7252-7074-9 (paperback) | ISBN 978-1-7252-7075-6 (hardcover) | ISBN 978-1-7252-7076-3 (ebook)

Subjects: LCSH: Spiritual direction. | Christian leadership. | Organizational change.

Classification: BV652.1 M4 2021 (print) | BV652.1 (ebook)

JANUARY 7, 2021

Reproduced from Transforming Experience in Organisations, 1st Edition by Susan, Long, published by Routledge. © *Susan Long 2016* reproduced by arrangement with Taylor & Francis Books UK.

John Bazalgette and Rebekah O'Rourke (https://www.rebekahorourke.com/) in *Transforming Experience in Organisations*, 1st Edition by Susan Long, published by Routledge used with permission.

Reproduced with permission from Barrett Values Centre— https://www.valuescentre.com/

Poetry by Marlene Marburg used with permission— https://www.marlene.marburg.com.au

Axial Age Graphic by Mike Anderson used with permission

Anthroprocene Graphic by Ray Troll Art https://www.trollart.com/— used with permission

Contents

List of Tables x
List of Figures xi
Foreword by Wilkie Au xiii
Preface xvii
Acknowledgments xix

Introduction 1
    The *Kardia* of Leadership 4
    Religion: One Aspect of Spirituality 6
    Moving from the Individual to the Corporate 7
    The Journey of this Book 9

Chapter 1: Spiritual Direction in the Ignatian Tradition 15
    The Practice of Spiritual Direction 15
        Who or What is God? 17
    Ignatian Spirituality and the Spiritual Exercises 20
        The Spiritual Exercises 21
        Annotations for Spiritual Direction 24
    The Art of Discernment 28
    Ignatian Spiritual Direction 32
        Spiritual Consciousness 34
        Interior Freedom 35

Chapter 2: Spirituality, Leadership and Organizational Development 39
    Why Integrate Spirituality, Leadership and Organizational Development? 39
    A Brief Overview of Leadership Theory 43
        Adaptive Leadership Practice 46
    Organizational Development Theory and Ignatian Spirituality 49
    The Life, Death Resurrection Cycle 53
        Power Expending—Diagnosing the Doubt in a Team 58
    The Transforming Experience Framework and Spiritual Direction 60

CONTENTS

Chapter 3: Spiritual Direction, Spiritual Formation and Consciousness 64
    Spiritual Direction and Leadership Consciousness 67
    Stages of Spiritual Formation and Leadership Consciousness 70
        Week One Dynamic of Spiritual Formation
           and Levels of Consciousness 72
        Week Two Dynamic of Spiritual Formation
           and Levels of Consciousness 74
        Week Three Dynamic of Spiritual Direction
           and Levels of Consciousness 76
        Week Four Dynamic of Spiritual Direction and Levels
           Consciousness 77
    Stages of Spiritual Formation and Organizational Consciousness 78

Chapter 4: Spiritual Direction and Leadership 85
    Spiritual Formation, Spiritual Direction and Leadership 86
        Spiritual Direction as a Reflective Process for Leaders 88
        Leadership Identity and Relationship with God 88
        Ternary Leadership and Relationship with God 92
    Healed by Love, Self-esteem, Differentiating 94
        Disruption and Vulnerability 94
        Indifference in Ignatian Spirituality 96
        Disordered Tendencies and Vulnerability 98
    Called to Service 99
        Relationship with Jesus, with Self and with God 100
        Vulnerability, Personal Power and Creativity 103
        Becoming Christ 105
        Who is God?—Connectedness with Source 109
    Discernment and Spiritual Direction 114
        Noticing the Inner Critic and a Change in Perspective 115
        Driven or Drawn and a Culture of Excessive Busyness 118
        Following Your Call 119
    Committed, Confirmation in Suffering, Anointed 120
        Vulnerability as a Basis for Leadership—Strengthened by/and in the
           Face of Suffering 121
    Living the Call to Leadership 123
        Being on the Spiritual Journey and Making Meaning 123
        Has Spiritual Direction Supported Your Leadership Development? 124

Chapter 5: Spiritual Direction and Organizational Development 127
    Stage One Personal Mastery: Survival, Relationship, Self-esteem 128
        From Corporate Shame to Shared Identity 128
        Relationship Consciousness 131
        Group Spiritual Direction for Leadership Teams 133
    Stage One: Towards Transformation via Vulnerability 135

Contents

Stage Two: Internal Cohesion: Transformation, Adaptability, Continuous Learning 137
    Spiritual Formation as Different to Teaching Skills 137
Organizational Development and Communal Discernment 139
    Internal Cohesion and Interconnectedness 142
Stage Three: External Cohesion, Making a Difference 144
    Life-Death-Resurrection Cycle 145
    Maintaining Consciousness of Original Purpose and Primary Spirit 149
Stage Four: Working in the Spirit—Lasting Change 151

Chapter 6: The Role of the Spiritual Director in Leadership and Organizational Development 155

Role of the Spiritual Director in the Domain of Person 157
    A Compassionate Gaze as a Disposition in the Role of Spiritual Director 163
Role of the Spiritual Director and the Domain of System 166
    Centrality of God/Source in the Spiritual Direction System 170
Role of the Spiritual Director and the Domain of Context 171
    Spiritual Direction in the Workplace 172
Role of the Spiritual Director and the Domain Source 175

Chapter 7: Spiritual Direction for the Twenty-First Century 178

Spiritual Direction and the Experience of Personhood for Leadership and Organizational Development 179
    Interconnectedness as an Enabling Dynamic for Leadership and Organizational Development 180
    Changing context for Spiritual Direction 181
Challenges and Opportunities of a Changing Context for Spiritual Direction and Leadership and Organizational Development 182
    Spiritual Direction—a Feminine Ministry in a Patriarchal Container 183
Difficulties of Clericalism 185
Moving from a Culture of Dependency to Professionalization 187
Impact of Formal Spiritual Direction Training Programs 187
The Future 188

Conclusion 189
Bibliography 191
Index 199

List of Tables

Table 1: The dynamic and content of the Spiritual Exercises
Table 2: Epistemology specific to the Ignatian spirituality methodology for action research/organizational development.
Table 3: Stages of spiritual formation and leadership consciousness.
Table 4: Healthy/unhealthy motivations levels one–three of consciousness.
Table 5 Seven levels of organizational consciousness.
Table 6 Positive focus and negative focus aspects of levels one to three of SLOC.
Table 7: Dynamic of Week Two of the Spiritual Exercises and levels four and five SLOC.
Table 8: Sally's transition through the process of spiritual direction.
Table 9: Word frequency for interviewees and their relationship with God, Jesus and love.
Table 10: Positive focus and negative focus aspects of levels one to three of SLOC.
Table 11: Dynamic of Week Two of the Spiritual Exercises and levels four and five SLOC.
Table 12: Comparison male/female membership spiritual direction community.

List of Figures

Figure 1: Graced aspects of the Weeks of the Exercises
Figure 2: Identifying movements of the Spirit
Figure 3: Consolation and desolation
Figure 4: Dynamic and flow of the Week Two meditations
Figure 5: The timeline of the advent of philosophy/religion across the great cultures
Figure 6: The geologic history of Earth–Artwork © Ray Troll, 2020 (used with permission)
Figure 7: Life-death-resurrection cycle
Figure 8: Power expending elements of the LDR
Figure 9: Addressing doubt in the team
Figure 10: Transforming experience into authentic action through role
Figure 11: Seven levels of consciousness and the seven stages of psychological development
Figure 12: Process of spiritual formation and seven levels of consciousness
Figure 13: Barrett's seven levels of consciousness and the dynamic of spiritual formation in the Spiritual Exercises
Figure 14: Life, death and resurrection cycle and the Seven Levels of Consciousness
Figure 15: Characteristics of binary and ternary leadership styles
Figure 16: Sally role drawing
Figure 17: Life, death and resurrection cycle and the Seven Levels of Consciousness
Figure 18: Transforming experience into authentic action through role
Figure 19: "The Compassionate Gaze of Christ" Illustration by Lynda
Figure 20: Spiritual direction system
Figure 21: The spiritual direction system for the director
Figure 22: Spiritual direction system incorporating leadership and organizational development
Figure 23: Pot bound

Foreword

Today, the call for renewed leadership comes from both the young and the old. Speaking on behalf of the young at the UN Climate Action Summit in 2019, Greta Thunberg, a seventeen-year-old Swedish activist, gave an impassioned cry for enlightened leadership in response to the dire threat of global warming. Sounding an urgent plea for action, she challenged world leaders to go beyond business as usual and mere technical solutions and to respond with bold new leadership inspired by passionate conviction. Thunberg's words went viral and reverberated throughout the world.

Similarly, Pope Francis called for transformative leadership in his 2019 Christmas address to the Roman Curia, the administrative unit of the Holy See that assists the Pope in governing the Catholic Church. His challenge resembled Thunberg's rebuke of world leaders for their complacent leadership in dealing with the climate crisis. The Pope reminded the church leaders that they must grow and govern in a way that reflects ongoing interior transformation. Citing the words of Cardinal John Henry Newman,[1] Francis reminded them that growth requires ongoing change: "Here below to live is to change, and to be perfect is to have changed often." The Pope insisted that Newman was not talking about "changing for change's sake, or following every new fashion, but rather about the conviction that development and growth are a normal part of human life." Francis emphasized that "for Newman *change was conversion*, in other words, interior transformation," not merely external change, like "simply putting on new clothes, but remaining exactly as we were before." For the sake of personal transformation, Francis strongly encouraged church leaders to let themselves to

---

1. Newman, *Essay on the Development of Christian Doctrine*, 20; in Francis, *Christmas Greetings to the Roman Curia*, para 5.

"be challenged by the questions of the day and to approach them with the virtues of discernment."

In this compelling work, Dr. Bernadette Miles argues convincingly that leadership comes from within and that spiritual direction can play an important role in organizational development and systemic change. Clearly, this message resonates with Pope Francis's exhortation to the Roman Curia: the kind of effective leadership needed to revive moribund structures and practices must emanate from a place of interior transformation and discernment. In this, Pope Francis revealed his identity as a Jesuit and as a son of Ignatius of Loyola, who in the sixteenth century devised the Spiritual Exercises as a means of forming leaders who were guided by a discerning heart. Miles' use of the Spiritual Exercises of St. Ignatius as a means of forming transformative leaders is fitting and historically consistent with Ignatius' own strategy for bringing about the renewal he deemed critically needed in society and in the church.

Spiritual direction in the Ignatian tradition focuses on the active presence of God in the world today and the importance of discerning how one is being uniquely called to join with God in covenant partnership. The operative questions for discernment are: "What is God about in the world?" and "How can I best contribute to God's project in the world today?" Transformational leadership, as suggested by Miles, is linked to a partnership with God. Contextualizing this central Ignatian vision of leadership for the present age, Miles rightly asserts that the ongoing relevance of Ignatian discernment in spiritual direction into the twenty-first century requires a paradigm shift from a focus on an individual's personal salvation to a care for all creation and a new consciousness of the interconnectedness of all creation.

Miles offers an innovative way to integrate spirituality with the workplace and to foster creative organizational leadership. Going beyond training centered on managerial skills and role performance, the model of transformative leadership presented here requires that leaders undergo deep, personal transformation in order to be effective change agents. This kind of leadership that "comes from within" can have a positive impact on organizations. Because only transformed people can transform others, effective agents of system change must be committed to an ongoing process of consciousness-raising that elevates their intrapersonal, interpersonal, and societal awareness. They must integrate an awareness of the "shadow" (the unconscious) in both individual and group life. In this work, Miles

Foreword

makes a forceful case for why the training of such transformative leaders requires a holistic formation that integrates the head, heart, and soul of the person. It cannot be purely academic but must involve an ongoing reflection on one's experience. This experiential mode of learning, commonly referred to as *praxis,* is a key component of Ignatian andragogy. Miles calls this process *kardia,* the name she has given to the spiritual formation center in Melbourne, Australia that she cofounded.

This book is a fine work of creative synthesis—weaving together key notions from such diverse fields as leadership and organizational theory, depth psychology, psychoanalytic and socio-analytic theory, spiritual formation and Ignatian spiritual direction—to make a cogent and coherent case for how spiritual direction in the Ignatian tradition can make a unique contribution to the formation of leaders of organizations.

>Wilkie Au, PhD.
>Professor Emeritus
>Dept. of Theological Studies
>Loyola Marymount University
>Los Angeles, CA, USA

Preface

THE RATIONALE FOR THIS book arose from my twenty years working as a spiritual director and formator of spiritual directors in the field of Ignatian spirituality. I have a background in business management and a Master's degree in Applied Science (organizational dynamics) from which the two disciplines of spirituality and organizational development blended naturally, culminating in PhD research on this topic. In my ministry as a spiritual director, I began to notice that spiritual direction had a direct impact on the way people engage in leadership and that there are subsequent benefits to their workplace. When Malcolm who is a leader in secondary education, commented that his engagement with spiritual direction "not only changed my life through the work we have done in Ignatian spiritual direction, but you have changed the life of my school community … the values and principles of Ignatian spirituality permeate all that I do, and through this, has impacted the work and culture of my organization", I wanted to discover how.

Spiritual direction is based on the premise that we are totally interconnected through the Ground of our Being, the Source of all Life, the Mystery within, and further that we can co-create our world with this Mystery and discern our pathway forward. Therefore, before I begin, I need to be clear in my understanding of God, which underpins the ministry of spiritual direction and the context of this book.

I believe this Mystery (which I call God) permeates the whole of creation whether or not we name it, notice what might be seen as evidence of it, or believe in a religious interpretation of what or who Mystery is. Further, I believe that I can have a relationship with Mystery, and this impacts all that exists, all I do, and all I am. I align with Teilhard de Chardin's proposition:

Preface

God is dynamically interior to creation, gradually bringing all things to their full being by a single creative act spanning all time.[2] Every element is an overflow of God, who makes things to make themselves.[3] God acts from within, at the core of each element, by animating the sphere of being from within.[4]

Therefore, I am not asking *whether* spirituality and relationship with Mystery have relevance in the workplace, rather I work from the premise that Mystery *is already present* in all things, regardless of whether we are conscious of this presence.

This book is an exploration of what happens when a relationship with Mystery is taken consciously into our working lives through spiritual direction—and how that influences leadership potential, style and capacity and organizational development.

---

2. Teilhard de Chardin, *Christianity and Evolution*, 26 in Delio, *Emergent Christ*, 37.
3. Edwards, *How God Acts*, 47 in Delio, *Emergent Christ*, 37.
4. Delio, *Emergent Christ*, 37.

Acknowledgments

For my husband, Bushy and his constant reminders to get back to work on my writing. For his generous support and encouragement over the many years of study that have contributed to this work, I am deeply grateful. To my four sons, their partners and my seven grandchildren, thank you for your patience and understanding especially with the reduced time I have been able to spend with you all.

The each of the participants in the research who agreed to be interviewed and share their sacred and deeply personal experiences, thank you. This work would not have been possible without your generosity of spirit.

I am grateful to the academic supervisors who accompanied me throughout the research including Professor Susan Long, Dr. Marlene Marburg, Rev. Dr. Alan Niven, and Rev. Dr. Michael Smith SJ.

Words will not be able to fully acknowledge the contribution of Dr. Marlene Marburg. Marlene is my colleague, friend, mentor, supervisor, and has been an unfailing support to me at every stage of the research.

I acknowledge with gratitude the generosity of The Barrett Values Centre (www.valuescentre.com), Michael Anderson (https://www.mike-anderson.biz/), Ray Troll (https://www.trollart.com/), Marlene Marburg Marburg, (http://www.marlenemarburg.com.au/), Anthony Siow, John Bazalgette and Rebekah O'Rourke (https://www.rebekahorourke.com/) for permission to include their work in my manuscript.

I would also like to acknowledge the contribution of the Commonwealth Government to this research through a Research Scholarship funded by the Research Training Program, and the University of Divinity and Stirling Theological College for providing the facilities and resources to undertake this research.

To each of you and all of you, my heartfelt thanks.

Introduction

My interest in the topic of this book was sparked at the 2010 Conference of Spiritual Directors International (SDI) held in San Francisco, where spiritual directors were charged with responsibility for listening within the world as it moves through a process of irreversible transformation. I resonated with the keynote speaker and cosmologist, Brian Swimme, who claimed the era of industrial religion is passing, and that a new consciousness grounded in love is emerging. I was challenged to recognize that though religious institutional structures have served the world well in the past by developing and enabling education, healthcare and social justice systems that are accessible to all, these institutions are now too small for the challenges the world faces today. It seems that the work of religious institutions of the past is coming to completion, as they no longer have the resources to tackle the global issues that are emerging in the twenty-first century. Who could have predicted that ten years later in 2020 we would see the whole world shut down with the pandemic COVID 19, which has forced global shut down and social isolation?

I was left with two questions: What might organizational systems need in order to support transformation into new consciousness? What role might the ministry of spiritual direction have as new discoveries begin to emerge? The deeper question of how spiritual direction might impact organizational systems settled into my thinking and raised my curiosity.

Structural change is not "just about replacing one mindset that no longer serves us with another. It's a future that requires us to tap into a deeper level of our humanity, of who we really are and who we want to be as a society."[1]

---

1. Scharmer and Kaufer, *Leading from the Emerging Future*, 1.

Strengthening Spirit–Releasing Potential

> We have entered an Age of Disruption. Yet the possibility of profound personal, societal, and global renewal has never been more real. Now is our time.
>
> Our moment of disruption deals with death and rebirth. What's dying is an old civilization and a mindset of the maximum "me"— maximum material consumption, bigger is better, and special-interest-driven-decision-making that has led us into this state of organized irresponsibility, collectively creating results that nobody wants.[2]

Transformational change requires new ways of listening, recognizing that the "success of our actions as change-makers does not depend on *what we do* or *how* we do it, but on the inner place from which we operate."[3] My experience of spiritual direction supports the theory that leadership comes from within and that spiritual direction can play an important role in systemic change.

I first experienced spiritual direction in the year 2000 when I began making the *Spiritual Exercises*[4] in daily life. I clearly recall leaving my initial spiritual direction session and being astonished by the depth of attentiveness my spiritual director gave me in exploring my experience, in particular how she invited me to speak about my personal faith. I hadn't heard of spiritual direction or the *Spiritual Exercises* before beginning this journey, and I had no idea what to expect. When my spiritual director introduced herself by phone a week earlier, she suggested that before we met, I might consider what I wanted from God. I had no idea how to answer that question. My understanding of God was probably best described as Sunday Catholic with an insurance policy for life after death. Yet, I had a profound longing to explore what lay within my deeper self, my spiritual self. Spiritual direction seemed like it might become an entry point for a clearer focus on this work.

Spiritual direction is an ancient tradition that seeks to facilitate the exploration of a deeper relationship with all aspects of personhood and uncover *what makes your heart sing*. In the Ignatian tradition and woven

---

2. Scharmer and Kaufer, *Leading from the Emerging Future*, 1.

3. Scharmer and Kaufer, *Leading from the Emerging Future*, 19.

4. In this work I use the Literal Translation of the *Spiritual Exercises* of Saint Ignatius, otherwise known as the Autograph, by Puhl, *Spiritual Exercises of St Ignatius*. The annotations are the first twenty numerated paragraphs in the text of *The Spiritual Exercises*. Paragraphs 21 to 370 are classified as notations. In this work, a number in square brackets designates the annotations and notations, for example [19].

Introduction

through the framework of the *Spiritual Exercises*, there is an invitation to grow in one's relationship with God through four seasons of prayer, which Ignatius calls Weeks. In the company of a spiritual director the Exercises offer a compilation of meditations, prayers and contemplative practices through which one learns to live a discerning life. The role of the spiritual director is to accompany another (the directee) as they explore their experience of God and begin to uncover their interior world.

Though I did not have any of this language to articulate what I was looking for when I began the *Spiritual Exercises*, these definitions fitted well with my search for meaning at the time. Before spiritual direction and engaging in the Exercises I had no idea that I could have a personal relationship with God. My faith was a childhood faith based on creeds, doctrine and obedience. When I took the time to consciously connect with God through contemplative prayer, I discovered that the Mystery within was waiting to connect with me. In the words of Thomas Merton:

> One opens the inner doors of one's heart to the infinite silences of the Spirit, out of whose abysses love wells up without fail and gives itself to all.[5]

The environment provided by my spiritual director enabled me to speak about things I didn't know were in me, such as my deep desires, my life journey, relationships, fears, hopes, my understanding of God and my deep faith story. Nothing seemed unwelcome in the session and my spiritual director had a way of noticing and affirming the things that were important to me. Marlene Marburg describes the spiritual direction process that expresses and embodies this intentional companioning:

> At a broader level, the directee speaks from a culture and is formed through her own speaking. Speaking helps her to integrate intellectual and affective dimensions of her spirituality. The process and product of speaking in spiritual direction helps the speaker to reflect on the self and to own those reflections through speaking them and to use the tool of communication to create a new platform of awareness before moving forward to find opportunities to enhance relationship with God and to integrate learning's in relation to the sharing focus in spiritual direction.[6]

---

5. Merton, *Love and Living*, 21.
6. Marburg, *Spiritual Direction*, 2.

The process of spiritual direction, the skills of the director and the discipline of making the Exercises provided the architecture of prayer that enabled me to reframe my life story and discover the potential within. As a consequence, I began to take more active leadership in all areas of my life, as a mother, wife, friend, business manager and database consultant, and now as a leader in the field of spiritual direction. When a person enters the spiritual direction process and opens herself or himself to the Mystery within, the invitation to strengthen the spiritual self can release potential and free them in new ways for leadership, whether or not they hold a formally appointed leadership position.

The Kardia of Leadership

If you dare
to put your heart in there
it will catch fire
and when hearts are aflame
there is an exposition
no more daring
just sparks of the dream
showering stardust
awakening[7]

Leadership does not necessarily or automatically rest with those appointed to hierarchical positions; rather it exists everywhere in organizations, communities, families and in all aspects of life. Leadership motivates and inspires people to tackle tough challenges and thrive, creating a vision for the future and inspiring others to follow that vision. Leadership may be distributed and therefore displayed not only by those in senior positions or management roles, but also by people across an organization, often in previously unrecognized ways. Ronald Heifetz et al., suggest,

> What is needed from a leadership perspective are new forms of improvisational expertise, a kind of process expertise that knows prudently how to experiment with never-been-tried-before relationships, means of communication, and ways of interacting that will help people develop solutions and surpass the wisdom of today's experts.[8]

7. Marburg, *Grace Undone: Passion*, 85.
8. Heifetz et al., *Practice of Adaptive Leadership*, 3.

Introduction

There are many ways to describe leadership and as many styles of leadership as there are leaders, and though the role and expression of leadership might change, the core process is the same. Kevin Cashman identifies three fundamental aspects of effective leadership:

- *Authenticity:* Well developed self-awareness that openly faces strengths, vulnerabilities and developmental changes.
- *Influence:* Meaningful communication that connects with people by reminding self and others of what is genuinely important.
- *Value Creation:* Passion and aspiration to serve multiple constituencies—self, team, organization, world, family, community—to sustain performance and contribution over the long term.[9]

Blending these concepts enables a working definition of leadership as *authentic influence that creates value* and is *leadership from the inside out*. Mastery of leadership is not solely about achieving things, rather it is concerned with one thing, "consciously making a difference by fully applying more of our potential. As leaders, the more we can unleash our whole capabilities—mind, body, spirit—the more value we can create within and outside of our organizations."[10] This is consistent with Otto Scharmer and Katrina Kaufer's understanding of the importance of strengthening our *inner place* as a fundamental aspect of leadership. In the Christian setting, this could be understood as strengthening the *kardia* of leadership. *Kardia* is the *soul* of a person or the center of all physical and spiritual life in a person. Choosing to lead from the *kardia, as* Ruth Haley Barton explains,

> is a vulnerable approach to leadership, because the soil is more tender than the mind or the ego. This is the place where we don't have all the answers—or at least not necessarily when everybody wants them! It is a place where we are not in control; God is. It is a place where the quickest way is not always the best way, because the transformation that is happening in us is more important than getting where we think we need to go.[11]

A key aspect of Ignatian spirituality and the *Spiritual Exercises* is the fundamental belief that God is present in our world and active in our lives,

---

9. Cashman, *Leadership From the Inside Out,* 24.
10. Bill George, former Chairman and CEO of Medtronic in Cashman, *Leadership From the Inside Out,* 25.
11. Barton, *Strengthening the Soul of Your Leadership,* 210.

and that through prayer and discernment we can work with God to co-create our future. Leadership is exercised in partnership with God, and is dependent on our willingness to become more spiritually and ethically aware as to how we participate in both constructive and destructive behaviors.

Religion: One Aspect of Spirituality

Using the word "God" immediately places this book within a theological setting and will bring with it many different layers of meaning to each reader. Spirituality is *a priori* to religion and is concerned with the ongoing evolution of all creation. Spirituality has an unlimited breadth of charisms such as Mercy, Ignatian, New Age, Monastic, Creational, spiritual but not religious, and others not named here. Though I believe that it is possible to adapt this book to any secular or religious setting, I will speak from a Christian perspective and use that language. My hope is that readers of this book will note this perspective and in turn use their own language with freedom and creativity as spiritual teacher Adyashanti suggests,

> The number one mission of any religious teaching is to open us up to the direct experience of mystery and awe. As soon as we forget that, we then get into sustaining institutions, thinking that dogma is more important than religious awe, and many other agendas start to take over institutionally. [12]

Richard Rohr puts this simply: "God is always bigger than the boxes we build for God, so we should not waste too much time protecting the boxes."[13] Spiritual direction seeks to support others in exploring their experience of mystery and awe and therefore it is essential that the spiritual director does not impose their own theological frameworks or religious belief system. Working at the level of spirituality "includes the intellectual, emotional and relational depth of human character, as well as the continuing capability and yearning for personal development and evolution."[14] Rachel Naomi Remen explains,

> the spiritual is not the religious. A religion is a dogma, a set of beliefs about the spiritual and a set of practices which arise out of those beliefs. There are many religions and they tend to be

---

12. Adyashanti, "Return to the Heart of Christ Consciousness."
13. Rohr, *Everything Belongs*, 25.
14. Benefiel, *Soul at Work*, 9.

mutually exclusive. That is, every religion tends to think that it has "dibs" on the spiritual -- that it's "The Way". Yet the spiritual is inclusive. It is the deepest sense of belonging and participation. We all participate in the spiritual at all times, whether we know it or not.[15]

An underpinning belief of Ignatian spirituality is that the Creator will deal "directly with the creature, and the creature directly with his Creator and Lord."[15] This means that within this tradition the spiritual director's primary purpose is to facilitate the relationship between the directee and Mystery, not to teach doctrine or dogma.

This exploration of how spiritual direction can support leadership and organizational development, assumes that those coming to spiritual direction will have some sense of Presence, Mystery, God or Source of life, and be active in working with humanity in shaping our world. The use of the word Presence, Mystery, God or Source in this book is intended to be inclusive of, and respectful towards other language used.

Moving from the Individual to the Corporate

Ignatian spirituality is an apostolic spirituality that evolved from the experience of the co-founder of the Society of Jesus, St Ignatius of Loyola (1491–1556). Ignatius lived by the knowledge that God is at work in the world and that each of us can personally experience God. He further believed that we are able to discern and make choices that lead us towards God and godliness and to create a better world.

When Swimme charged spiritual directors at the SDI Conference with the responsibility of being the ears of the universe to listen for the revelation of God, this resonated with me deeply as an Ignatian spiritual director. I wanted to respond to Swimme's challenge to reframe the task of spiritual direction:

> The task of spiritual direction is to deconstruct the maladaptive story that humans are living out of. The central task of spiritual direction is to create a culture that amplifies life's hum . . . to learn that Earth is not a collection of resources but a community of life that the human is invited to join.[16]

---

15. Remen, "On Defining Spirit," para. 5.
16. Swimme in Ellmann, "Seeking God Everywhere and Always," 20.

Strengthening Spirit–Releasing Potential

Spiritual direction is a way of listening to the community of life to help the world listen for a way of being that is creative and not destructive. For St Irenaeus *The glory of God is a human person fully alive.* The spiritual director listens to help the directee find a pathway forward that brings life, both for the directee and for the world. The Jewish mystical tradition recognizes "each human being as a creative spark awaiting more kindling on his or her soul journey."[17] I am interested in how this creative spark can be nurtured and unleashed within individuals and within the heart of organizational life.

Alistair and Joshua Bain describe this creative spark as the *primary spirit* of an organization. They define primary spirit as that which breathes life into an organization, the animating principle. Primary spirit is "absolutely fundamental to organizational existence" and "is the underlying meaning for people connecting around a particular primary task."[18] Margaret Benefiel suggests that "[o]rganizations, like individuals, have souls that transcend and support their practical activity."[19]

When the primary spirit or soul of an organization is aligned with the primary spirit or soul of individuals who work and lead within the organization at all levels, this creates potential space for the creative spark of God to be released, and in turn generates abundance and new life. In a time when scarcity seems to be the dominant narrative in our religious institutions,[20] a focus on abundance is essential. Judith Cannato argues that "[b]esides recognizing that there are institutions or other collective forces that have strayed off course, losing their bearings, it is also necessary to recognize that we live in a time of unprecedented resourcefulness and creativity."[21] In this time of rapidly accelerating change, according to Alfred Darmanin, we are creating "organizations never imagined before. And changing organizations require changed leadership. This in turn requires creative leaders, capable of inventing new and original ways of seeing reality, creating new energy and life into the organization."[22]

---

17. Zevit, "Exploring the God-Field," 356.
18. Bain and Bain, *Note on Primary Spirit*, 100.
19. Benefiel, *Soul at Work*, 26.
20. Miles, "Ignatian Spirituality, Apostolic Creativity and Leadership," 35–41.
21. Cannato, *Field of Compassion*, 4.
22. Darmanin, "Ignatian Spirituality and Leadership," 13.

Introduction

The world needs transformational leadership that can inspire positive energy that enables and sustains change. Stephen Denning describes transformational leaders as having the capacity to

> change the world by generating enduring enthusiasm for a common cause. They present innovative solutions to solve significant problems. They catalyze shifts in people's values and ideologies. They demonstrate willingness to sacrifice personal interests when necessary. . . . They don't just generate followers: their followers themselves become leaders.[23]

In this book, I identify the ways in which creative transformational leaders can be supported through the practice of spiritual direction and describe the effect this has on both the leader and the institution.

The Journey of this Book

Chapter 1: Spiritual Direction in the Ignatian Tradition

Spiritual direction in the Ignatian tradition provides abundant resources and tools to support leadership and organizational development. I introduce foundational aspects of Ignatian spirituality, the Spiritual Exercises and the Discernment of Spirits, and the question: Who or what is God? I then make a brief comparison between spiritual direction and psychoanalysis, identifying the centrality of a person's relationship with God in spiritual direction as the primary difference between the two disciplines. Spiritual direction raises spiritual consciousness and develops interior freedom.

Chapter 2: Spirituality, Leadership and Organizational Development

Why integrate spirituality, leadership and organizational development? This chapter offers a critical overview of current literature in the fields of spirituality, leadership and organizational development. I begin by considering a brief history of spirituality in the workplace, then give an overview of leadership theory, explore the concept of transformational and adaptive leadership and highlight the importance of listening skills in leadership

---

23. Denning, *Secret Language of Leadership*, 22.

practice. I introduce systems theory, unconscious and unconsciousness in groups and organizational systems, and explore the relationship between Ignatian spirituality and organizational development. Drawing on the *Transforming Experience Framework*[24] *(TEF)* and Richard Barrett's *Seven Levels of Consciousness,*[25] the concept of developing leadership and organizational consciousness through the practice of spiritual direction is introduced.

CHAPTER 3: SPIRITUAL DIRECTION, SPIRITUAL FORMATION AND LEADERSHIP CONSCIOUSNESS

Chapter 3 offers a brief overview of theories about consciousness and the unconscious. I introduce concepts of spiritual consciousness and organizational and leadership consciousness as developed by Richard Barrett. Spiritual formation is a process for developing a person's consciousness and by aligning the stages of spiritual fomation as presented in the Ignatian Spiritual Exercises, I offer a framework for identifying the stages of spiritual consciousness in leadership and organizational development.

CHAPTER 4: SPIRITUAL DIRECTION AND LEADERSHIP DEVELOPMENT

This chapter explores how spiritual direction influences the development of leadership potential for individuals who participated in this study. I situate their experience within the framework of levels one to three of Barrett's seven levels of leadership consciousness (SLLC) and dynamic of spiritual formation in the Week One of the Spiritual Exercises being stage one of spiritual formation.

Spiritual direction facilitates a process of spiritual formation, which in the Christian setting is impacted significantly by a person's relationship with God. In the early dynamic of spiritual formation, spiritual direction focuses on building a positive self-image in the light of the directee's relationship with God: when a person's self-image shifts, so too does their image of God. The spiritual director helps the directee to notice patterns

---

24. Long, *Transforming Experience in Organisations.*

25. Material from The Barrett Values Centre (www.valuescentre.com) on The Seven Levels of Consciousness have been included with permission.

that limit their freedom and encourages them towards knowing oneself as loved and lovable, even though they may not be perfect. A disposition of indifference is encouraged. Indifference in the Exercises is not regarded as an attitude of apathy or lack of concern, but a disposition of freedom from attachment to what influences decision-making. In the Week Two dynamic of spiritual direction a person's sense of call is illuminated, developing a clearer understanding of leadership capacity and style in parallel with development levels four and five of leadership consciousness.

The Week Three dynamic of spiritual direction deepens commitment to the call to leadership through confirmation in suffering, aligning with a deepening commitment to making a difference in the community. This aligns with level six of leadership consciousness where vulnerability becomes a basis for leadership where leaders are strengthened by/and in the face of suffering. In the Week Four dynamic of spiritual formation, spiritual direction supports leaders in living their call to leadership and service to humanity and planet Earth. Leadership is performed with compassion and humility with a focus on future generations, aligning with level seven—leadership consciousness.

Chapter 5: Spiritual Direction and Organizational Development

Chapter 5 considers spiritual direction from the perspective of system, context and organizational development. Spiritual direction enhances organizational development by raising organizational consciousness, exploring the data through the phases of spiritual formation and the seven levels of organizational consciousness. In the early stages of organizational consciousness, spiritual direction supports organizational development by developing relationship and self-esteem consciousness.

In the later stages of organizational consciousness, spiritual direction can support a group to move towards transformation, adaptability and continuous learning. Key elements of the spiritual direction process include communal discernment which supports the development of internal cohesion and awareness of interconnectedness. In the dynamics of stage three, organizational consciousness of making a difference and serving humanity and the planet, spiritual direction supports the group in coming to know the depth of its primary spirit and patterns of life, death and resurrection of the group.

Strengthening Spirit–Releasing Potential

Chapter 6: The Role of the Spiritual Director

This chapter looks at spirituality, leadership and organizational development from the perspective of the role of spiritual director. This role is influenced significantly by the director's experiences of personhood. The director's capacity to hold the directee with compassion and love, without judgement, and to listen in-depth to the directee's experiences of life, death and resurrection, are central to the role of the spiritual director. Spiritual formation that supports and enables the director's role includes a deep exploration of the director's own experiences, their knowledge of discernment of spirits, a well-developed trust in God, and the capacity to keep out of the way when the directee is working directly with God. Confidentiality and clear boundaries around the spiritual direction dynamics are essential in creating an effective working environment.

Changing contexts for the ministry of spiritual direction in the twenty-first century are revealing new challenges, pathways and opportunities. The experience of interconnectedness with God/Source and between the directee and director permeates every aspect of the role of spiritual direction. Shared connection at the level of the experience of God/Source takes the spiritual direction session to a place of compassion, respect, graciousness and a wisdom that leads both the director and the directee towards freedom.

Chapter 7: Spiritual Direction for the Twenty-First Century

This chapter summarizes the benefits of how spiritual direction can support leadership and organizational development. I identify challenges that emerge from the changing context of spiritual direction and leadership and organizational development including:

- spiritual direction being a feminine ministry located in a patriarchal container;
- the difficulties of patriarchy and clericalism;
- moving from a culture of dependency to professionalization;
- the impact of formal spiritual direction training programs.

Introduction

I explore and identify opportunities for developing the ministry of spiritual direction to be a resource for leadership and organizational development and industry-specific formation programs for spiritual direction.

Chapter 1

Spiritual Direction in the Ignatian Tradition

Giving the Spiritual Exercises

Let there be nothing
between pen and point;
nothing between you and God.
Let the poetry of prayer open
your heart right down the sternum.

Let God have God's way with you.
Let God be the you God wants to be.

If I am to have one love, one desire
it is to feel all there is,
and to witness your sense of yourself
as a firework fountain bursting
the night sky.[1] (Marlene Marburg)

The Practice of Spiritual Direction

SINCE THE BEGINNING OF human history, women and men have sought the accompaniment of others to explore their relationship with the Source of life. Approaches to the ministry of spiritual direction share a common factor—the art of tending the sacred within. Norvene Vest states,

---

1. Marburg, *Grace Undone: Passion*, 117.

Strengthening Spirit–Releasing Potential

> God is indeed Mystery, and every form of religion is an effort to respond faithfully to the mystery of the sacred by whatever name. The sacred breaks through into human experience in many ways, and humans respond variously to the awesome experience of the holy.[2]

Mystery is that which the "created" world knows partially and seeks to know more. St. Paul writes in the first letter to the Corinthians: "For now we see in a mirror, dimly, but then we will see face to face. Now I know only in part; then I will know fully, even as I have been fully known." (1 Cor 13:12 NRSV)

In the Christian tradition, the role of the spiritual director (the director) is to accompany another (the directee) as they deepen their relationship with God, learn about themselves and explore God's infinite interest in us. Thomas Merton identifies that the purpose of spiritual direction:

> is to penetrate beneath the surface of a [person's] life, to get behind the façade of conventional gestures and attitudes which [s/he] presents to the world, and to bring out [his/her] inner spiritual freedom, [his/her] inmost truth, which is what we call the likeness of Christ in [the] soul.[3]

I would take Merton's description one step further. Spiritual direction supports Christians not just to take on the *likeness* of Christ, but also to respond to the call to take on the *role* of Christ, becoming Christ in the world today. In the Ignatian tradition, while the directee discovers their own gifts and limitations in the light of their relationship with God during the spiritual direction session, they are also encouraged to go one step further and ask the question; how does this relationship with God manifest in the world? Or, as Marburg asks in her poem *Giving the Spiritual Exercises*, how can we "let God be the you God wants to be"?[4] In opening oneself to a participative relationship with God, a person becomes God's self-communication. Marburg explains,

> Ignatian spiritual direction offers contemplative and generative listening and questioning wherein the spiritual director and the spiritual directee are attentive and responsive to their interior experience of Mystery in their midst. Ignatian spiritual direction contemplatively and actively seeks to help a person grow in

---

2. Vest, *Tending the Holy*, vii.
3. Thomas Merton in Vest, *Tending the Holy*, 126.
4. Marburg, *Grace Undone: Passion*, 117.

relationship with God as Mystery in all things, at the same time as nurturing a deepening personal sense of identity, vocation and mission.[5]

This book is premised on the existence of God so before I introduce the foundations of Ignatian spirituality and the art of listening through the practice of spiritual direction, I need to underpin this book by identifying, as far as is possible, who or what I understand God to be.

Who or What is God?

To engage fully in spiritual direction a person must have some sense that there is a Presence within creation that breathes life into our existence, and that we can relate to this Presence as One which draws us towards freedom, hope, love and truth. Some religions call this God, but for many people, using the word God to describe Presence carries with it a history and meaning no longer tenable by some or useful for others.

Defining God is problematic because to define anything or anyone is to set limits upon or mark out its boundaries. For the same reason we often have to be satisfied with a 'working definition' of spirituality within, and tailored to, a specific context or phenomenon. Armstrong writes that God is a reality that must go beyond all we can think and know; therefore, it is not possible to simply define God. God transcends definition. Jewish Rabbi Maimonides (1135–1334 CE) argues, "You cannot even say that God exists because our notion of existence is so limited that it cannot possibly apply to God."[6] For the priests of India in the tenth century BCE, "Ultimate Reality" was known as the Brahman: "'The All'; the whole of reality; the essence of existence; the foundation of everything that exists; being itself. The power that holds the cosmos together and enables it to grow and develop."[7]

The Brahmin priests developed a form of religious discourse called the Brahmodya, which is a ritual competition in which the contestants each sought "to find a verbal formula that expressed the mysterious ineffable reality of the Brahman. The contest always ended in silence when contestants

---

5. Marburg, "Landscapes of Contemporary Spiritual Direction in Australia," 28.
6. Armstrong, *Case for God*, 534.
7. Armstrong, *Case for God*, 370.

were reduced to wordless awe. In the silence they felt the presence of the Brahman."[8]

I know the experience of meeting a mysterious ineffable reality, which I call God, both in my work as a spiritual director witnessing it in others, and in my own life experience. It is an experience that is always difficult to articulate. Wilfred Bion, in his psychoanalytic work "uses the deliberately empty sign "O" to point towards this unspeakable reality that he says can be "intersected with" but not grasped."[9] Bion says,

> "O" does not fall in the domain of knowledge or learning . . . it is darkness and formlessness but it enters in the domain of K[nowing][10] when it has evolved to a point where it can be known through knowledge gained by experience, and formulated in terms derived from sensuous experience.[11]

In spiritual direction the unspeakable reality Bion refers to as "O" is brought into consciousness and explored by helping the directee to speak in sensuous though imprecise terms about their experience of God. This exploration attempts to understand and create some knowledge about God and self for the sake of the directee.

In Jewish tradition the name given is YHVH and is understood to be deliberately unspeakable. As soon as poetic words such as Source, Origin, Savior, Gaia, King, Yahweh, Father, or God are used, an interpretation, a meaning and image have been added to the experience that is mysteriously present. John Caputo states,

> Whatever it is you say God is, God is more. The very constitution of the idea is deconstructive of any such construction . . . the very formula that describes God is that there is no formula with which God can be described.[12]

In this book I use the words God, Presence, Mystery and Source interchangeably with the expectation that the reader will have his or her own language and understanding of what or who this Mystery is. Rather than

---

8. Armstrong, *Case for God*, 370.
9. Mawson, "Introduction," 33.
10. Bion proposes a schema of affective links, L, H & K or Love, Hate and Knowing in emotional relationships. "K" stands for knowing and the ability to think about, and hence tolerate better, the frustrations of coming to know. Bion, *Learning from Experience* and Fisher, "Emotional Experience of K," 43.
11. Bion, *Attention and Interpretation*, 26.
12. Caputo, *On Religion*, 115 in Armstrong, *Case for God*, 316.

impose their own understanding of God upon a directee, the spiritual director enables the directee to clarify for themselves the image of the God which most naturally emerges from their relationship, and work with the directee in allowing God to support them in strengthening their spiritual self. The spiritual self permeates all dimensions of the self being "that unseen part of who we are that provides our physical self with insight, intuition, and other ways of knowing and being beyond what our five senses experience in the physical world."[13]

Working with a person's experience of God and image of God is essential to the spiritual direction process. If the directee has an image of a controlling God, one to be feared or one that will judge every action taken, then the directee will not trust that God desires to enable each of us to fulfil our potential, but might believe that God wants to destroy what is not perfect. Katherine Dyckman et al. explain,

> Humans develop and order experience through images. Granted that no image of God is adequate, it is important to discover how one relates to God. Naming God implies a corresponding self-image. If God is a tyrant, I am oppressed; if God is a beneficent, I am gifted.[14]

Images of God are not necessarily static and will change over time as our image of self and understanding of our world changes. In the past, my image was of God the Father with a long white beard sitting on a throne, watching my every move, counting my errors, delighting in my successes, and ready to judge me on the last day. I learned about this God in primary school and carried this image into my 40s without realizing it, until one day I participated in a lecture on the cosmos. The facilitator opened up the vastness of creation and the wonder of the universe and challenged us to consider a God who set all of creation in motion and continues to co-create with us. An old man with a beard sitting on a throne with a magic wand bringing life into being over seven days, no longer made sense. My old image of God was shattered. My consciousness was raised to a new awareness and God, once a judge looking on from the edges, became a God inviting me to collaborate in the ongoing evolution of life. I was challenged to become responsible for my own beliefs and capacity to work with God.

---

13. Kirk, "Caracolores."
14. Dyckman et al., *Spiritual Exercises Reclaimed*, 105.

I have not been able to define God in containing or limiting ways since that day; God is present in all that exists, God is deeply within me and I in God. Perhaps this was my first call into the second Axial Age consciousness (as described later in this book) of religion and God. As my image of God is released from a static set of beliefs encased in doctrine and dogma, I am also released to become more fully myself. I resonate with John Fowles definition in his novel *The French Lieutenant's Woman*: "There is only one good definition of God: the freedom that allows other freedoms to exist."[15]

Ignatian Spirituality and the Spiritual Exercises

Ignatian Spirituality is taking
your graces,
your inspirations,
your holy desires
to serve God,
and transforming them into action
in everyday life.[16]

All human beings are gifted with a human spirit, which both enables and compels them to search for identity, meaning and a sense of belonging in their world. Spirituality involves a conscious attempt to engage in practices that allow the exploration, reflection and integration of one's deepest values, sense of meaning and purpose into daily life. Christian spirituality involves making a choice for growth by embracing a personal relationship with Jesus Christ and by being centered on the Gospels and forming community as the Body of Christ, following his example of what it means to be fully human.

Ignatian Spirituality evolved from the experience of St Ignatius of Loyola (1491–1556) as he reflected upon and recorded the way in which he interacted with life's struggles and joys. Ignatian Spirituality is deeply rooted in the Christian tradition as an apostolic spirituality described as "a spirituality of choice at the level of faith."[17] That means my relationship with God will impact my decision-making and will ultimately free me to become apostolically effective in the world. To be apostolically effective is

---

15. Fowles, *French Lieutenant's Woman*, 86.
16. Attributed to George Schemel—source unknown.
17. Borbely et al., *Focussing Group Energies*, 3:1.

to live a life of self-giving love in service of others, following the example of Jesus Christ. A fundamental characteristic of Ignatian spirituality is the experience of "finding God in all things" [33] and at the heart of Ignatian spirituality are the Spiritual Exercises.

The Spiritual Exercises

> *I move progressively to wholeness*
> *into the mystery of God's creative love*
> *inviting me into a love response*
> *to a "friendly separation"*
> *from all that might cause me*
> *to lose my freedom [23]. (Mary Ward)*[18]

The tools and dynamic process inherent in the Exercises pervade every part of the ministry of a spiritual director in the Ignatian tradition. The *Spiritual Exercises* text is a compilation of meditations, prayers, and contemplative practices developed by Ignatius to enable others to deepen their relationship with God and become apostolically active in the world.

Ignatius states that the Spiritual Exercises have "as their purpose the overcoming of self and the ordering of one's life on the basis of a decision made in freedom from any disordered attachment." [31] Ignatius believes that we need to exercise our spirit if we want to be healthy spiritually and become familiar with attachments that might prevent us from being open to God's invitation to love and freedom.

The full Spiritual Exercises can be made in an enclosed retreat over approximately 30 days [20] or a retreat in daily life over 30–36 weeks [19]. The retreat is separated into four phases or Weeks of the spiritual journey. Each of these Weeks is not literally one week in length; Week is the name given to describe each phase or season of the spiritual journey within the Exercises. Schemel and Roemer identify the dynamic of the Four Weeks of the Spiritual Exercises as: Purification—Illumination—Confirmation in Suffering—Confirmation in Joy.[19]

---

18. The Principle and Foundation as adapted by Mary Ward founder of the Institute of the Blessed Virgin Sisters (Loreto Sisters), 1585. Ignatius invites the exercitant to pray with the Principle and Foundation at the beginning of the Exercises to challenge them to consider his or her purpose in life.

19. Roemer and Schemel, *Beyond Individuation to Discipleship*, 30–33.

Marburg re-contextualizes the dynamic of the Exercises in a framework of love that identifies two distinct movements within the Exercises:

> Weeks One and Two are about being loved and called, the character of God's initiative towards a person; Weeks Three and Four are about the character of human response to God's initiative, that is, being committed and loving. The overall dynamic therefore can be expressed as: Loved—Called—Committed—Loving.[20]

The dynamic movement of spiritual formation within the Exercises progressively raises a person's consciousness through the felt experience of God's loving, working, creative, presence within us and around us and in all creation. Table 1 below illustrates the dynamic and content of the Exercises as they unfold during the retreat.

	Week One	Week Two	Week Three	Week Four
Dynamic	Loved Purification	Called Illumination	Committed Confirmation in Suffering	Loving Confirmation in Joy
Content	We come to know ourselves as loved sinners who, within the gaze of God who loves us unconditionally, recognize and understand our own part in the destruction of life; and that there is nothing we can do to attain this love or alternatively to stop God from loving us. The invitation to transformation is to know that God's love is freely given waiting for all to receive it.	Focuses on a personal relationship with Jesus and how this impacts our own apostolic and creative potential, by clarifying our identity and vocation before God. The invitation to transformation is to come to know ourselves as called and gifted.	Looks more closely at our capacity to stay focused and faithful to the call even in the light of suffering. Can we stay faithful to the invitation of God to service even if the cost is high?	Offers an invitation to incarnate our consolation. To bring into fruitful being the graces, gifts and desires that flow from our relationship with God.

Table 1—*The dynamic and content of the Spiritual Exercises*

20. Marburg, "Poetry and Grace," 17.

Alhough the Exercises are prayed in a linear process, each of the Weeks can have the character of all or some of the movements that occur in an ongoing spiral process. Marburg articulates the orientation of the exercitant (the term given to the one making the Exercises) towards God as they move through the experience of making the Exercises from four aspects (Figure 1):

- the experience of person through each of the four Weeks
  Anticipation—Risk—Vulnerability—Surprise

- the character of God's initiative towards that person
  Loved—Called—Dedicated—Loving

- the person's experience of encountering God
  Known—Desired—Valued—Commissioned

- the person's response to God's initiative
  Wonder—Presence—Self-abandonment—*Ministry*[21]

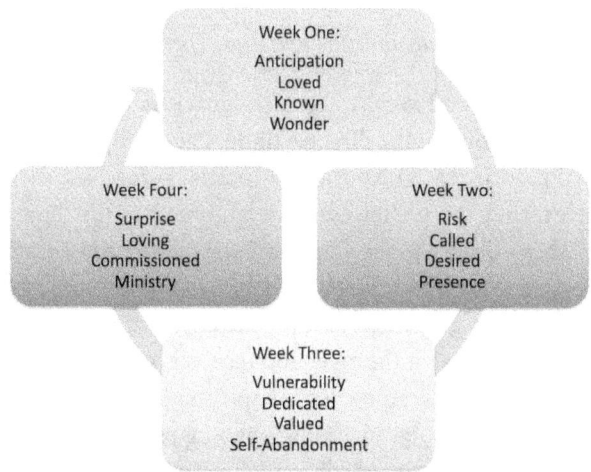

Figure 1: Graced aspects of the Weeks of the Exercises [22]

Dynamic movements found within the full Spiritual Exercises offer a continuing process of growth for any person engaged on the spiritual journey.

21. Marburg, "Poetry and Grace," 15–19.
22. Marburg, "Poetry and Grace," 19.

A person who lives an Ignatian spiritual life would over time and through ongoing formation revisit and deepen each of these graces time and again. Grace can be defined as God's self-communication to the world.[23] Marburg explains:

> Grace is not some independent endowment external to life but is deeply integrated with life. The Exercises are a framework to help a person grow in the graced awareness of any impediments to full human flourishing. This includes all dimensions of personhood: physical, sexual, psychological, spiritual, social, intellectual, affective and moral, in no particular order or hierarchy.[24]

Ignatius names the purpose of the Exercises as being "the conquest of self and the regulation of one's life in such a way that no decision is made under the influence of any inordinate [or disordered] attachments." [1] A person formed in Ignatian spirituality becomes conscious of what keeps them attached to aspects of the self that prevent them from choosing freedom for themselves and for others. These attachments might be to things such as success, money, fear, or relationships.

Annotations for Spiritual Direction

At the beginning of the Exercises Ignatius provides twenty annotations to help both the director and the directee understand the goals of the Exercises and to maintain an open disposition towards themselves, each other and God whilst making the Exercises. Puhl summarizes this approach: "The purpose of these observations [annotations] is to provide some understanding of the spiritual exercises which follow and to serve as a help both for the one who is to give them and for the exercitant."[25] Though Ignatius wrote these annotations for the giver and receiver of the Spiritual Exercises, they also form the basic framework for spiritual direction in the Ignatian tradition in its many settings including ongoing regular spiritual direction, retreat direction and occasional spiritual direction.

Drawing on the annotations, in the following I articulate the disposition for the director and the directee in the dynamic relationship of spiritual direction.

23. Rahner, *Foundations of Christian Faith*.
24. Marburg, "Poetry and Grace," 345.
25. Puhl, *Spiritual Exercises of St Ignatius*, 1.

Spiritual Direction in the Ignatian Tradition

i. In spiritual direction we seek to become aware of disordered affections and attachments so that we might work with God to make decisions that free us to become apostolically effective in the world. "Affections can be in harmony or disharmony with one's personal integrity. Disordered affections conflict with one's deepest humanity, unfolding spirituality and growth in spiritual freedom."[26] Spiritual direction seeks to support the directee in uncovering and releasing disordered affections [1].

ii. The spiritual director will be brief, to the point, and allow the directee to share freely from their experiences without imposing their own opinions and interpretations on the directee's experience. "For it is not much knowledge that fills and satisfies the soul, but the intimate understanding and relish of the truth." Interior knowledge is to be valued to a greater extent than intellectual knowledge [2].

iii. God will reveal Godself more clearly in symbols and affective knowledge rather than in concise conceptual knowing. The task of the spiritual director is to pay attention and express respectful reverence when the directee is touched by affective knowledge [3]. [27]

iv. The Spiritual Exercises separate the spiritual journey into four seasons of the soul called Weeks. Identifying which season the directee is experiencing in the spiritual direction session will help the director to work with, be present to, the directee and not move a directee beyond his or her own experience. This allows the directee to take the time they need to fully experience the graces being given at each stage of the spiritual journey, rather than pushing them along a prescribed path. When making the Spiritual Exercises it is expected that the exercitant will move through these stages progressively; this is an ongoing, dynamic cyclic process that continues throughout the spiritual journey and in ongoing spiritual direction as follows:

> *Week One*: A first week person may not yet know that they are loved and lovable.
>
> *Week Two*: The second week person will be discerning their identity and sense of call as to how they will live their lives and serve God.

---

26. Dyckman et al., *Spiritual Exercises Reclaimed*, 57.
27. Smith, "Annotations," 3.

Week Three: In the season of the third week, a person will deepen their understanding of their identity, vocation and mission in the light of suffering and the cost of the call.

Week Four: The fourth week person will be fully alive, living their call and both experiencing and demonstrating a generative stance in life. [4, 11, 18].

v. Both the director and directee need to have a magnanimous disposition and a trust that God will deal directly with the directee. It is important for the directee to be enabled to deal directly with God. The director's role is to remain balanced and help the directee to discern and respond to God's unique and personal invitation to them [5, 15].

vi. The directee will move between consolation[28] and desolation and be affected by spiritual experiences on a regular basis. If no movements are apparent, it will be helpful to enquire about what is happening in the directee's life and prayer. In this time the director will seek to be more active in the way they work with the directee. [6, 7].

vii. When a directee is in desolation, a gentle approach is essential. The director, by encouraging and supporting the directee, will help the directee to uncover what might be holding them in desolation [7].

viii. When directees bring experiences to the spiritual direction session that might be helped by the Rules for Discernment, give these Rules as appropriate. It is more helpful to give each Rule as they match the directee's experience; this way the learning will be embedded into their own experience. The Rules for Discernment are not appropriate for a person at the beginning of their spiritual journey. These Rules require self-knowledge and some experience in discerning the way the Spirit moves a person towards freedom [8 & 9].

ix. A person who is advanced in the spiritual journey is more likely to be tempted by what appears to be a "good" thing rather than drawn towards what might be considered a "bad" thing such as laziness or dishonesty. The temptation of doing too much good may lead a person away from freedom, for example, over-commitment to work, prayer,

---

28. Ignatius names as consolation a movement towards God which is evidenced by an increase in hope, love, peace and an increase in faith and joy [316]. "Desolation is those movements that lead to darkness of soul, turmoil of spirit, inclination to what is low and earthly, restlessness rising from many disturbances and temptations which lead to want of faith, want of hope, want of love, and a movement away from God" [317].

SPIRITUAL DIRECTION IN THE IGNATIAN TRADITION

or taking on roles that are beyond their skills or time availability. The director needs to be aware of any tendencies the directee might have towards over-commitment, especially when they are going ahead with great fervor [10 & 14].

x. When there is no spiritual movement in the directee, check whether they are giving adequate time to prayer, or too much time to prayer. Help them to find a balance that is realistic and helpful to their lifestyle and other commitments [13].

xi. Help the directee to actively work against desolation and move towards consolation in their decision-making. In the time of consolation, one remembers and stores up a supply of strength against the day of desolation; remind the directee of times when they have experienced consolation and help them to draw strength from this when in desolation [13].

xii. The director may not influence the decision-making of the directee, rather they must remain at balance, providing a space where the directee can explore and discern the best pathway forward for them individually. If there were a choice between pride, riches and honor, or poverty, insults and humility, it would be better to move them towards poverty, insults and humility to find the pathway forward that leads to freedom [16].

xiii. Confidentiality is essential to the spiritual direction relationship. This must be made clear at the beginning of the relationship. The director should not share spiritual direction conversation outside of the relationship. The director should not pry into personal matters of the directee unless it is specifically at the service of the directee and his/her relationship with God [17].

The annotations are followed by the Presupposition that the director's disposition is to put a good interpretation on what their directees present at the spiritual direction session, to see goodness in the directee and trust that God also sees this. If the directee brings material into the session that seems fallacious, the director should help the directee explore this, rather than correct or impose their interpretation on the issues brought into the session [33]. An Ignatian spiritual director will be well versed in the art of discernment.

The Art of Discernment

The art of discernment is essential to the ministry of spiritual direction. The word "discern" comes from the Latin verb *discernere* that means to sift through or to sort out. Maureen Conroy suggests that "developing a discerning heart is both an art and a skill"; a place where the artist mode allows us to "pay attention to the mystery and beauty of God's personal love for us" and the skillful stance enables the sifting and sorting of experiences to help us become aware of our unredeemed self, that is the part of the self that might retreat from God and the invitation of love.[29] Discernment can be used as a tool to make concrete individual important decisions or can be understood as a way of living in love with God where one's whole life is directed towards God. William Barry notes that discernment has at its purpose achieving "union with God in action."[30]

Franz Meures identifies three dimensions of attentiveness for spiritual discernment:[31]

i. Attentiveness to God and God's revelation: "That is we listen to the Gospel, we pray, we contemplate the Cross. All those symbols, texts, rituals that bring us into contact with what God is for us and what He [sic] said to us."[32]

ii. Attentiveness to our own interior movements: "What is going on inside me? What are my thoughts, my feelings, my plans, my aspirations, my daydreams, my night dreams? So, all that I can find in the inner space of my soul [sic]"[33]

iii. Attentiveness to the external reality: What is going in the world, what are the facts and limitations of reality?

Ignatius provides Rules for Discernment to support the director and the directee in understanding how spiritual movements operate. These rules are not laws to be obeyed; rather they are guidelines that help us identify how diverse "spirits" operate. Ignatius describes the Rules for Discernment as:

---

29. Conroy, *The Discerning Heart*, xi.
30. Barry, *Letting God Come Close*, 125.
31. Meures, "Affective Dimension of Discerning and Deciding," 60–77.
32. Meures, "Affective Dimension of Discerning and Deciding," 74.
33. Meures, "Affective Dimension of Discerning and Deciding," 74.

Rules for understanding to some extent the different movements produced in the soul and for recognizing those that are good to admit them and those that are bad, to reject them [313].

The spiritual director helps the directee to sift and sort through interior motions, affections, and desires. Ignatius uses the term "affections" to indicate "the direction of one's heart in a way that feelings, as subjective responses to stimuli, cannot."[34] Affections can emanate from past experiences, can be felt in the present and in turn stimulate further affections. Affections can be aligned with one's values and personal integrity or conflict with one's integrity and therefore be disordered.

Following a person's deepest desire is central to the practice of spiritual direction. Ignatius understood that the will of God could be found in our deepest and most authentic desires. "God speaks directly into our desires, communicating to us as a schoolmaster teaches."[35] Desire is "an inclination towards some object accompanied by a positive affect. The quality of the desire is determined by the object whereas its intensity comes from its affect."[36] Desires generate physical energy and passion and animate our spirituality. Fears on the other hand are the negative pole of desire. Desires can also be conflicting, for example: I might want to lose weight, which aligns with my value of good health, but I love to eat pasta. My desire for pasta then conflicts with my desire for good health. Like affections, desires need to be brought into consciousness and discerned. At the deepest level of knowing (beneath ego) there is no conflict. Harnessing the energy of our desires and becoming aware of the direction towards which a particular desire is moving us is part of the work of spiritual direction and central to Ignatian spirituality and discernment.

Ignatius recognizes we will experience movements of the spirit in different ways, depending on the direction we are headed in different aspects of our lives. He suggests that we are either moving from bad to worse, away from God and away from freedom, or from good to better, towards God and towards freedom. So, we first need to recognize the direction that our life is moving; from good to better, or bad to worse? It should be underlined here that a person might be moving towards hope, love and freedom in one aspect of their life, and simultaneously into enslavement and despair

---

34. Dyckman et al., *Spiritual Exercises Reclaimed*, 57.
35. Da Camara, *Pilgrim's Testament*, 40.
36. Kinerk, "Eliciting Great Desires," 3.

in another. For example, I might devote my life to the service of the poor whilst at the same time be afflicted with a gambling addiction. Where I am caught in destructive patterns of behavior, "bad spirit" might encourage me: "Today will be your lucky day, you just need one more win." And "good spirit" will niggle me: "You really don't want to go to the casino." In aspects of my life where I am moving from good to better, then I can expect bad spirit to cause disturbance and disquiet, and "good spirit" to encourage and console (Figure 2).

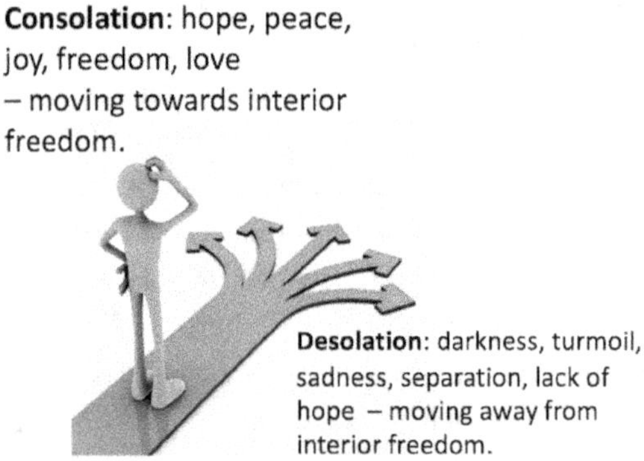

Consolation: hope, peace, joy, freedom, love
– moving towards interior freedom.

Desolation: darkness, turmoil, sadness, separation, lack of hope – moving away from interior freedom.

Figure 2: Identifying movements of the Spirit

Once I have recognized the direction towards which my life is moving, I then need to understand and notice movements of spiritual consolation and desolation. Spiritual consolation is an interior movement identified by an increase in faith, hope, love, joy and peace, and a movement towards interior freedom. Spiritual desolation is a movement away from freedom and characterized by an increase in turmoil of spirit, disturbances, sadness, darkness, lack of faith and a lack of hope (Figure 3).

Spiritual Direction in the Ignatian Tradition

Moving bad to worse
away from God
into enslavement and despair

Moving from good to better
towards God
and hope, love, freedom, joy

| Bad spirit will console and encourage continuation of particular **pattern** of behavior | Good Spirit will disturb and challenge –'are you sure you really want to do this?' | Going from bad to worse (e.g.. addictive patterns of behaviour) | Going from good to better (e.g., moving towards freedom and service of others) | Good Spirit Will console and encourage | Bad Spirit Irritate, disturb, cause disquiet, 'who do you think you are?' |

In the words of Ignatius:

In the case of those who go from one mortal sin to another, the enemy is ordinarily accustomed to propose apparent pleasures. He fills their imagination with sensual delights and gratifications, the more readily to keep them in their vices and increase the number of their sins.

With such persons the good spirit uses a method which is the reverse of the above. Making use of the light of reason, he will rouse the sting of conscience and fill them with remorse. [314]

In the case of those who go on earnestly striving to cleanse their souls from sin and who seek to rise in the service of God our Lord to greater perfection, the method pursued is the opposite of that mentioned in the first rule.

Then it is characteristic of the evil spirit to harass with anxiety, to afflict with sadness, to raise obstacles backed by fallacious reasonings that disturb the soul. Thus he seeks to prevent the soul from advancing.

It is characteristic of the good spirit, however, to give courage and strength, consolations, tears, inspirations, and peace. This He does by making all easy, by removing all obstacles so that the soul goes forward in doing good.[315]

Figure 3: Consolation and desolation

Discernment in the dynamic of Week Two of the Exercises is not concerned with choosing good from bad, rather it is making a choice between two goods. For example: Will I take a position of leadership in my organization or will I give my time to completing a PhD? Neither option will necessarily have a bad outcome, so how do I begin to sift and sort and come to know which is the greater good—or the *magis*? "*Magis* (Pronounced "*mah-jis*") is Latin for "more" or "better" and invites individuals to ask the questions: What more can I do for God? What more can I do for others?" *Magis* does not necessarily imply actually doing more, rather it means which course of action will produce the greater good, which at times could mean doing less, and thus be the "better."

Discernment is not a simple process. The spiritual director will have integrated aspects of discernment into their own lives, therefore making it a natural part of the way they listen in the spiritual direction session. Mark Thibodeaux states that true discernment teaches us to make honest assessments of our situation and to be self-aware. Discernment involves every aspect of our person "from emotion to analysis, from desire to resistance, from personal will to personal prayer."[37]

Ignatian Spiritual Direction

In spiritual direction, the director needs to be open to learning from others within a genuine learner's attitude, and not be tempted to become the teacher assuming that he/she knows the life-world, wisdom or meaning of central life-symbols of the book community. It is essential that the director allow meaning and truth to be discovered together in the process of listening to the directee's experience.

Listening within an Ignatian spiritual direction framework is to listen for the Transcendent at ever-deepening levels of human experience. Both the spiritual director and the directee, using all of their physical and spiritual senses while listening together for the movement of God within the shared conversation of the directee's experiences in life, seek the pathway that leads to freedom at the deepest level of truth and self-transcendence.

Enhancing our awareness of subjectivity is a core aspect of Ignatian spiritual direction. In the practice of Ignatian spiritual direction, which is based on the framework and dynamics of the Spiritual Exercises, Ignatius reminds the director and the directee that we are "creatures" formed by our "Creator", God. Ignatius instructs the director to trust entirely that God, the Creator and Lord, will communicate God's self-impassioning to the person, disposing her towards the way in which she will be better able to serve God in the future [15].

Christians believe that God exists as the source of all life. We are invited into relationship with God through contemplation and prayer and through this relationship we come to trust in God as we learn God's ways with us. It is this trust that takes the practice of listening to a depth that makes spiritual direction unique. When the director and the directee actively trust what they recognize as truth coming from God, the listening paradigm shifts to a place where letting go of fear becomes possible and releases a person to participate in the transformative process. Marburg describes this God:

---

37. Thibodeaux, *God's Voice Within*, 1.

> The universe as revelation of God makes God accessible and knowable to a meaningful extent. God relates to the world as present dynamic lover of all things, and is the source of being, knowing and loving. God is present, sustaining the unfolding human experience of wholeness, the integration of body, mind and spirit. From this is inferred that God desires the unity of all things.[38]

Bion in his work as a psychoanalyst wanted to know "how we know what we know"[39] claiming that it is possible to encounter "Absolute Truth", "Ultimate Reality" or "Reverence and Awe," which he names as "O". Grotstein explains,

> "O" is perhaps Bion's most far-reaching conception. It designates an ineffable, inscrutable, and constantly evolving domain that intimates an aesthetic completeness and coherence. He refers to it by different terms, "Absolute Truth," "Ultimate Reality," or "reverence and awe." When preternaturally personified, it is called "God."[40]

Grotstein continues,

> Bion left behind the preconceptions of the psychoanalytic establishment and ventured inward in a soul-searching, mystic journey [which then]. . . led him to transcend the positivistic certainty of psychoanalytic ontic determinism and "messianically" return it to its proper home in numinous parallax and doubt, where the mystic and relativistic "science of man" truly resides. Bion thus forged a psychoanalytic metatheory based on an epistemology of elements, functions and transformations relating to the mental emotional processing of Truth and ultimately on the fundamental universality of "O."[41]

Thus truth resides in the individual rather than institutional law, dogma or doctrine. This book explores how raising consciousness of the phenomena of "O" can impact leadership and organizational development. In other words, how can spiritual direction support leaders in seeking truth that in turn transforms and supports organizational development?

---

38. Marburg, "Poetry and Grace," 21.
39. Grotstein, "Bion's 'Transformation,'" 109.
40. Grotstein, "Bion's 'Transformation,'" 110.
41. Grotstein, "Bion's 'Transformation,'" 111.

John Dominic Crossan coined the idea of God's "companionship of empowerment" as it asserts itself in a dynamic living relationship of discovery and freedom, of "self-appropriation and self-transcendence."[42] It is not a static goal or something to be attained, but perhaps could be understood as the raising of spiritual consciousness.

Spiritual Consciousness

The depth of personal formation that the director has undertaken is essential to the quality of the shared listening in the spiritual direction interview. As Rohr states, "to discover the truth you must become the truth" and further "when you are transformed others will be transformed by you."[43] Spiritual formation is the process of awakening spiritual consciousness and a deepening self-awareness.

The concept of spiritual consciousness originally developed from Howard Gardner's work on multiple intelligences in which he identifies seven types of intelligence: verbal-linguistic, logical-mathematical, visual-spatial, musical-rhythmic and harmonic, bodily-kinesthetic, interpersonal and intrapersonal.[44] Robert Sternberg introduces two other forms of intelligence about which Gardner mused: spiritual intelligence and existential intelligence. "Spiritual intelligence involves a concern with cosmic or existential issues and the recognition of the spiritual as the achievement of a state of being."[45] John Mayer contends that spiritual consciousness is a better term than spiritual intelligence as "intelligence implies abstract reasoning, whereas the phenomena classified as 'spiritual' are better understood as experiential, personalized and connoting heightened awareness of the Ultimate in relation to awareness of self and others."[46] Mayer identifies key components of spiritual consciousness:

- *Attending* to the unity of the world and transcending one's existence;
- *Consciously entering* into heightened spiritual states;
- *Attending* to the sacred in everyday activities, events, and relationships;

---

42. Crossan in O'Murchu, *Jesus in the Power of Poetry*, and in Marburg, "Poetry and Grace," 85.
43. Rohr, *What the Mystics Know*, 4.
44. Gardner, *Frames of Mind* in Lovat, "Practical Mysticism," 5.
45. Sternberg, "North American Approaches to Intelligence," 426.
46. Elkins et al., "Toward a Humanistic–Phenomenological Spirituality," 6.

- *Structuring consciousness* so that problems in living are seen in the context of life's ultimate concern; and [47]
- *Desiring* to act, and consequently, acting in virtuous ways (to show forgiveness, to express gratitude, to be humble, to display compassion).[48]

Consciously entering a "heightened spiritual state allows one to structure consciousness in a way that enhances and sharpens one's sense of knowing and understanding," [49] and requires the use of the language of mysticism.

The Ignatian spiritual director sees life through the eyes of the mystic, which is "to awaken the profound presence of the unitive Spirit, which then gives us the courage and capacity to face the paradox that everything is—ourselves included."[50] Spiritual consciousness and mysticism are not limited to those who belong to a formal religion, but are central to all human experience. A key aspect of spiritual consciousness is interior freedom.

Interior Freedom

In Week Two of the Exercises the exercitant contemplates the early life of Christ, considers what underpins Christ's decision-making, and is asked to begin looking at the way they make choices for themselves. The Two Standards is one of the meditations given and Figure 4 below shows the context in which the meditation is given.

---

47. The descriptor "ultimate concern" was coined by Paul Tillich in his book: *Dynamics of Faith*. Marburg describes "ultimate concern" as "*the convergence of all desires (and values and loves) into one integrating desire, without the embodiment of such, life would be compromised*" (verbal communication 2017).
48. Mayer, "Spiritual Intelligence," 48.
49. Lovat, "Practical Mysticism," 7.
50. Rohr, *What the Mystics Know*, ix.

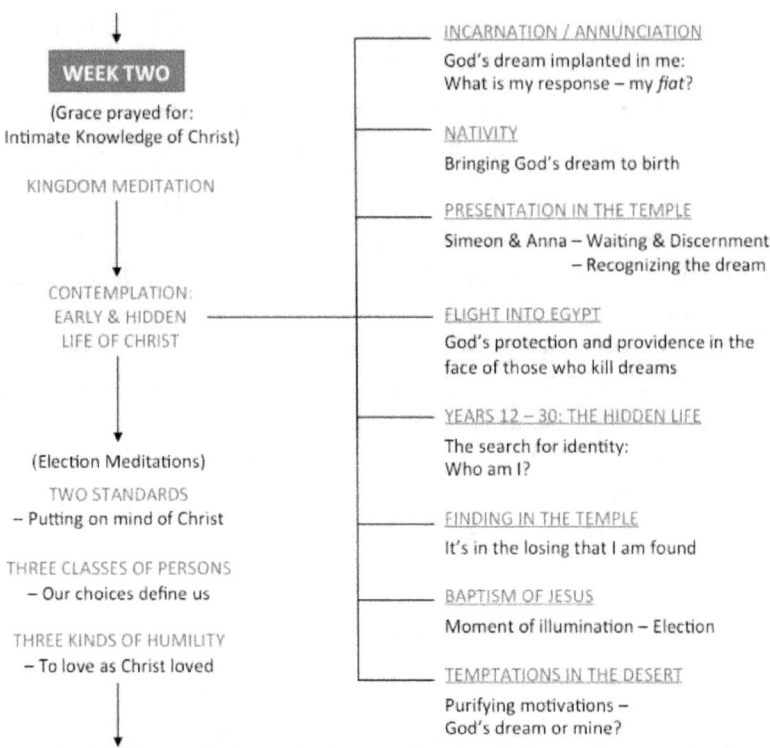

Figure 4: Dynamic and flow of the Week Two meditations[51]

Drawing on his experience as a soldier, in the meditation on the Two Standards, Ignatius describes the imagery of a battlefield and invites the exercitant to choose the standard or flag of the army the exercitant will fight under. "One that of Christ our Commander-in-Chief and our Lord, the other that of Lucifer, the deadly enemy of our human nature." [138] Ignatius suggests in the meditation that if we are faced with a choice between: pride, honor and riches (the standard of the enemy); or humility, poverty and humiliation, (the standard of Christ); we should choose humility, poverty and humiliation. At first this may seem absurd, but in fact a deep understanding of this dynamic is fundamental to the disposition of the spiritual director.

It is not wrong to desire positions of honor, wealth or to be well thought of, but if such desires are the primary influence on decision-making, it is likely they will lead a person towards enslavement and away from what is

---

51. Siow, "Dynamics and Flow in the Second Week" (used with permission).

most deeply desired. If our valency is pride, then our pride will ultimately destroy us, if it is gluttony, gluttony will destroy us.

One of the first questions for discernment then asks, "is the focus on me, my ego, my pride, or is the focus on God and the greater good of all and freedom?" If we choose the latter, even though it might appear at first that we are choosing humiliation and poverty, this decision will most likely lead us towards freedom and be the most life-giving decision we can make; life-giving for each of us, and for the whole of creation. The spiritual director knows that each of us face such decisions every day within our own personal dynamics. They might ask their directee: What are you at war with within yourself, within your relationships and within the world? Could you choose poverty, humiliation and humility over riches, honor and pride rather than going to "war"?

It needs to be clarified that poverty, insults and humiliation are not in themselves good. They will be destructive when they are imposed on others. The meditation on the Two Standards is an invitation to look at how avoiding the experience of poverty, insults and humiliation might inhibit the capacity to actively choose freedom. In human societies, we have been led to believe that honor, riches and pride are essential to success yet, with the help of developments in the fields of psychology and psychodynamics, we might now be able to see that this stance promotes a narcissistic individualism which can be destructive.

> The narcissism and individualism present in the late twentieth-century establishment has, through its values of self, greed, consumerism, acquisition and exploitation, promoted the emergence of perversion through the process of turning a blind eye.[52] . . . A narcissistic society promotes the development of an increasingly perverse society, or at least increases major pockets of socially enacted perversion.[53]

Throughout the *Spiritual Exercises*, Ignatius brings the exercitant's attention to the way in which they make decisions that work against potential perversion. Ignatius focuses on individual, social and global sin. Spiritual direction in the Ignatian tradition seeks to unearth blocks to good discernment and good decision-making at every level. The disposition prayed for in the Two Standards—of risking choosing poverty, humiliation and insults

---

52. Long, *Perverse Organisation*, Loc. 90 citing Hoggett, *Partisans in an Uncertain World*; Steiner, *Psychic Retreats*, Gettler, *Organisations Behaving Badly*.

53. Long, *Perverse Organisation*, Loc. 600.

over honor, pride and riches—is the disposition that lies at heart of the question: *How can spiritual direction support leadership and organizational development?*

Chapter 2

Spirituality, Leadership and Organizational Development

Why Integrate Spirituality, Leadership and Organizational Development?

THE BENEFIT OF CONSCIOUSLY integrating spirituality into the workplace is being discussed widely and a practice rationale is under consideration. One significant contributor to this topic Margaret Benefiel (together with her colleagues), recognizes that "our relationship to work is an integral part of our self-concept, greatly affecting not only the quality of our lives in the workplace but also at home.[1]

> One of the greatest challenges facing leaders today is the need to develop new business models that accentuate SRW [spirituality and religion in the workplace], spiritual leadership, employee well-being, sustainability, and social responsibility without sacrificing profitability, revenue growth, and other indicators of financial performance (the so-called triple bottom line, or "People, Planet, Profit).[2]

Spiritual direction is one way in which spirituality can be integrated into organizational life, offering a unique resource to support leaders in the

---

1. Benefiel et al., "Spirituality and Religion in the Workplace," 175–87.
2. Fry, "Maximising the Triple Bottom Line" in Benefiel et al., "Spirituality and Religion in the Workplace," 176.

workplace as they begin to integrate spirituality into leadership and organizational development.

While secular institutions are being challenged to integrate spirituality into organizational development, it is important to note that religious institutions are also being challenged to evolve and enter second Axial Age thinking.

German philosopher Karl Jaspers first coined the term "Axial Age"[3] to describe the time between approximately 800–200 BCE when human consciousness made a deep spiritual evolutionary change, and the great religions of Taoism, Confucianism, Monotheism, Hinduism, Buddhism, Jansinism and Greek rationalism emerged, laying the spiritual foundations of humanity simultaneously and independently. Religions emerged from a human desire to pursue the Divine or Ultimate ground of meaning and express this desire in different ways. The archetype of the Axial period is the solitary monk, for example: the Hindu sanyasi, the Buddhist monk, the Jewish prophet, and then later the Christian monk, leading to the beginning of individualization and the rise of individual consciousness. In 1949 Jaspers claimed that the levels of spirituality and wisdom attained during the Axial Age had not yet been surpassed, with many religions still living from foundations laid in the axial period.[4]

The introduction of mass communication, technology and particularly the Internet, is drawing humanity into a second Axial Age (first suggested by Cousins in 1994).[5] Karen Armstrong explains,

> All over the world, people are struggling with these new conditions and have been forced to reassess their religious traditions, which were designed for a very different type of society. They are finding that the old forms of faith no longer work for them; they cannot provide the enlightenment and consolation that human beings seem to need. As a result, men and women are trying to find new ways of being religious. Like the reformers and prophets of the first Axial Age, they are attempting to build upon the insights of the past in a way that will take human beings forward into the new world they have created for themselves.[6]

---

3. Jaspers, *Origin and Goal of History*,
4. Vigil, "Theology of Axiality and Axial Theology," 168.
5. Cousins, *Christ of the 21st Century*; Vigil, "Theology of Axiality and Axial Theology"; Armstrong, "New Axial Age."
6. Armstrong, "New Axial Age," para. 1.

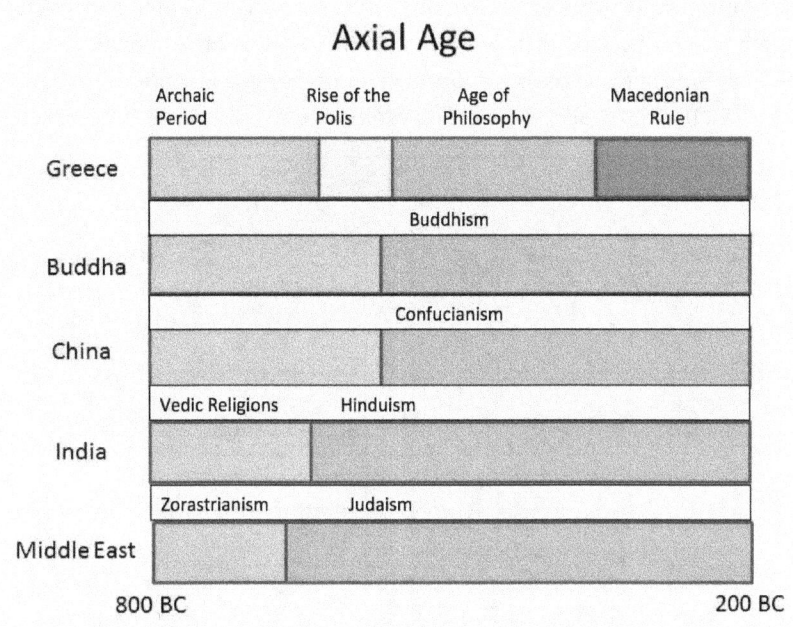

Figure 5: The timeline of the advent of philosophy/religion across the great cultures[7]

Many people come to spiritual direction struggling with religious frameworks that no longer work for them. The difficulty for individuals and groups who wish to take religious belief seriously in the twenty-first century is that institutional religion seems to remain in the first Axial Age where an individual's personal salvation remains as the central purpose of religion. The new Axial Age calls forth a reawakened consciousness of the interconnectedness of all creation, an appreciation of the central purpose of evolution and a vision of the whole of creation as the core of religious truth. Transition into a second Axial Age in the twenty-first century is accompanied by another major era shift for humanity from the Holocene Epoch to the Anthropocene Epoch.

Today's scientists are arguing that a new geological epoch, the Anthropocene, needs to be declared because "humans are altering the planet, including long-term global geologic processes, at an increasing rate." [8]

Though the Anthropocene has no agreed start-date, some proposals identify the spread of agriculture and deforestation, the Industrial

7. Artwork ©Mike Anderson, "Axial Age" (used with permission).
8. Waters, "Anthropocene," para. 1.

Revolution, and radioactive elements dispersed across the planet by nuclear bomb tests in 1950 as marker events. There are also "other signals that can be identified such as plastic pollution, soot from power stations, concrete, and even the bones left by the global proliferation of the domestic chicken."[9]

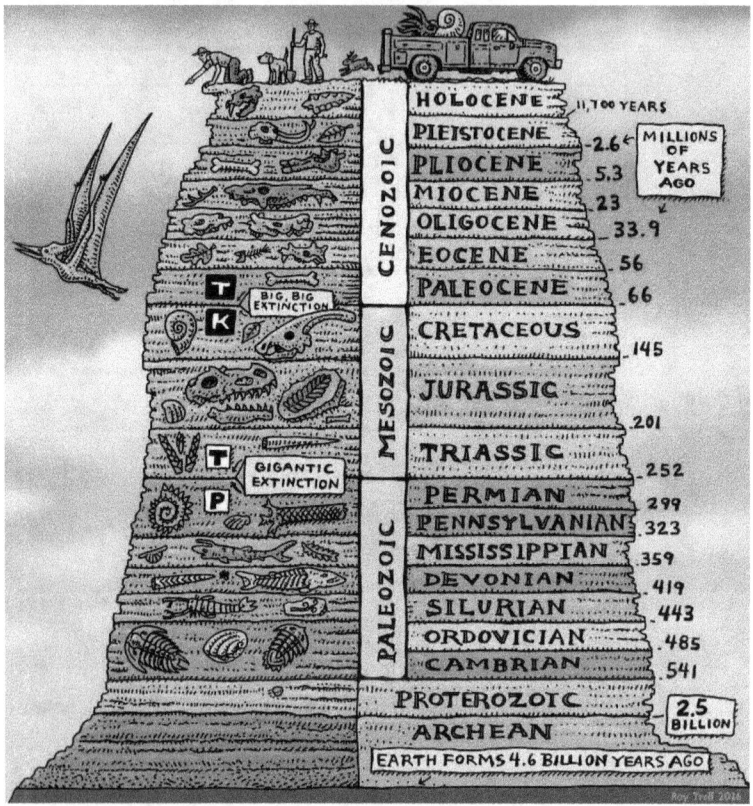

Figure 6: The geologic history of Earth—Artwork © Ray Troll, 2020 (used with permission)

The epoch we are leaving, the Holocene, has seen 12,000 years of stable climate since the last ice age during which all human civilization developed (Figure 6). Experts argue,

> the striking acceleration since the mid-20th century of carbon dioxide emissions and sea level rise, the global mass extinction of species, and the transformation of land by deforestation and development mark the end of that slice of geological time . . . . The

9. Carrington, "Anthropocene Epoch," para 2.

Earth is so profoundly changed that the Holocene must give way to the Anthropocene.[10]

This indicates simultaneous and massive changes in the physical geological aspect of Earth and the spiritual consciousness of Earth. Thomas Aquinas recognized that "a mistake about creation is a mistake about God,"[11] and so it follows that a change in our understanding of creation requires a change in our understanding of God. Such a change would argue that faith can no longer be merely for the benefit of individuals or small sections of our community, it must be about care for all creation.

One benefit spiritual direction can offer leadership and organizational development is that it supports individuals and groups to navigate the transition to second Axial Age consciousness and can raise consciousness to the consequences of the Anthropocene Epoch, the details of which are still emerging. My hope is that religious institutions remaining in first Axial Age thinking will evolve with the encouragement of spiritual direction and adaptive leadership styles. Like religion and spirituality, leadership theories also have a history of evolution.

A Brief Overview of Leadership Theory

Leadership theory has evolved from the early belief that great leaders are born, not made, through to the contemporary understanding that leadership is transformational and relational. A brief history of the evolution of leadership theory can be categorized into six phases:[12]

i. *Great Man Theory (1840s):* Great leaders are born not made, and only a man [and not a woman] could possess the characteristics required to be a leader.

ii. *Trait Theory (1930s–1940s):* What type of person makes a good leader? By analyzing mental, physical and social characteristics of a leader, traits such as intelligence, creativity and other values were identified as central to recognizing who might be a leader.

---

10. Carrington, "Anthropocene Epoch," para 3.
11. Thomas Aquinas is quoted by Delio, *Christian Life in Evolution,* 14:01.
12. This material is a brief summary of Leadership-Central.com: "Where Leaders Expand and Share Their Knowledge."

iii. *Behavioral Theories (1940s–1950s):* What does a good leader do, or what key behavioral patterns result in effective leadership? By focusing on the behavioral characteristics of leaders as opposed to their mental, physical and social characteristics, an assumption that leaders could be made (not just born) emerged. Behavioral theories divided leaders into two categories: those concerned with task and those concerned with people.

iv. *Contingency Theories (1960s):* Leadership emerges from within the context; leadership behaviors succeed in specific situations. There is no single way of leading; leadership style is situational, that is, human traits that enable leadership are related to the situation in which the leader exercises leadership.

v. *Transactional Leadership (1970s):* Leadership is concerned with power and influence and is characterised by transactions made between leaders and followers in a reward/punishment paradigm, seeking to motivate followers by appealing to their self-interest.

vi. *Transformational Leadership (1970s):* Leaders and followers raise each other to higher levels of motivation and morality, identifying opportunities for life-giving change, creating a vision for transforming people and organizations.

Transformational leadership theory introduces personal formation as central to visionary leadership and requires a disposition that is open to being challenged and a willingness to be changed.

Transformational leadership is an ongoing process and occurs "when one or more persons engage with others in such a way that leaders and followers raise one another to higher levels of motivation and morality."[13] Higher levels of morality and motivation move the focus from individual success or egocentric leadership to a more eco-centric leadership style where shared vision, social responsibility, and empowerment of others are central to the purpose of leadership.

William Bass identifies four somewhat different but related components of transformational leadership: Charisma (or idealized influence), inspirational motivation, intellectual stimulation and individualized consideration or individual attention.[14] Transformational leadership the-

---

13. Burns, *Leadership*, 20.

14. Covey, "Transformational Leadership Report," 5; Burns, *Leadership*; Bass, *Leadership and Performance*.

ory (TL) introduces the importance of awareness, beginning with (and growing) the leader's self-awareness in recognizing thoughts, feelings, what motivates decision-making, values, passions and how these influence leadership roles. The transformational approach to leadership endeavors to minimize the competition model in favor of a relationship model, raising consciousness in the organization and developing a culture of collaboration rather than an approach of command and control.

> Transformational Leadership inspires wholeness of being, so your thoughts, feelings and actions are consistent. It is about leading with an integrity and authenticity that resonates with others and inspires them to follow. Not only does it inspire others to follow, but to become leaders themselves.[15]

Though the concept of transformation within organizational development is an important one for enabling change, the idea that leaders have responsibility for transforming others can be somewhat problematic. Steven Covey proposes that transforming people is the central goal of transformational leadership.

> The goal of transformational leadership is to "transform" people and organizations in a literal sense—to change them in mind and heart; enlarge vision, insight, and understanding; clarify purposes; make behavior congruent with beliefs, principles, or values; and bring about changes that are permanent, self-perpetuating, and momentum building.[16]

The risk here is that transformation might be limited to a particular mold or idealized position that the leader has in his mind and which followers are obliged to accept. Transformational leadership is likely to be more successful if the goal is to support others in becoming who they truly are in a process of self-actualization wherein their creativity, desires and individual capacities are encouraged and supported through the inclusion of a spiritual dimension in the transformation process.

If within the organizational dynamic leaders and followers understand the nature and dynamics of their dependence on each other, a collaborative approach to leadership is possible. Although empirical research confirms that transformative leadership influences follower and

---

15. Covey, "Transformational Leadership Report," 10.
16. Covey, *Principle-Centred Leadership*. 287.

organizational performance,[17] there are also criticisms including that it "lacks sufficient identification of the situational context variables on leadership effectiveness."[18]

The concept of inspirational leadership may be more comprehensible than transformational leadership. While transformational leadership is concerned with transforming followers into high performers, inspirational leadership aims to inspire followers to higher achievements.[19] Inspirational leadership is about inspiring others "to face and overcome [the] rigors of the journey."[20] The locus of power in inspirational leadership is shifted from the leader to the follower and leader.

Adaptations and specializations have developed within transformational and inspirational leadership theory. In 1994, Heifetz *et al* introduced the concept of adaptive leadership.[21]

Adaptive Leadership Practice

Adaptive leadership is "the practice of mobilizing people to tackle tough challenges and thrive."[22] Drawing on principles found in molecular biology, adaptive leadership identifies that organizational change:

- requires successful adaption building on the past rather than jettisoning it;
- occurs through experimentation;
- relies on diversity;
- generates loss; and
- takes time.[23]

17. McCleskey, "Situational, Transformational, and Transactional Leadership," 120; Diaz-Saenz, "Transformational Leadership."

18. McCleskey, "Situational, Transformational, and Transactional Leadership," 120; Diaz-Saenz, "Transformational Leadership"; Yukl, "Evaluation of Conceptual Weaknesses."

19. Lee, "Transformational Leadership," para. 17, citing Adair, *The Inspirational Leader*; Avramenko, *Inspiration at Work*.

20. Adair, *Inspirational Leader*, 107 in Lee, "Transformational Leadership," para 25.

21. Heifetz et al., *Practice of Adaptive Leadership*; Heifetz and Laurie, "Work of Leadership."

22. Heifetz et al., *Practice of Adaptive Leadership*, 14.

23. Heifetz et al., *Practice of Adaptive Leadership*, 14–16.

In the practice of adaptive leadership, the leader identifies the difference between technical problems that the organization must tackle, and challenges that invite adaptation and change in people's beliefs, habits and priorities. Leadership, when seen in this light, requires openness to learning and willingness for change and to be changed.

This is where spiritual direction can be most effective. With a working knowledge of discernment as embedded in Ignatian spirituality, spiritual direction supports leaders in maintaining an adaptive disposition where the focus on the "problem" can become a focus on "challenge". The role of discernment in spiritual direction for leadership and organizational development is explored in more detail later in this book.

Heifetz *et al* identify six principles of adaptive leadership:

i. get on the "balcony" and observe what is going on around you;

ii. identify the adaptive challenge;

iii. regulate distress;

iv. maintain disciplined action;

v. give the work back to the people; and

vi. protect leadership voices from below, "don't silence whistle-blowers, creative deviants and others exposing contradictions."[24]

Working through an adaptive challenge will bring about some losses and raise anxiety and fear within the organization. "Practicing adaptive leadership is difficult on the one hand and profoundly meaningful on the other; it is not something you should enter into casually."[25] An adaptive challenge requires the leader to consider the question: "in what new ways of thinking and acting are you willing to engage on behalf of what you believe most deeply?"[26] A sense of purpose is at the core of the disposition of the adaptive leader, highlighting the need to have an understanding of their personal dynamics:

> You are a system as complex as the one you are trying to move forward. To understand your personal system, you have to take stock of many different things: your personality, life experiences, cognitive and other skills, and emotional makeup. You also need

---

24. Heifetz et al., *Practice of Adaptive Leadership*, 60–61.
25. Heifetz et al., *Practice of Adaptive Leadership*, 41.
26. Heifetz et al., *Practice of Adaptive Leadership*, 233.

to appreciate that your behaviors and decisions stem not just from forces within yourself as a system but also from forces acting on you in any given organizational situation.[27]

If an organization is seeking to evolve and develop new models for the twenty-first century and ready for the new Axial Age, an adaptive leadership style is essential. The question remains though: How does a leader develop the capacity to know him or herself intimately and trust their sense of purpose in order to be able to take up the challenge of transformational and adaptive leadership? While individual reflection is helpful towards this goal, doing the inner work of self-awareness though personal accompaniment such as spiritual direction can enable a leader to consciously develop their leadership capacity.

An organization set on maintaining a status quo woven around their own success might not be open to, or even conscious of leadership styles that invite and enable change. Spiritual direction can support an organization to become aware of closed thinking.

To facilitate change, one must be able to stay centered in the tension of conflicting ideologies desires while at the same time become aware of closed thinking. This can be difficult to navigate and requires self-knowledge and a willingness to be changed. The methods of listening offered in spiritual direction and discernment can support leaders and organizations as they relinquish redundant and unhelpful patterns of behavior and thus enable new vision to emerge. The task in spiritual direction is not to avoid destructive dynamics, but to identify them, learn from them and act against what does not bring life and freedom.

In this book I model spiritual direction as a method and container for listening that enables growth in self-awareness for individual leaders and promotes patterns of organizational behavior in which relationship with God is central to the listening paradigm. Discernment is a valuable tool in organizational development. When this is enhanced with an understanding of systems theory, spiritual direction becomes a valuable tool in supporting organizational development. By integrating systems theory as organizational dynamics are explored within the spiritual direction conversation, the leader can develop insights and allied skills that facilitate organizational development and change.

Open systems theory is based on the knowledge that organisms, as well as human organizations and societies are more or less open systems,

---

27. Heifetz et al., *Practice of Adaptive Leadership*, 180.

consisting of a number of component systems that are interrelated, interdependent and interconnected to the environments of which they are part. Each sub-system has boundaries separating them from other systems and subsystems.[28]

In the case of an organization, some people occupy roles, form relationships and conduct activities not only within their part of the system but also within other parts of the system and sub-systems. Systems import and export things such as materials, information, other people, emotions and money. "Systems psychodynamics, therefore, provides a way of thinking about energizing or motivating forces resulting from the interconnection between various groups and sub-units of a social system,"[29] and expands the idea of a leader as a position or role in a system subject to its dynamics. The study of an open system, therefore, involves paying attention at each level of the system to conscious and unconscious processes, including boundaries, relationships and the environment surrounding it.

Organizational Development Theory and Ignatian Spirituality

Organizational development (OD) "is a process of continuous diagnosis, action planning, implementation and evaluation, with the goal of transferring knowledge and skills to organizations to improve their capacity for solving problems and managing future change."[30] Organizational development theory originated in the 1930s from human relations studies in which psychologists identified that work behavior and motivation are influenced by organizational structures and behaviors. Kurt Lewin introduced the idea of feedback, a valuable tool in addressing social processes, to organizational development theory in the 1940–50s and first coined the phrase "action research"[31] in his 1946 article *Groups, Experiential Learning and Action Research*:

> The research needed for social practice can best be characterized as research for social management or social engineering. It is a type of action-research, a comparative research on the conditions and effects of various forms of social action, and research leading

---

28. Bertalanffy, *General Systems Theory* in Stacey, *Strategic Management and Organisational Dynamics*, 58.
29. Neumann, "Systems Psychodynamics," 57.
30. Glanz et al., "Health, Behaviour and Education," para 1.
31. Smith, "Infed."

to social action. Research that produces nothing but books will not suffice.[32]

In more recent times, the work of organizational dynamics "has expanded to focus on aligning organizations with their rapidly changing and complex environments through organizational learning, knowledge management and transformation of organizational norms and values."[33] Kate McArdle and Peter Reason note the connection between action research and organizational development:

> Action Research and organization development are close cousins. We argue that in remembering the way OD is in many ways born of action research we can emphasize OD not only as a process of organizational improvement but also as a process of mutual and liberating inquiry.[34]

Ignatian spirituality in itself is a form of action research. David Coghlan, an Irish Jesuit steeped in Ignatian spirituality and Professor Emeritus in organizational change and action research at Trinity College Dublin states,[35]

> Ignatian spirituality presents a contribution to action research that explicitly addresses the experiential knowing that comes from religious faith and how that knowing leads to practical knowing that is in harmony with the presentational and propositional knowing of the Christian community.[36]

According to Coghlan, when research is undertaken in the spirit of Christian faith, action research and Ignatian spirituality can contribute to each other in four ways:

i. Ignatian cycles of action and reflection can be juxtaposed with action research cycles;

ii. Extended epistemology includes knowledge born of grace and being in love with God;

---

32. Lewin, *Resolving Social Conflicts*, 202–3.
33. Glanz et al., "Health, Behaviour and Education."
34. McArdle and Reason, "Action Research and Organizational Development," 133.
35. This section draws on two papers written by David Coghlan: "Ignatian Spirituality as Transformational Social Science" and "Seeking God in All Things."
36. Coghlan, "Ignatian Spirituality as Transformational Social Science," 103.

Spirituality, Leadership, Organizational Development

iii. Four territories of experience (desires, plans, actions and outcomes) are contained in the Spiritual Exercises and the Ignatian tradition of spiritual direction;[37]

iv. First, second, and third person practice/inquiry provide a working framework.

Through the Spiritual Exercises, which form the basis of Ignatian spirituality, Ignatius offers a method of prayer for reflecting on our experience so as to become conscious of how God is present "in our story: in the past, in the present and in the intimations of our future."[38] Within each Exercise, the exercitant explores four territories of experience: desires, plans, actions and outcomes within the overall dynamic of the *Exercises* moving the exercitant towards inner freedom and apostolic action. Each experience of prayer, reflection and action leads to the starting point for the next Exercise.

Table 2 below shows how Ignatian spirituality and the practice of conscious intentionality developed by Bernard Lonergan can be understood as both an epistemology, specific to the Ignatian spirituality and as a methodology that can support research and organizational development. Drawing on the dynamic of the Spiritual Exercises, Lonergan developed his Method in Theology, the key:

> being "self-appropriation," that is, the personal discovery and personal embrace of the dynamic structure of inquiry, insight, judgement, and decision. By self-appropriation, one finds in one's own intelligence, reasonableness, and responsibility the foundation of every kind of inquiry and the basic pattern of operations undergirding methodical investigation in every field.[39]

---

37. Coghlan, Ignatian Spirituality as Transformational Social Science," 95.
38. Coghlan, Ignatian Spirituality as Transformational Social Science," 93.
39. Lonergan, *Method in Theology* 3–25.

Knowing	Action research/ organizational development	Conscious intentionality	Ignatian spirituality
Experiential	The knowledge arising as we encounter the realities around us.	*Experiencing*	Knowledge born of personal encounter with God the through intentional reflection on desire, scripture, life and realities around us.
Presentational	The knowledge expressed in our giving form to this experiential knowing, through elements such as language, images, music, painting.	*Understanding—insight*	Knowledge expressed through elements such as spiritual conversation, images of God, art, poetry, music.
Propositional	The knowledge distilling our experiential and presentational knowing into theories, statements and propositions.	*Judging—reflective insight*	The knowledge distilling our experiential and presentational knowing into coming to know what God wants of me through the discernment of spirits.
Practical	The knowledge that brings the other three forms of knowing to full fruition by *doing* appropriate things, skillfully and competently.	*Acting—Decision*	The knowledge that brings the other three forms of knowing to full fruition by *doing*—how I incarnate my consolations. [40]

Table 2—*Epistemology specific to the Ignatian spirituality methodology for action research/organizational development.*[41]

40. To incarnate one's consolations is to actively choose to move towards what gives peace, hope, joy and an increase in faith, making decisions that are congruent with what moves a person closer to God and therefore become apostolic in their way of life.

41. Adapted from: Coghlan, "Ignatian Spirituality as Transformational Social Science"; Heron, *Co-operative Inquiry*; Reason and Torbet, "Action Turn."

The central process of action research in organizational development is to explore and enhance our awareness, understanding and skills in each of the four territories of experience: intentionality, planning, action and outcomes.

When Ignatian spirituality is integrated with systems theory and a working knowledge of unconscious processes in organizations, this provides a framework for spiritual direction as a reflective practice for leadership and organizational development.

The Life, Death Resurrection Cycle[42]

In my work as a spiritual director, and for many of the participants in my research, we have drawn on concepts within a program developed in the 1980s called the Ignatian Spiritual Exercises for the Corporate Person (ISECP). Though the originators of this program might not recognize my work as a reflection of their original intention, I need to acknowledge the original source of this material which came from a retreat attended by Fr Michael Smith SJ in 1987. The underpinning philosophy of the program is that for Christian organizations "to be a true corporate person, a group must be united to God as a group;" and further "what is not consciously structured will be unjustly structured."[43]

> Saint Ignatius speaks frequently and urgently about the necessity of being free from disordered affections and inordinate attachments in our decisions. To neglect this area of the unconscious in our spiritual journey, as individuals or as a group, is courting the most crude deceptions right at the heart of apostolic spirituality in its decision-making structures, processes and attitudes. ISECP spends considerable time and energy on these unconscious dynamisms and influences.[44]

My experience of working as a spiritual director with leaders and groups using material from ISECP has contributed significantly to the

---

42. The information from this section is a synopsis of the work of James Borbely SJ, George Schemel SJ, John English SJ, Judith Roemer, and Marita Carew in their work *Focussing Group Energies: Common Ground for Leadership, Organization, and Spirituality*. Borbely et al. acknowledge the work of © 1977 Management Design Inc. (MDI) consultants on change and design.

43. Borbely et al., *Focussing Group Energies*, 1:xii.

44. Borbely et al., *Focussing Group Energies*, 1:iii.

emergence of this book, in particular, the life-death-resurrection cycle (LDR—Figure 7), which is a vitality curve for diagnosing where an organization is currently in their life cycle:

> The life-death-resurrection cycle is built on the assumption that all of life is characterized by a pattern of life, death and resurrection . . .We know that every rock, every plant, every tree, every individual, and every organization will be characterized by a series of life, death, resurrection rhythms.[45]

Drawing on the work of ISECP, what follows is my adaptation and interpretation of the LDR. In a similar way to systems theory, the LDR looks at group life as a living organism. Life emerges as fragile and if the conditions are right, will move into a period of growth, chaos, flourishing and struggles, while becoming stronger and more complex; then eventually, aspects of life will begin to diminish and finally life will die; remnants of what was life become fertilizer for new life already emerging. With every new life-form comes the potential to co-create with God, bringing a fresh dimension of change in the evolution of the universe.

> Evolution shows us that change is integral to new life. Given a sufficient amount of time, life evolves. To evolve is not only to change but to become more complex, to unite in such a way that new forms of life emerge and diverge.[46]

We can choose whether we work together with God in facilitating change that is life-giving, building up the body of Christ, or defending against change by staying attached in the past. I see Jesus as one of the greatest change agents to enter the history of humanity. He challenged the status quo and facilitated change by focusing on two important aspects of how we live in relationship with each other in truth and love:

- The truth will make you free (John 8:32 NRSV)
- You shall love the Lord your God with all your heart, and with all your soul, and with all your mind . . . You shall love your neighbor as yourself." (Matt 22:37–39 NRSV)

---

45. Borbely et al., *Focussing Group Energies*, 3:27.
46. Delio, *Emergent Christ*, 2.

By following Jesus' example and moving consciously together in truth and love, "we can become agents of change, serving the development of a community of life grounded in love."[47]

Figure 7: Life-death-resurrection cycle[48]

For a group to work together effectively and harness creative energy, there is a need to understand that the group has a life and work that is more than the sum of the life and work of its individuals. This creative energy gives the group power to perform the functions it was created to do. In the LDR, power in a group is understood to be "the free commitment of individuals to goals and objectives they have freely chosen."[49]

The LDR is a sociological model for the life-cycle of a collaborative team naming the important dimensions of group life, indicating where those dimensions may cause intra-group conflict, and signaling how to address those conflicts when they occur. If the LDR cycle of the group "is not understood or consciously attended to by the team and the leader, various

---

47. Miles, "Incarnating Our Consolations," 38.

48. The *life-death-resurrection cycle* is based on the *vitality curve* designed by Cada et al., *Shaping the Coming Age of Religious Life*, 77, in Borbely et al., *Focussing Group Energies*, 1:37.

49. Borbely et al., *Leadership, Spirituality and Organisational Practice*, Mod 3, 15.

unconscious forces may contribute to destructive interpersonal conflict within the group and lead to its dissolution."[50] The LDR cycle begins with the primary spirit or myth of the group.

Primary Spirit—Myth: The life of a new group or organization will begin with a dream, a vision or an idea. When two or more people join this vision, the foundational myth and the LDR cycle of this new group has begun. There is a shared passion, or primary spirit that breathes life into the foundational story or myth, around which the group coalesce and new life is created. This foundational myth is essential to the ongoing life of the group. The primary task of any group leader then is to keep the myth alive and focused. The main goal of the leader is to keep the group in touch with their identity as a group through their myth, and to ensure that all decision-making flows from, and is aligned with the myth.

If the myth changes, a new group will have formed. It is important for the group to be conscious of this change and to check that the new myth is the connecting point for all members of the group. If this is not made clear there will be confusion within the group and a disintegration of commitment will result. Likewise, when a new member joins the group, he/she should encounter the deep myth of the group, and if that aligns with their own deep beliefs and desires, it will be possible to become part of the collaborative team.

> Collaborative ministry evolves from a deep center, a primary spirit that attracts diversity and creativity in which individuals commit to shared goals and objectives to which they have freely chosen. Primary spirit as an attractor creates a strong and clear internal boundary; external boundaries are permeable and welcoming. The felt sense of shared roots increases with proximity to the center, but there is freedom and space for people to move in and out. [51]

The myth of the group will be permeated with the "primary spirit" of the group. Primary spirit exists before values and gives meaning to primary task. It is that part of an organization which is life-giving to the individual, group or organization.[52] All groups have a primary spirit, and when this is confused, they will find avoidance and corruption of the task that the group is meant to be doing.

50. Borbely et al., *Leadership, Spirituality and Organisational Practice*, Mod 3, 5.
51. Miles, "One Body, One Spirit, One Mission," 59.
52. Bain and Bain, "Note on Primary Spirit," 100.

Beliefs and Assumptions: The LDR cycle assumes that when a group first forms, it begins to shape its belief system. Belief systems are the stories we tell ourselves to define our personal sense of "reality" and make sense of the world around us. A belief system is the set of precepts by which a person lives daily life, governing thoughts, words, and actions. When the belief systems of group members are not aligned, or are in opposition, value conflicts can ensue. It can be very difficult to repair damage done within a group when this level of conflict arises. The belief system emerges from the myth and should be consistent with the myth. If this is not the case, there will be constant confusion and conflict, making the group impossible to lead. The LDR cycle specifically refers to groups who form within a specific belief system. Groups can function effectively with a variety of belief systems where a belief system is not primary to their identity.

As the group starts to take shape, assumptions are formed. These assumptions are the stable patterns of expectations that members of the group share consciously and unconsciously. An assumption is something we take for granted—something you believe to be the case, even without proof.

Goals and Objectives: "A goal is a transcendent reality: never fully articulated and never fully attained. It is something to which we aspire. Objectives, on the other hand, are measurable. We decide to accomplish particular projects within a particular length of time."[53] Goals must flow from and be aligned with the primary spirit and myth of the group. IS-ECP recognizes that a collaborative ministry team will have two goals: a transcendent goal which articulates their identity in God and is the reason this group exists; and an apostolic goal which makes concrete the way in which this team will achieve this goal and to whom and with whom they will minister.

Objectives are developed from the goals. They articulate what you will do to make your goals concrete. They can be evaluated and reviewed regularly.

Programs: Programs are what the group does and where the group spends most of its time, energy, money and other resources.

Decisions: The group makes decisions related to standard operating procedures, budgets, management issues, employing staff etc., and keeps the group operating.

---

53. Borbely et al., *Focussing Group Energies*, 3:38.

The core hypothesis of the LDR cycle is that money can't buy the "free commitment" that comes from a deep alignment with the myth, goals and objectives of a group, from which all activities flow.

Power Expending—Diagnosing the Doubt in a Team

When an organization is in the process of establishing its mission and growing, it is building up energy, growing stronger, and it might seem that the possibilities are endless (the utopian flaw). In the life of a group or an organization there will be periods of regression, suspended growth. At different stages, parts of the group will be thriving and other parts moving into doubt and disintegration. Some things need to be let go and new things allowed to be birthed, but if this is not done consciously, commitment will be eroded in the group. The first signs of erosion of free commitment will come in the form of doubt (Figure 6).

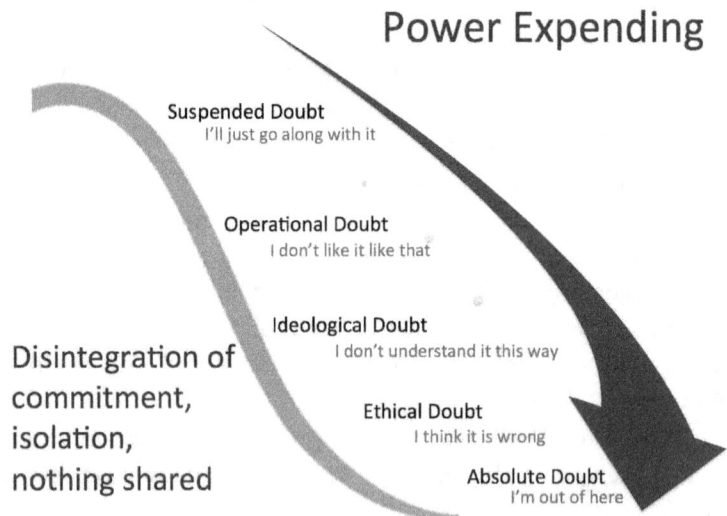

Figure 8: Power expending elements of the LDR cycle.

When doubt begins to creep into a team, the natural tendency might be to ignore or dismiss it. This might be the most dangerous thing that a leader can do. If the group has the courage to listen to doubt when it emerges, they can regather their original purpose and desires and strengthen their work.

When doubt is ignored it can erode and destroy the group. The more deeply doubt is allowed to penetrate, the more destructive and painful it will be to address. By addressing doubt when it first appears in the team, the group can become conscious of the team falling into total disrepair at the level of absolute doubt. Through evaluation, doubt can be returned to the power building side of the grid where the commitment is generated. The principle is that, at whatever level the doubt takes place, we tend, address or take care of the doubt by evaluating one level lower on the opposite side of the grid. For example, if the doubt is an operational doubt, then together we need to go back to the objectives, one level lower on the power building side. We don't return to the program level on the same level, but we go back to the objectives and take a look at them to see whether the way we decided to program the work is the best way (See Figure 9).

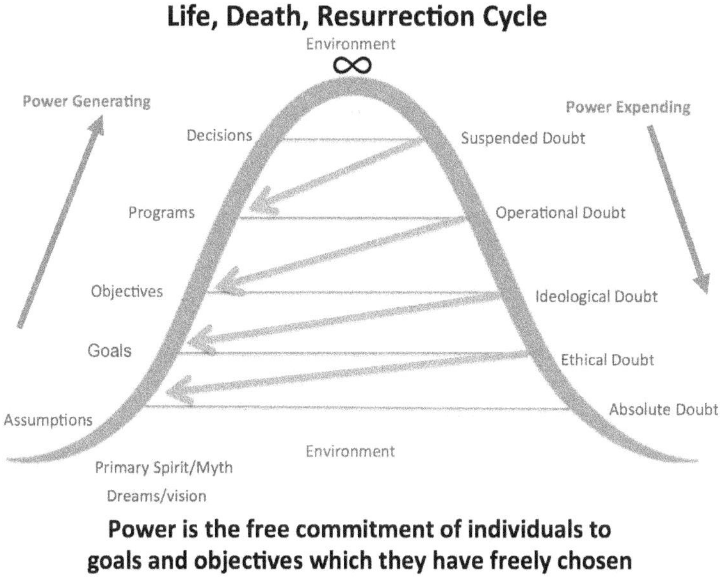

Life, Death, Resurrection Cycle

Environment ∞

Power Generating — Decisions, Programs, Objectives, Goals, Assumptions, Primary Spirit/Myth, Dreams/vision

Power Expending — Suspended Doubt, Operational Doubt, Ideological Doubt, Ethical Doubt, Absolute Doubt

Environment

Power is the free commitment of individuals to goals and objectives which they have freely chosen

Figure 9: Addressing doubt in the team[54]

Change is a natural part of group life. Some groups or aspects of group life need to die but when change to the core identity of the group happens without group consensus, there will be a loss of commitment of individuals and

---

54. Adapted from Borbely et al., *Leadership, Spirituality and Organisational Practice*, Mod 3, 13.

power and energy will be drained from the mission. Spiritual direction in a group setting can provide a safe container for the group to address doubt in the team as it arises, and thereby support organizational development.

The Transforming Experience Framework and Spiritual Direction

The Transforming Experience Framework (TEF) developed by the Grubb Institute provides a lens for the discipline (education, formation, research and practice) of spiritual direction to consider organizational dynamics and the role of leadership. The TEF is a framework for exploring how "people can take authentic action through taking up role."[55] The TEF (Figure 10) places role as the intersecting element of four domains of experience: person, system, context and Source. Role in work systems is not a simple position description or set of instructions, it is complex and dynamic and will be influenced by the person taking up the role, the system in which it is located, the context in which it is found and its relatedness to Source. Using the TEF framework supports an integrated investigation into the role holder's experience of:

i. being a person;

ii. being in a particular system;

iii. being in a particular context; and

iv. connectedness to Source.

---

55. Long, "Transforming Experience Framework," 2.

Spirituality, Leadership, Organizational Development

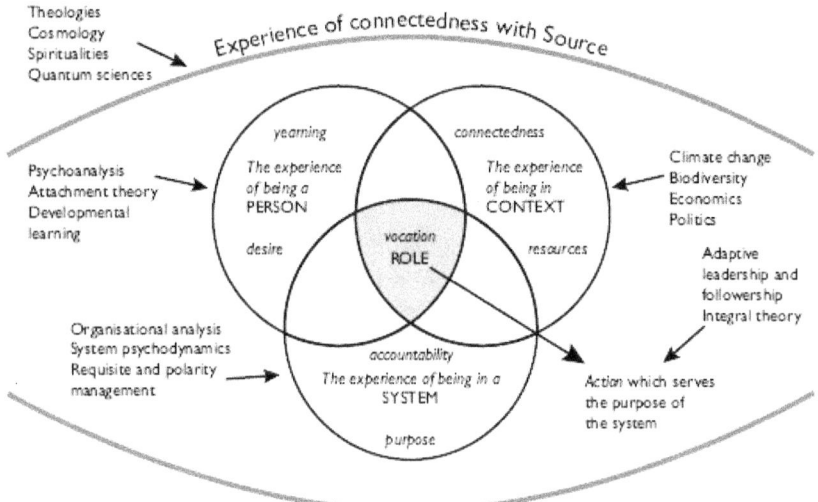

Figure 10: Transforming experience into authentic action through role (TEF)[56]

When exploring the experience of being a person, the writer helps the role holder to consider their relatedness to others. This relatedness can be understood as

> a nexus or network of relationships that centre in the person ... [within whom] are carried one's personal images of parents, siblings, colleagues, aspirations and fears. Fundamental to the experience of being a person is the experience of desire, the underlying impetus that drives us to work at transforming ourselves and the world we live in.[57]

The experience of being in a system is the exploration of the way in which "people come together in systems in order to fulfil their needs and desires: in work systems, this includes the need to produce products and services."[58] Systems are differentiated from other systems by boundaries and are centered on shared purpose. Social systems include dimensions such as families, work organizations, departments, teams, neighborhoods and countries.[59]

56. Long, "Transforming Experience Framework," 5.

57. Bazalgette et al., "Absolute in the Present," 106 in Roberts and Bazalgette, "Daring to Desire," 143.

58. Long, "Transforming Experience Framework," 8.

59. See pp. 48–49 above for a discussion of systems theory.

The domain of *context* is the environment within which the social system occurs and includes what might impact the role holder's experience. The environment includes "physical, political, economic, social, historical, international, and emotional context for the system."[60]

The fourth domain, connectedness with Source, is perhaps the most vague and indefinable aspect of the TEF. Bazalgette notes that organizational consultants working with clients using the TEF rarely bring the concept of Source into the conversation: "A lot of people tell me they just don't know how to talk about connectedness to Source in the framework, and so choose to leave it out."[61] In spiritual direction the domain of connectedness with Source is the primary focus. The practice of interviewing and listening in spiritual direction intentionally focuses on the interviewee's experience of Source and how this permeates and influences the domains of person, system, context and then role.

Bazalgette makes the following observations about the domain of Source:

- Source is not a distinct domain; it is connected and runs throughout. Though we may not be working and seeking to purposely and consciously make sense of Source, we are never not working with Source.

- Source is about connectedness and permeates the TEF. Instead of asking "what" Source is, we might instead ask, "What is the nature of connectedness?"

- What is the Source of my experiences—what are the deeply shared connected values and beliefs that keep the current experience/show on the road? What are the experiences of authority, faith, belief, loving, lovable-ness and values through the experiences of being a person, in a system, in a context, that are driving the here-and-now occurrence? In systems, we constantly test whether we are capable of loving or being loved—that is at the Source, the deepest levels of what is really happening here, on this "mortal coil" of human experience.

- When we consciously work with our nature of connectedness to Source, we find resources for transformation as we are working with the literal root or creative Source of the experiences and occurrences.[62]

---

60. Long, "Transforming Experience Framework," 9.
61. Bazalgette, "Connectedness With Source," 224.
62. Bazalgette, "Connectedness With Source," 224–25 (paraphrased).

The TEF intentionally leaves the definition of Source open so that the role holder may bring his or her own interpretation. Likewise, the spiritual director must also have an open stance to directees and understanding of what Source is to them, not imposing their own theology or doctrines onto the directee. Long hypothesizes that Source is the unconscious:

> The associative unconscious is a network and a process of unconscious thinking that belongs to the system and its context, rather than to the individual person. We cannot apprehend it as a whole, we can only, as it were, dip into it through our collective associations. It is accessed through free association, reverie, meditation, the arts, music, and other collective endeavors that suspend ego. It can be a source of reaching towards truth, beauty, and transcendence into a place of greater good. It can also bring forward associations of human frailty, vulnerability, cruelty, and horror.[63]

Connectedness to Source occurs in both conscious and unconscious processes. We are always connected with the Source of all life. What spiritual direction and the TEF offer is a framework in which we can raise consciousness to this connectedness. Bazalgette and Irvine recognize:

> Connectedness with Source is always present to the extent that when it is taken into account the full range of available resources becomes evident, especially in terms of human imagination, inventiveness, resourcefulness, and resilience. Where this potential collective resource is ignored or suppressed, the result is that the organizations and institutions become fragile, brittle and [they] under-perform. They are at risk.[64]

Whereas psychoanalysis is an attempt to bring the unconscious into consciousness, spiritual direction seeks to bring connectedness with Source into consciousness. In the next chapter, I explore the concepts of the unconscious, consciousness and how they relate to spiritual formation and spiritual direction.

---

63. Long, "Transforming Experience Framework," 92.
64. Bazalgette, "Connectedness With Source," 219.

Chapter 3

Spiritual Direction, Spiritual Formation and Consciousness

SPIRITUAL DIRECTION PRACTICED IN the Ignatian tradition has the capacity to change a person's consciousness. Consciousness is defined as:

- the quality or state of being aware, especially of something within oneself;
- the state or fact of being conscious of an external object, state or fact;
- awareness, especially concern for some social or political cause.[1]

Many attribute the discovery of the unconscious mind to Sigmund Freud (1856–1939).[2] However, as eighteenth-century German romantic philosopher Friedrich Schelling (1775–1854) sought to understand the somewhat unknowable entity we call God, he developed the concept of the unconscious in a systemic way, recognizing the unconscious as "the source of creative power."[3] Schelling postulates "the existence of an unconscious as a substrate prior to consciousness. This unconscious is ground to self-consciousness, ground to existence and a necessary substrate."[4]

> Most people turn away from what is concealed within themselves
> just as they turn away from the depths of the great life and shy

---

1. Merriam-Webster Dictionary, "Consciousness."

2. In this section I borrow from Long's history of the unconscious in *Transforming Experience in Organizations,* 31–106.

3. Ffytch, *Foundation of the Unconscious*; McGrath, *Dark Ground of the Spirit,* in Long, "Transforming Experience Framework," 37.

4. Long, "Transforming Experience Framework," 37.

away from the glance into the abysses of that past which are still in one just as much as the present.[5]

Schelling grapples with the unconscious and the concept of God as the source of creation.

> Building on the premise that philosophy cannot ultimately explain existence, he merges the earlier philosophies of Nature and identity with his newfound belief in a fundamental conflict between a dark unconscious principle and a conscious principle in God. God makes the universe intelligible by relating to the ground of the real but, insofar as nature is not complete intelligence, the real exists as a lack within the ideal and not as reflective of the ideal itself.[6]

Schelling offers a theology of omniscience where God is understood to be all-knowing and all-powerful: Schelling indicates that if you are not perfect, you cannot reflect God. Ignatian spirituality challenges this assumption on the premise that we can have a personal and intimate relationship with God, who is all-loving, and that our call to perfection is to reflect this Love into the world. Grappling with the "fundamental conflict between a dark unconscious principle and a conscious principle in God"[7] within human experience, as described by Schelling, is at the heart of discernment and the work of spiritual direction which is grounded in faith rather than science. The practice of spiritual direction is based on the premise that whether we are conscious or unconscious of the presence of God, we are in communication with God, and God is in communication with humanity at all times—that is the nature of God.

Sigmund Freud (1856–1939) rejects the teleological emphasis found in Schelling's work, preferring to align with the emerging sciences of the time. He develops the idea of the unconscious as "a dynamic system of the mind where threatening thoughts (instinctual representatives) are kept from consciousness, but not from having an impact on other thoughts, feelings and behaviors."[8]

Carl Jung (1875–1961) then introduces the concept of the collective unconscious. Whereas the "personal unconscious contains repressed ideas, traumas and injuries, the shadow self and inferior function of the

---

5. Schelling, *Ages of the World*, 93–94 in Long, "Transforming Experience Framework," 37.

6. *Encyclopedia of the Romantic Era*, 1001.

7. *Encyclopedia of the Romantic Era*, 1001.

8. Long, "Transforming Experience Framework," 50.

Strengthening Spirit–Releasing Potential

personality . . . the collective unconscious refers to inherited contents that are the same for everyone." [9] Jung "believed that the unconscious was the source of creativity beyond repressions."[10] In my experience of spiritual direction, I have consistently witnessed the release of creativity in people as they dare to explore the depth of their own experiences in light of their relationship with God. Sally's story is a common story for many I have accompanied in spiritual direction:

> When Sally first came to spiritual direction, she was in a work role that was draining all her energy. Though she loved the work, the dynamics of her work relationships were unhealthy and exhausting. Sally believed that if she worked harder, it would get better.
>
> As we explored Sally's relationship with God in spiritual direction, Sally begins to notice that it was not God who is asking her to work harder. In fact, when she sat in prayer with God, the invitation was to slow down and breathe. In slowing down, Sally discovered that she had been responding to unspoken demands in the workplace, that perhaps she was placing on herself. Part of her work role was to write creative pieces and she loved to do this, but rarely gave herself the time to do this well. Sally discerned that she would start to give a higher priority to her writing and see what happened. She also discerned that she would make some time each day for reflection and meditation—just 15 minutes.
>
> After some time, Sally discovered that work was now life-giving instead of life-draining. Her work improved and she seemed to have more space in her day as she made space insider herself for God. Though there was still pressure at work, she responded differently and was able to discern the priorities with less stress. By releasing her creative energy, Sally also released spaciousness within herself that she had been crowding with stress and anxiety.

Bion (1897–1979) like Schelling, grapples with the concept of the unconscious as infinite. It is from Bion's perspective that we see the link between spiritual direction and unconscious processes. Spiritual direction explores the unconscious via the directee's experience of God or "O" as identified by Bion. Traditionally spiritual direction neither takes into consideration psychoanalytic theory, nor is it conducted within a therapeutic setting.

---

9. Long, "Transforming Experience Framework," 52.
10. Long, "Transforming Experience Framework," 53.

The practice of spiritual direction has for years resisted being identified as therapy and has avoided psychoanalytical language. However my experience is that, without the scientific language of psychoanalysis spiritual directors have sought to uncover the source of creativity (cf. Jung) and the experience of Ultimate Reality (cf. Bion), by exploring what is concealed within ourselves (cf. Schelling) and the unconscious processes that invest people in disordered patterns of attachment. Similarities between therapy and spiritual direction are many. As we come to know more about psychodynamic processes, the spiritual director becomes more knowledgeable and adept at working with human experience. Susan Long, following Freud's thinking on the unconscious from which psychoanalysis developed, notes: "We tend to think and speak of *the* unconscious: a mysterious unknown terrain that influences us from the inside. Yet, it is not so much a hypothetical place as it is a function or state of mind: unconsciousness."[11] Spiritual direction supports the development of consciousness in which the directee attends to disordered patterns of behavior whilst exploring their relationship with God.

Spiritual Direction and Leadership Consciousness

Building on the work of Maslow's hierarchy of needs, Richard Barrett developed a model to describe seven levels of consciousness and how they correspond to stages of psychological development (Figure 11). Barrett recognizes that "an authentic, full spectrum leader must understand and master his or her personal dynamics as well as the cultural dynamics of the organization, business unit or division he or she leads."[12] This is consistent with the process of self-awareness that is developed through the process of spiritual formation.

---

11. Long, "Transforming Experience Framework," 31.
12. Barrett, "Seven Levels of Leadership Consciousness," 1.

Strengthening Spirit–Releasing Potential

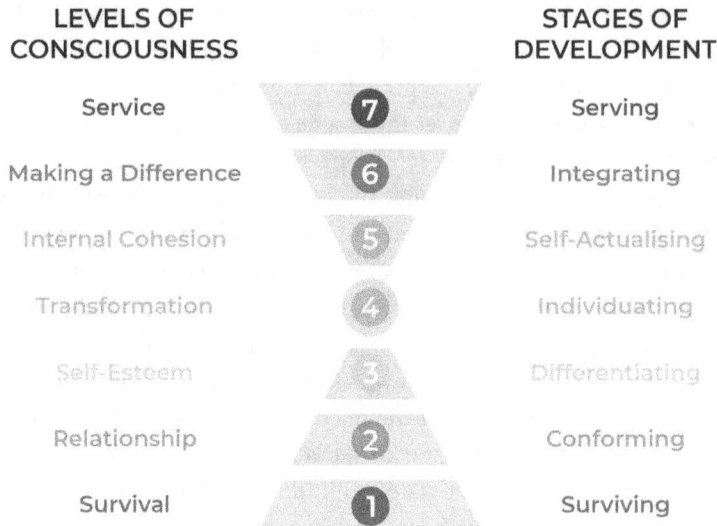

Figure 11: Seven levels of consciousness and the seven stages of psychological development[13]

Maslow presents a hierarchical schema of human needs beginning with psychological needs and the basic instinct to survive; second is safety and security; third, love and belonging, social and relationships; fourth, esteem needs, ego-centric need to achieve, responsibility and reputation; and fifth, self-actualization, personal growth and reputation.[14] Barrett, aligning his thinking with Maslow's, contends that every human being, and all human group structures evolve and grow in consciousness in seven well-defined stages aligned with our basic needs: survival, relationship, self-esteem, transformation, internal cohesion, making a difference and service.

Neither Maslow's hierarchy of needs nor Barrett's SLOC acknowledge and incorporate the centrality of relationship in all aspects of human development. Pamela Rutledge notes, "None of Maslow's needs can be met without social connection and collaboration."[15]

> Connection is a prerequisite for survival, physically and emotionally. Needs are not hierarchical. Life is messier than that. Needs are, like most other things in nature, an interactive, dynamic system, but they are anchored in our ability to make social connections.[16]

13. © Barrett Values Centre (used with permission).
14. Maslow, "Theory of Human Motivation."
15. Rutledge, "Social Networks," para. 1.
16. Rutledge, "Social Networks," para. 7–8.

Presenting the model of SLOC as a hierarchy creates the illusion that once we have climbed the hierarchical ladder, we will have arrived at the pinnacle with the work done, whereas for individuals and groups, the process of developing consciousness is more cyclic and emergent than definitive and hierarchical. Although raising of consciousness through spiritual formation is progressive and at times follows the hierarchy presented by Barrett, it is more dynamic and cyclic than either schema indicates.

Interconnectedness and relationship with Source are central to the experience of spiritual direction. Placing interconnectedness and relationship with Source at the center of the spiritual formation process, as well as awareness of Barrett's levels of consciousness, allow the dynamic nature of spiritual formation to be represented more fully (see figure 12 below).

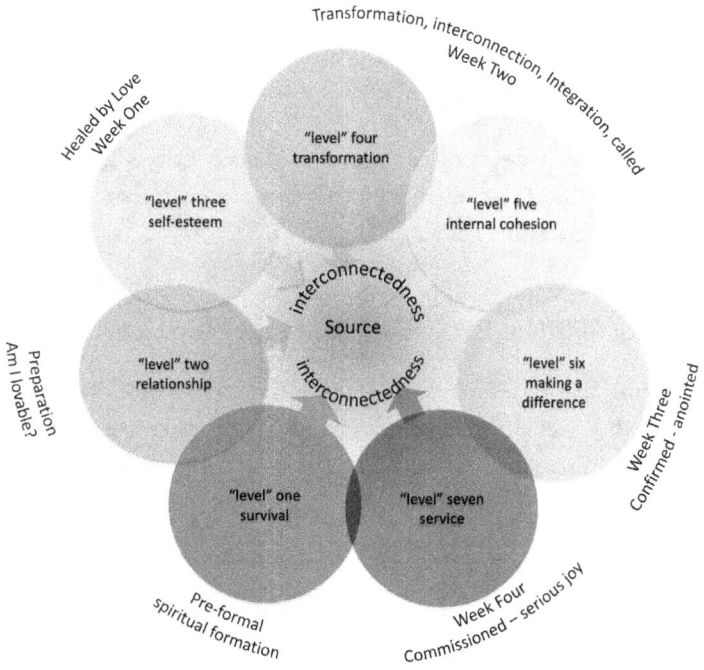

Figure 12: Process of spiritual formation and seven levels of consciousness

I integrate the formative dynamic of spiritual formation as articulated in the Spiritual Exercises, with Barrett's seven levels of leadership and organizational consciousness, thus creating a framework to understand the different stages in leadership and organizational development as they occur in the process of spiritual direction (see figure 13 below). Integrating these two frameworks offers an interpretive framework that resonates with the dataset in this book.

DYNAMIC OF SPIRITUAL FORMATION IN THE SPIRITUAL EXERCISES	LEVELS OF CONSCIOUSNESS		STAGES OF DEVELOPMENT
Week Four – serious joy	Service	7	Serving
Week Three – called, anointed	Making a Difference	6	Integrating
Week Two – transformation, interconnection, integration	Internal Cohesion	5	Self-Actualising
	Transformation	4	Individuating
Week One – healed by love	Self-Esteem	3	Differentiating
Preparation – am I insignificant or have I been created to be loved and to love?	Relationship	2	Conforming
Not thinking about Exercises or spiritual formation	Survival	1	Surviving

Figure 13: Barrett's seven levels of consciousness and the dynamic of spiritual formation in the Spiritual Exercises [17]

Barrett articulates aspects of each level of consciousness for leaders and organizations, which I briefly introduce below and then elaborate on in the following chapters as they emerge.

Stages of Spiritual Formation and Leadership Consciousness

Spiritual direction raises a person's consciousness to a deeper understanding of how their personal dynamics operate within their relationship with God. Spiritual direction can transform the inmost dimension of the human being, the *kardia*:

> *Kardia* is Greek for "heart" or "mind," and encompasses both . . . It is a word which holds a breadth of personal meaning including: mind, soul, interiority or inner self, desire, intention. It refers to the place in which a person experiences him or herself as authentic and centered. [18]

---

17. Adapted from Barrett, "Barrett Seven Levels Model."
18. Marburg and Miles, "Application to the Australian Ecumenical Council," 4.

Spiritual Direction, Spiritual Formation and Consciousness

Spiritual formation Spiritual Exercises stages	Positive Focus/*Negative Focus*	Levels of Consciousness		Stages of Development	Leadership Characteristics
Week Four: Commissioned, called—serious joy	Service to humanity and the planet: compassion, humility, future generations.	Service	7	Serving	Wisdom/Visionary: Service to society, humanity and the planet. Focus on ethics, social responsibility, sustainability, and future generations. Displays wisdom, compassion and humility.
Week Three: Confirmation in the call to serve in the face of suffering.	Making a difference in the community: actualizing meaning, collaboration, intuition, mentoring, empathy.	Making a Difference	6	Integrating	Mentor/Partner: Strategic alliances and partnerships, servant leadership. Focus on employee fulfilment, mentoring and coaching. Displays empathy and utilizes intuition in decision-making.
Week Two: Transformation, interconnection, integration	Finding meaning in existence: integrity, alignment, authenticity, creativity, passion, honesty, trust.	Internal Cohesion	5	Self-Actualizing	Integrator/Inspirer: Strong cohesive culture, and a capacity for collective action. Focus on vision, mission and values. Displays authenticity, integrity, passion, and creativity.
	Continuous growth and development: adaptability, continuous improvement, courage, team-player.	Transformation	4	Individuating	Facilitator/Influencer: Empowerment, adaptability, and continuous learning. Focus on personal growth, teamwork and innovation. Displays courage, responsibility, initiative, and accountability.
Week One: Healed by love, self-esteem, differentiating.	Building a sense of self-worth: pride in self, self-reliant, self-discipline, positive self-image. *Arrogance, status, power, glamour, rigidity.*	Self-Esteem	3	Differentiating	Manager/Organizer: High performance systems and processes. Focus on strategy, performance, excellence, quality, productivity and efficiency. Displays pride in performance.
Preparation for Exercises: Am I lovable.	Harmonious relationships: family, friendship, belonging, open communication, ritual. *Blame jealousy, judgement, conflict, gossip.*	Relationship	2	Conforming	Relationship Manager: Employee recognition, open communication, and conflict resolution. Creates employee and customer loyalty and treats people with dignity.
Pre-spiritual formation	Physical survival and safety: health, nutrition, financial stability, self-defense. *Violence, greed, corruption, territorial.*	Survival	1	Surviving	Crisis Manager: Financial stability, organizational growth, and employee health and safety. Displays calmness in the face of chaos, and decisiveness in the midst of danger.

Table 3—*Stages of spiritual formation and leadership consciousness.*[19]

19. Adapted from Barrett, "Seven Levels of Leadership Consciousness," 1–5.

Transformation of the *kardia* influences a person's leadership capacity and their leadership style. As discussed earlier, Barrett proposes Seven Levels of Leadership Consciousness (SLLC) as a model for understanding how leadership styles change as levels of consciousness and psychological development progress. I align the formation process of the Spiritual Exercises with Barrett's SLLC (Table 3) to provide a framework for understanding leadership development for each of the participants in this research.

Week One Dynamic of Spiritual Formation and Levels of Consciousness

When an individual or a group are in survival mode the primary task is to ensure that basic psychological and physical needs are met (Table 4). For example, at level one consciousness, it is unlikely that the group or individual is able to consider spiritual formation. In the first three levels of consciousness as articulated by Richard Barrett there are healthy and unhealthy motivations which parallel early stages of spiritual formation.

	Healthy Motivations	*Unhealthy Motivations*
3 Self-esteem	Feeling a sense of personal self-worth.	Underlying anxieties about not being respected and not being enough.
2 Relationship	Feeling a sense of love and belonging.	Underlying anxieties about not being accepted and not being loved.
1 Survival	Feeling secure and safe in the world.	Underlying anxieties about not being safe or secure and not having enough.

Table 4—Healthy/unhealthy motivations levels one–three of consciousness.[20]

> The unhealthy behaviours derive from the existential fears of the leader's ego: not having enough money, protection or security to satisfy the ego's need for safety; not having enough love, caring or acceptance to satisfy the ego's need for belonging; and not having enough power, authority or status to satisfy the ego's need for respect or recognition. These personal fears play out in the context of the organisation as personal entropy and significantly impact the Cultural Entropy® scores of the organisation, thereby undermining its performance.[21]

20. Barrett, "Seven Levels of Leadership Consciousness," 2.
21. Barrett, "Seven Levels of Leadership Consciousness," 2.

When a leader is working in basic survival mode, Barrett identifies the characteristics of leadership as a crisis manager where financial stability, organizational growth, and employee health and safety are paramount. The leader displays calmness in the face of chaos, and decisiveness in the midst of danger. Unhealthy aspects of survival leadership consciousness might be exploitation, over-control, violence, greed, corruption, and territorial behavior. Though these characteristics may also be understood as relational, they do not have a positive effect on relationship. At level one leadership consciousness, survival is the primary focus and it is unlikely that a person working at this level of consciousness would seek spiritual direction.

The first step in the spiritual formation process aligns with level two leadership consciousness where the focus is on developing healthy relationships. In preparing to make the Spiritual Exercises, the spiritual director supports the exercitant in exploring the question: Am I lovable? Am I created to be loved and to love? The exercitant must have some belief that they are loved and lovable to God before they are able to enter the formation process. At level two consciousness, groups and individuals become more aware of the importance of healthy relationships, building open communication, loyalty, and customer and employee satisfaction. A healthy relationship with God is an essential first step in the spiritual formation process. When a person is ready to enter a conscious relationship with God, their image of God and their image of self are questioned.

The focus of the Week One of the Exercises and early spiritual formation stages is to be healed by love while at the same time encountering the problem of evil in the world and understanding our own part in the destruction of life. The exercitant faces their own need for healing from the effects of fear, guilt and weakened self-image, insights facilitated by an encounter with unconditional love from God. Level three consciousness is the development of self-esteem for both individuals and groups where high performance, best practice and healthy processes and systems are developed.

Before entering the transformative process of the Week One dynamic of spiritual formation, directees will have moved beyond Barrett's first level of leadership consciousness, which is the state of survival or crisis management. A moment of disruption or crisis in a person's life can be the catalyst that draws them to consider spiritual direction for support. Scharmer and Kaufer name disruption as a time of opportunity: "the more the old formal system is disrupted and moves toward collapse, the more we will see new patterns of connection and self-organized collaboration emerge."[22] This is true in both individual and corporate settings, creating an opportunity not just to help the person in recovery from crisis, but also to change old frameworks and build a new understanding of their identity, vocation and mission. In the dynamic of Week One, spiritual direction deliberately seeks to uncover interior patterns of disorder rooted in the psyche of a person, and so begin the transformative process. Leaders working at level two consciousness in a healthy way do not run away or hide from their emotions, whereas the unhealthy aspect is to remain defensive and closed:

> When leaders hold subconscious fears about not belonging, they are afraid to deal with their own or others' emotions, they avoid conflicts, are less than truthful in their interpersonal communications, and resort to manipulation to get what they want. They either try to mask their true emotions behind humour or they protect themselves by blaming others when things go wrong.[23]

Week Two Dynamic of Spiritual Formation and Levels of Consciousness

In the Week Two dynamic of spiritual formation the focus is on transformation, integration and interconnection. When the spiritual director works in the dynamic of Week Two of spiritual formation, a sense of call is illuminated. This develops a clearer understanding of leadership capacity and style. By clarifying their identity and vocation before God, the focus of Week Two of the Spiritual Exercises is on a personal relationship with Jesus and how this influences the exercitant's apostolic and creative potential. The invitation to transformation is for exercitants to come to know themselves as called and gifted. This parallels levels four and five of leadership consciousness where transformation, integration and interconnection become central leadership characteristics.

When the directee transitions from the dynamic of Week One to Week Two of spiritual formation, the directee begins to move beyond unhealthy aspects of their own behavior, becoming more conscious of what inhibits their freedom in making decisions. Barrett identifies a similar movement in level 4 leadership consciousness:

---

22. Scharmer and Kaufer, *Leading from the Emerging Future*, 127.
23. Barrett, "Seven Levels of Leadership Consciousness," 4.

> The unhealthy aspects of the first three levels of consciousness begin to dissipate at level 4 consciousness as the leader learns to let go of his or her fears. This may require substantial self-leadership work. The ego must confront the subconscious fear-based beliefs learned in childhood about not feeling safe, not feeling loved, and not feeling respected, and either manage, master, or release them. These are the fears that keep us locked into the motivations of the first three levels of consciousness that represent our deficiency needs.[24]

Spiritual direction in the dynamic of Week Two of spiritual formation shows a strong correlation to what Barrett describes as level four leadership consciousness:

> As the subconscious fears diminish, the leader's ego becomes free to take on the higher motivations of the soul. The soul yearns to find meaning in life through a cause or purpose that lies close to its heart. It wants to find fulfilment by giving its unique gift and exploring its own creativity. At level 4 consciousness the ego begins to learn how to blend its motivations with those of the soul.[25]

Spiritual direction supports a growing awareness of influences on their decision-making, clarifying a unique sense of self, and bringing into consciousness a sense of personal vocation and purpose in the world. Within level four consciousness, individuals and groups are open to transformation, empowerment, adaptability, and continuous learning. The focus is on personal growth, teamwork and innovation.

Level five consciousness is evidenced by internal cohesion and the development of a strong cohesive culture and the capacity for collective action. Leaders with level five consciousness focus on vision, mission and values and display authenticity, integrity, passion, and creativity.

> The inspirational leader is a self-actualized individual who builds a vision and mission for the organisation that inspires employees, customers, and society. They promote a shared set of values and demonstrate congruent behaviours that guide decision-making throughout the organisation. They demonstrate integrity and are living examples of values-based leadership. They walk their talk. They build cohesion and focus by bringing values alignment and mission alignment to the whole company. In so doing, they enhance the company's capacity for collective action. They exploit

---

24. Barrett, "Seven Levels of Leadership Consciousness," 3.
25. Barrett, "Seven Levels of Leadership Consciousness," 3.

opportunities for collaboration. By creating an environment of openness, fairness, and transparency, they build trust and commitment among their people. The culture they create unleashes enthusiasm, passion, and creativity at all levels of the organisation. They are more concerned about getting the best result for everyone rather than their own self- interest. They are focused on the common good. They are creative problem solvers.[26]

In the fourth and fifth levels of consciousness Barrett suggests that unhealthy behaviors begin to dissipate, and the focus moves from safety to transformation and internal cohesion:

> As the subconscious fears diminish, the leader's ego becomes free to take on the higher motivations of the soul. The soul yearns to find meaning in life through a cause or purpose that lies close to its heart. It wants to find fulfilment by giving its unique gift and exploring its own creativity. At level 4 consciousness the ego begins to learn how to blend its motivations with those of the soul.[27]

When a directee comes to spiritual direction with an awareness of their own brokenness and expressing a trust and confidence that God is a benevolent God, they will begin to ask: how can my own skills and gifts be released for the service of others? The focus shifts from self-awareness towards supporting the directee in naming their identity, vocation and mission, and clarifying their unique vocation and leadership style.

Week Three Dynamic of Spiritual Direction and Levels of Consciousness

In Week Three of the Spiritual Exercises the exercitant meditates on the passion and death of Jesus. The challenge here is to be able to enter the experience of suffering and remain committed to following Christ and finding the strength to carry out one's mission. Can they stay faithful to the invitation of God to continue serving when the cost is high? Willing to be vulnerable and stay true to purpose, even in the face of death, becomes a core leadership value in Week Three. This correlates with level six leadership consciousness where leaders work as mentor/partners and are motivated by their need to make a difference in the world, aligning with level six of leadership consciousness.

---

26. Barrett, "Seven Levels of Leadership Consciousness," 6.
27. Barrett, "Seven Levels of Leadership Consciousness," 3.

In level six of consciousness Barrett recognizes: "When we uncover our soul's purpose, we can establish a mission and a vision for our lives and tap into our deepest levels of passion and creativity . . . we begin to make a difference in the world."[28]

> They are true servant leaders in that they recognize and focus on building a working environment where individuals can find their passion and fulfil their potential. . . . They recognize the importance of environmental stewardship and will go beyond the needs of compliance in making their operations environmentally friendly. . . . They care about their people, seeking ways to help employees find personal fulfilment through their work.[29]

At level six, leaders display empathy and utilize intuition in making decisions and the leader's own ego and agenda become secondary. Interviewees identify that the experience of vulnerability through suffering strengthened their identity as a leader.

Week Four Dynamic of Spiritual Direction and Levels Consciousness

In Week Four of the Exercises the exercitant is invited to incarnate their consolation by bringing into fruitful being the graces, gifts and desires that flow from their relationship with God. This movement aligns with level seven of consciousness in which making a difference becomes a way of life. The Week Four dynamic of spiritual direction is about living the call to leadership in service of humanity and the planet, with a sense of deep joy and hope through compassion and humility, and with a focus on future generations. The exercitant will experience deep joy which Marburg describes in her poem:

> *serious joy*[30]
> You know about serious joy
> deep in the chambers of the heart.
> It can't be ignored.
> It is a piece of God's own heart
> thrown to you with dart precision.
> And when it pierces your heart,

---

28. Barrett, "Seven Levels of Leadership Consciousness," 3.
29. Barrett, "Seven Levels of Leadership Consciousness," 6.
30. Marburg, *Grace Undone: Passion*, 118.

God sings the sound
consoling you, filling you
as if with an angel's soft sigh.
Rilke says a smile goes somewhere.
I imagine it touching the atmosphere—
its pink helium making the world
lighter, more buoyant,
spinning the universe.

Week Four aligns with level seven in Barrett's SLOC, which is to be a wisdom figure with a global vision and a holistic perspective on life. Level seven leaders focus on ethics, social responsibility, sustainability, and future generations. They display wisdom, compassion, and humility:

> For them, the world is a complex web of interconnectedness, and they know and understand their role. They act with humility and compassion. They are generous in spirit, patient and forgiving in nature. They are at ease with uncertainty and can tolerate ambiguity. They enjoy solitude and can be reclusive and reflective. Level 7 leaders are admired for their wisdom and vision.[31]

Stages of Spiritual Formation and Organizational Consciousness

The concept of organizational consciousness is an emerging paradigm within the study of organizational development. David Bohm suggests that we have to "share our consciousness and be able to think together, in order to do intelligently whatever is necessary."[32] Organizational consciousness is "the organization's capacity for reflection; a centering point for the organization to 'think' and find the degree of unity across systems; and a link to the organization's identity and self-referencing attributes. It operates at three stages: reflective, social, and collective consciousness."[33] For organizational consciousness to have an impact on organizational development it must be both reflective and anticipatory. When an organization has the capacity to reflect on the past and at the same time look forward to the future it wants to create, the organization can become conscious of patterns of life, death and resurrection that lie within, and thereby raise awareness of what might be holding back any potential for flourishing. Spiritual direction provides

31. Barrett, "Seven Levels of Leadership Consciousness," 5.
32. Bohm, "On Dialogue," 16.
33. Barrett, "Seven Levels of Leadership Consciousness," 1.

a process for exploring organizational life that is simultaneously reflective and anticipatory.

As mentioned previously, ISECP develops organizational consciousness by increasing the organization's capacity for self-reflection and discernment through structured exercises, creating a centering point for the organization to think, reflect and identify degrees of unity and disunity across systems, thereby developing the organization's identity and self-referencing attributes. Barrett provides a framework for understanding organizational consciousness naming seven well-defined levels which he groups into three stages:

Stage one—personal mastery:

- level one: survival—pursuit of profit and shareholder value
- level two: relationship—relationships that support the organization
- level three: self-esteem—high performance systems and processes

Stage two—internal cohesion:

- level four: transformation—adaptability, continuous renewal and learning
- level five: internal cohesion—shared vision, values building community

Stage three—external cohesion:

- level six: making a difference—strategic alliances and partnerships
- level seven: service– service to humanity and planet; social responsibility[34]

Though Barrett proposes a linear model of organizational consciousness, organizational consciousness does not necessarily begin with level one. When an organization is founded on an altruistic purpose, they might begin with attributes of organizational consciousness located in level six of making a difference and level seven of service. However they may not have the skills and attributes located in the earlier levels of consciousness such as basic business needs. Developing organizational consciousness is an ongoing and cyclic journey. Table 5 below details Barrett's SLOC.

34. Barrett, "Seven Levels of Organisational Consciousness," 1.

Positive Focus/ Negative Focus	Levels of Consciousness		Stages of Development	Motivation
Service to humanity and the planet: compassion, humility, future generations, long-term perspective, ethics, compassion, humility.	Service	7	Serving	Social responsibility: Working with other organizations and the stakeholders of the organization in pursuit of societal objectives that enhance the sustainability of humanity and the planet, while deepening the level of internal connectivity inside the organization by fostering compassion, humility and forgiveness
Strategic alliances and partnerships: environmental awareness, community involvement, employee fulfilment, coaching/mentoring.	Making a Difference	6	Integrating	Strategic alliances and partnerships: Building mutually beneficial alliances with other organizations and the local community to protect the environment, while deepening the level of internal connectivity inside the organization by fostering internal cooperation between business units and departments.
Building internal community: shared vision and values, commitment, integrity, trust, passion, creativity, openness, transparency.	Internal Cohesion	5	Self-Actualizing	Internal cohesion strong cohesive culture: Enhancing the organization's capacity for collective action by aligning employee motivations around a singular mission, an inspiring vision and a shared set of values that create commitment and integrity, and unleash enthusiasm, creativity and passion.
Continuous renewal and learning: accountability, adaptability, empowerment, teamwork, goals orientation, personal growth.	Transformation	4	Individuating	Transformation adaptability and continuous learning: Giving employees a voice in decision-making and making them accountable and responsible for their own futures in an environment that supports innovation, continuous improvement, knowledge sharing, and the personal growth and development of all employees.
High performance: systems, processes, quality, best practices, pride in performance. *Bureaucracy, complacency.*	Self-Esteem	3	Differentiating	Self-Esteem High performance systems and processes: Creating a sense of employee pride by establishing policies, procedures, systems, processes and structures that create order and enhance the performance of the organization through the use of best practices. Focus on the reduction of bureaucracy, hierarchy, silo-mentality, power and status seeking, confusion, complacency, and arrogance.

Harmonious relationships: loyalty, open communication, customer satisfaction, friendship. *Manipulation, blame.*	Relationship	2	Conforming	Relationship Relationships that support the organization: Building harmonious relationships that create a sense of belonging and loyalty among employees and caring and connection between the organization and its customers. Focus on the reduction of internal competition, manipulation, blame, internal politics, gender and ethnic discrimination.
Financial stability: shareholder value, organizational growth, employee health, safety. *Control, corruption, greed.*	Survival	1	Surviving	Pursuit of profit and shareholder value: Creating an environment of financial stability, and focusing on the health, safety and welfare of all employees. Focus on the reduction of excessive control and caution, short-term focus, corruption, greed and exploitation.

Table 5 Seven levels of organizational consciousness.[35]

For effective organizational development to occur, the group needs to maintain continuous awareness of how skills and attributes located at each level of consciousness are operating within the group at any given time. Barrett contends that the most successful organizations will have full spectrum consciousness that displays positive aspects of all seven levels of organizational consciousness simultaneously. He describes the process:

> The "lower" needs, levels 1 to 3, focus on the basic needs of the business—the pursuit of profit or financial stability, building employee and customer loyalty, and high-performance systems and processes. The emphasis at these lower levels is on the self-interest of the organisation and its shareholders. Abraham Maslow referred to the needs of these three levels of consciousness as "deficiency" needs. An organisation gains no sense of lasting satisfaction from being able to meet these needs, but the leaders feel a sense of anxiety if these basic needs are not met.
>
> The focus of the fourth level is transformation—a shift from fear-based, rigid, authoritarian hierarchies to more open, inclusive, adaptive systems of governance that empower employees to operate with responsible freedom (accountability).
>
> The "higher" needs, levels 5 to 7, focus on cultural cohesion and alignment, building mutually beneficial alliances and partnerships, long-term sustainability, and social responsibility. Abraham Maslow referred to these as "growth" needs. When these needs are

35. Adapted from Barrett, "Seven Levels of Organisational Consciousness," 1–7.

met, they do not go away. They engender deeper levels of commitment and motivation.[36]

When organizational development is anchored in the group's relationship with God and a desire to be of service to the world, spiritual direction creates a holding environment where organizational consciousness can be explored and developed.

Barrett locates the business skills and capabilities required for ongoing management in the first stage of organizational consciousness. Organizations who focus exclusively on the satisfaction of needs at this level are not usually market leaders, are often internally focused and unable to adapt to change. "There is little enthusiasm among the work force, and there is little innovation and creativity. These organizations are often ruled by fear and are not healthy places of work. Employees often feel frustrated and complain about stress."[37]

Level of Organizational Consciousness	Healthy/Positive focus	Unhealthy/Excessive Focus
Level Three—Self Esteem	High performance: systems, processes, quality, best practices, pride in performance.	Bureaucracy, complacency
Level Two—Relationship	Harmonious relationships: loyalty, open communication, customer satisfaction, friendship.	Manipulation, blame.
Level One—Survival	Financial stability: shareholder value, organizational growth, employee health, safety.	Control, corruption, greed

Table 6 Positive focus and negative focus aspects of levels one to three of SLOC.[38]

The dynamic of spiritual formation in Week Two of the Spiritual Exercises aligns with levels four and five of organizational consciousness

36. Barrett, "Seven Levels of Organisational Consciousness," 3.
37. Barrett, "Seven Levels of Organisational Consciousness," 3.
38. Adapted from Barrett, "Seven Levels of Organisational Consciousness," 1–7.

(Table 7). The focus here is on transformation and continuous learning, adaptability and discernment.

Level of Organizational Consciousness	Spiritual Formation	Focus
Level Five	Week Two: Illumination, the call of Christ, corporate identity.	Building internal community: shared vision and values, commitment, integrity, trust, passion, creativity, openness, transparency.
Level Four		Continuous renewal and learning: accountability, adaptability, empowerment, teamwork, goals orientation, personal growth.

Table 7—Dynamic of Week Two of the Spiritual Exercises and levels four and five SLOC.[39]

> The focus of the fourth level of organizational consciousness is on adaptability, employee empowerment, and continuous learning. The critical issue at this level of consciousness is how to stimulate innovation so that new products and services can be developed to respond to market opportunities. This requires the organization to be agile, flexible and take risks.[40]

I now explore ways in which spiritual direction influences leadership development. The stories come from the experience of twenty-three leaders and spiritual directors who have received spiritual direction and offer their views and perspectives on the research question *How does spiritual direction influence leadership and organizational development* through individual interviews, group interviews or group discussions. I have used pseudonyms throughout.

I explore the influence spiritual direction has on leadership and organizational development, holding the Transforming Experience Framework (TEF) in mind as follows:

---

39. Adapted from Barrett, "Seven Levels of Organisational Consciousness," 1–7.
40. Barrett, "Seven Levels of Organisational Consciousness," 6.

1. the influence spiritual direction has on leadership development with a focus on person, role and Source;
2. the influence spiritual direction has on organizational development with a focus on person, system and context and Source; and
3. the role of the spiritual director in supporting the directee in leadership and organizational development.

I draw on the process of spiritual formation within the framework of the Spiritual Exercises and the Seven Levels of Leadership/Organizational Consciousness to articulate how spiritual direction supports leadership and organizational development (Figure 14).

Figure 14: Framework for understanding how spiritual direction can support leadership and organizational development

Chapter 4

Spiritual Direction and Leadership

Who do you say I am? Mark 8:29 NIV

LEADERSHIP IS A DISPOSITION held by a person in all aspects of their life and work. Leadership may also be understood as authority and responsibility given to a person appointed to a particular role such as CEO or Team Leader within a hierarchical system. Role facilitates action to serve the purpose of the system, and "any action that takes up the purpose of the system is called leader[ship]"[1] In this way then, "there is a mutuality and a consistent dance of followership and leadership."[2]

When a person is given a leadership role within an organization, their belief system, personal experience, psychological state, spirituality, desires, talents and skills contribute to their capacity to enact leadership within the context in which they work and the system to which they belong. Spiritual direction is a process that can help a person bring into consciousness elements that shape their disposition as a leader, and how this might affect the way he or she takes up leadership. Spiritual direction provides a framework for leaders to learn from their experience of their relationship with Source or what participants in this research name as God.

Spiritual direction facilitates a process of spiritual formation, raising a person's consciousness to a deeper understanding of how their personal dynamics operate within their relationship with God. People come to spiritual direction for a variety of reasons and at different stages in life. Some come at a time of crisis, others to discern a vocational call, deepen

---

1. Irvine, "Background to the TEF," 30.
2. Irvine, "Background to the TEF," 30.

their relationship with God, or experience the generative inter-subjectivity of spiritual direction. The process of spiritual formation is progressive and when leadership roles are explored in a spiritual direction session, consciousness of a person's leadership capacity and greater awareness of what influences their leadership style are raised.

Spiritual Formation, Spiritual Direction and Leadership

Spiritual direction provides a framework for individuals to reflect deeply on their inner life and in particular their relationship with God, which influences the way they engage in the world and take up leadership roles. For leadership to be adaptive, the leader needs to have an awareness of personal attachments, fears, limitations and preferences, thereby fostering the ability to be at balance when tackling tough challenges and risking possible failure. John names this clearly: "Once I got into spiritual direction I had more of a sense of who I was, what I was about, what I could do and what I couldn't do." John has held senior leadership positions for most of his working life without the support of spiritual direction. John recognizes a significant change in his own leadership style after entering spiritual direction and offers his observations on the way that spiritual direction can support leadership and organizational development:

> When someone has deliberately undertaken a course which helps them to understand themselves, and they have engaged with others in that pursuit of identity: "Who I am? What are the factors that influence me?" I think it gives a dimension that just technically learning about management styles, as important as it is, [does not]. It adds a certain edge to it, gives a certain dimension because it's centered particularly upon the person. Leadership sometimes comes out as the person who is given a leadership position . . . they can make the decisions and involve others as little or as much as they want to . . . That's leadership but to me it doesn't empower people.
>
> I think that the reason that might happen is because leaders have not really spent a lot of time reflecting upon their own inner workings, their own inner life. . . . Spiritual direction gives me a sense of who I am, how I relate to other people. How I deal with issues that impact me . . . I think that's an advantage . . . particularly within a Christian community . . . I'd be sent to a number of courses that dealt with leadership and management and it seemed . . . it was really about trying to get your office work organized

> so that you could pass papers across and out to someone else . . . paper management rather than people management . . . The person was left out . . . There was never any attempt to say: "Now are we heading in this direction . . . have we asked God to be part of this discussion?"

I asked John whether there is a difference when you check to see if God is in the direction you are heading?

> I think so . . . more serendipitous things happen. Things that you would have never had the foresight, and when these things happen you stand back and look at the whole process and you say "wow, that is beyond us. There is something of God in that graciousness." . . . I can be very efficient in my duties and tick off the tasks that I have but the most important task is: What can we do together? And if I am in a leadership role, how can I assist that person, what help can I be to that person? Without . . . taking over.
>
> Once I got into spiritual direction I had more of a sense of who I was, what I was about, what I could do and what I couldn't do. And as far as organizational things were concerned, I had to really rely on other people, people who could do the nitty gritty of things about organizing something and empower them to do it and work with them on that.

I asked John whether knowing your own self helps you to empower others—is that what you are saying?

> Yes. Because I have found knowing myself empowers me to be the person that I should be. I have spent too much of my life I think with cap in hand and doing the right thing and always a kind of fear that I might get it wrong and if I got things wrong then that would reflect badly on me. . . . Things really changed when I got involved in the whole process [of spiritual direction].

John recognizes that spiritual direction helped him understand that leadership is not about pushing papers around; it is about bringing himself fully to the role and empowering others. Spiritual direction supports the leader in developing interior freedom by exploring inner dynamics and reflecting on the past to notice what is helpful to their personal leadership style and what ought to be discarded. As John notes: "Spiritual direction gives me a sense of who I am, how I relate to other people, how I deal with issues that impact . . . me." He also names the importance of his relationship with God and self-reflection, which is a common theme for all participants.

Strengthening Spirit–Releasing Potential

Spiritual Direction as a Reflective Process for Leaders

Spiritual direction provides a safe place and a structure for leaders to reflect on their experience of leadership. Sarah recounts the difference between undertaking secular leadership courses and courses that had a focus on spiritual leadership. When the leadership course was supported with the reflective process of spiritual direction, Sarah felt able to take up her leadership role more fully, knowing more about her own dynamics in a lasting way:

> I am doing a responsible leadership subject at . . . University. . . . They will put up a lot of vignettes of various Harvard Professors . . . saying . . . how important reflection is. . . . In the course, yes reflection is very important, but they are not necessarily guiding people on *how* they can reflect. . . . It's all at the thinking, not the heart level . . . almost cerebral. Whereas in the Group Leadership Course and in the Discernment Course, which was backed up by spiritual direction, it really is able to take flesh, so it is authentic. It really gets into the system of *who I am* . . . it is that kind of lasting improvement of self.

Sarah echoes John in noting that spiritual direction offers a framework for reflecting on and coming to know *who I am* in the leadership role. Self-knowledge is also a key theme that the discussion group of spiritual directors identify.

Leadership Identity and Relationship with God

Spiritual direction creates a safe place where directees can allow themselves to be vulnerable and go deeply into the question of their identity as leader. There is a power shift in the way a directee sees him or herself as a leader when their relationship with God is brought into an awareness of their leadership style.

There is a correlation between a person's image of God and their image of self, and the ways in which this influences their leadership style. A person's image of self is the way in which they experience the self and is "made up of their attitude towards themselves; the extent to which they do or do not feel loved, valued, appreciated, competent and purposeful."[3] In conversation with experienced spiritual directors who were giving spiritual

---

3. Paulin-Campbell, "Impact of the Imaginal and Dialogical," 5.

direction to leaders during a leadership course, the impact of a person's image of God began to emerge:

> Martin: How you imagine yourself is how you are. If I imagine myself that I am a poor bastard or I am . . . hard done by, well that's actually how you will be. And that is linked very much with your image of God then. I am my imagination.

> Mary: We did quite a bit on image of God and how she saw God, because it . . . [came] out of her discovery of who she was, how she was relating, and linked into family stuff. . . . I think she knew it intellectually before . . . but something happened that it hit her, and she realized that was a barrier and a real block in her leadership but also actually in her inner world and her prayer . . . blocking her leadership.

> Joan: I think for one of my people, that is true in a very different way. It is the sense that God likes things to be nice, so let's keep things nice and that's what's holy. But her awareness over the weeks was opened up that actually . . . Jesus was not always nice and in fact quite abrasive. And that this was . . . part of what it might be to be a leader; that at times she might have to be that person who is abrasive or turns things upside down even though the others won't like it.

Spiritual direction brings into consciousness images projected onto God, and the effect a maladaptive image of God has on a person's leadership style. Ralph Hood *et al.*, observe, "levels of global self-esteem are positively related to adaptive God images (e.g., image of God as loving, nurturing, caring, or forgiving) and negatively related to maladaptive God images (e.g., images of God as rejecting, controlling, punishing or distant)"[4] The premise of spiritual direction is that in strengthening a person's relationship with God, he or she will clarify his or her own identity, vocation and mission:

- identity—who am I as a person;
- vocation—what is my deep call or purpose in life; and
- mission—how and with whom will I live out that purpose.[5]

---

4. Aten et al., *Psychology of Religion*, 137.
5. Roemer and Schemel, *Beyond Individuation to Discipleship*, 89.

It follows then that who or what the directee imagines God to be will have a direct influence on whom they see themselves to be.

> There is a dynamic interplay between image of God and image of self. As one shifts so does the other. As the image of God begins to shift through imaginal dialogue the experience of seeing oneself reflected in the eyes of an unconditionally loving God changes self-image.[6]

John Veltri describes an image of God as an "unreflected spontaneous attitude that influences my responses to God. Hence it can be a caricature, a stereotype, a hidden belief and it is influencing the stance I take when I am before God. It is intimately linked to my attitudes towards life and others. It is like a locked-in affective response."[7]

If a person comes for spiritual direction, the spiritual director can assume that to some extent the directee has a desire to consciously integrate their spiritual life with the rest of their life, (though the divide is an artificial one), to deepen their relationship with God and learn about themselves. It is important that the spiritual director clarifies with the directee who God is, at this time, for this directee.

> [Images of God are] formed by the early experience of significant relationships especially parental relationships and by the person's interpretation of God's role in the events and experiences of his/her life. It is also made up of knowledge about God gleaned from parents and other significant adults; catechesis and cultural images of God. It is the expectation that the person, out of all these experiences, brings to the relationship with God.[8]

Sally's image of God, image of self and leadership style changed considerably through the experience of receiving spiritual direction. Sally works as a minister of a large parish and came to spiritual direction exhausted and on the brink of a breakdown. Her image of God at the beginning of spiritual direction was "Taskmaster". If you work hard you will be loved. This image manifested in her leadership role as being stuck in working hard to look good for others. In an interview with Sally, she begins by speaking about her exhaustion from the pressures of work.

---

6. Paulin-Campbell, "Impact of the Imaginal and Dialogical," 1.
7. Veltri, *Orientations for Spiritual Growth*, 3.
8. Paulin-Campbell, "Impact of the Imaginal and Dialogical," 6.

> I start to think, what does God really want me to do, especially as a minister.... I have to do all the parish work, the administration, the visitation, the preaching whatever, but can I really minister [to] people and help them to get closer to God? ... I find that I drive them very hard to work out some program instead of really responding to God.
>
> What God wants is to have a closer relationship with Him, instead of working very hard.... I think God desires to get closer to us. He is not asking us to work very hard ... sometimes I was quite lost and confused, and I ask myself whether I am working for the Kingdom of God or whether I am working for my own glory? ... I work very hard just to prove myself, to prove to the others that I can be a good minister.... I can motivate people to do something. I can get the parish [to] develop some new programs. But I think for all these things, I get lost because I was doing something to prove that I can.
>
> [My spiritual director] spent much time ... to help me to go back to the love of God. How God is looking at me? ... The difficulty is I always listened to the voice of the bad spirit that I am not good enough. I haven't done it well. I haven't worked at something well.... I am driving myself very hard ... I have to work hard so that people would like me or would love me or ... would accept me. So, if I am still having this kind of thinking ... when I go back to work ... I will be back to the past. I will work very hard.

The spiritual direction sessions shifted Sally's image of God and transformed her leadership style from being driven and driving others towards a disposition of compassion towards self and others, and her understanding of authority transformed from a position of power to a disposition of love.

> He is God and not me; I am just working with God. I am just responding to Him, and only ... [when] I experience the compassionate love of God, then I can be a compassionate companion to work with others ... I can lead people in a compassionate way ... It has helped me to know more about my leadership style authority is not power but love ... the spiritual direction session has helped me to experience deeper the love of God so that I can love myself and I can have a greater capacity to love others in my leadership role.

Spiritual direction facilitates the exposure of a false or negative image of God being unconsciously lived out by Sally, suggesting that in a ternary style of leadership, spiritual direction facilitates an exploration of characteristics of the third element being held by the leader. The leader begins to realize how this may be impacting their perception of what they believe is being asked of them as a leader. Table 8 demonstrates Sally's transition from being stuck in a leadership style of working hard and trying to please others towards a more compassionate and loving leadership style as she journeyed with her spiritual director.

Image of God	Week One Healed by love	Week Two Transformation, integration, interconnection	Week Three Committed – anointed	Week Four Commissioned – serious joy	Image of God
Taskmaster – if you work hard you will be loved.	Stuck in working hard to look good for others – "I am driving myself very hard because I … have to work hard so that people would like me or would love me or would accept me."	He is God and not me; I am just working with God. I am just responding to Him, and only … [when] I experience the compassionate love of God then I can be a compassionate companion to work with others.	I can lead people in a compassionate way.	It has helped me to know more about my leadership style … authority is not power but love. The spiritual direction session has helped me to experience deeper the love of God so that I can love myself and I can have a greater capacity to love others in my leadership role.	God is love.

Table 8—Sally's transition through the process of spiritual direction.

Ternary Leadership and Relationship with God

Establishing a loving relationship with God is central to the dynamic of spiritual formation in Week One of the Spiritual Exercises. Alistair Mant's theory on ternary leadership highlights how a person's relationship with God might contribute to his or her leadership style. In his book *Leaders We Deserve*,[9] he identifies two distinct personality types when it comes to organizational leadership. The first is "binary" or a two-part relationship that involves me as the leader and the other,

> in which the individual is swamped, despite himself, by the interpersonal aspect of relationships. In this mode the main thing is to control, dominate or seduce the Other in the interests of personal survival.[10]

9. Mant, *Leaders We Deserve*.
10. Mant, *Leaders We Deserve*, 4.

The second personality type is "ternary," where this is a three-part relationship, involving me as leader, the other, and purpose:

> interpersonal power is regulated, some of the time anyway, by some "third corner"—an institution, a purpose or an idea. People who think this way value the third corner, see what life is about. Their instinct is to ask not, "Shall I win?" but rather, "What's it for?"[11]

Ternary leaders, Mant argues,

> Can run personal risks in the pursuit of some higher purpose and observe themselves, as from a great height, in their own interpersonal relationships. . . . The "third corner", be it an institution, a higher purpose or just an engaging idea, affords a certain graceful repose. In the ternary mode, it is actually possible to stop and think.[12]

In the binary form of leadership human beings interact in either survival or dominance mode. When a third element is introduced behavior is modified, mediated or otherwise understood by reference to some third abstracted element. Figure 15 shows the characteristics of binary and ternary leadership.

Two-part (Binary)	Three-part (Ternary)
interpersonal person power flight/fight (survival) conflict win/lose defence raiding	institutional role/task authority dependence (work) consensus share resolution building

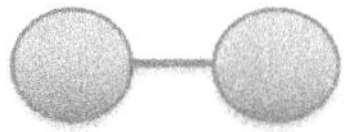

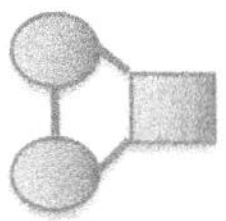

Figure 15: Characteristics of binary and ternary leadership styles. [13]

---

11. Mant, *Leaders We Deserve*, 5.
12. Mant, *Leaders We Deserve*, 6.
13. Mant, *Leaders We Deserve*, 11.

Healed by Love, Self-esteem, Differentiating

Before entering the transformative process of the Week One dynamic of spiritual formation, directees will have moved beyond Barrett's first level of leadership consciousness, the state of survival or crisis management. A moment of disruption or crisis in a person's life can be the catalyst that draws them to consider spiritual direction for support. As noted earlier, Scharmer and Kaufer name disruption as a time of opportunity: "the more the old formal system is disrupted and moves toward collapse, the more we will see new patterns of connection and self-organized collaboration emerge."[14] This is true in both individual and corporate settings and creates an opportunity not just to help the person in recovery from crisis, but also to change old frameworks and build a new understanding of their identity, vocation and mission. In the dynamic of Week One, spiritual direction deliberately seeks to uncover interior patterns of disorder rooted in the psyche of a person, and so begin the transformative process. Leaders working at level two consciousness in a healthy way do not run away or hide from their emotions, whereas the unhealthy aspect is to remain defensive and closed:

> When leaders hold subconscious fears about not belonging, they are afraid to deal with their own or others' emotions, they avoid conflicts, are less than truthful in their interpersonal communications, and resort to manipulation to get what they want. They either try to mask their true emotions behind humour or they protect themselves by blaming others when things go wrong.[15]

Disruption and Vulnerability

A major life disruption such as loss of a relationship, loss of physical capacity, or loss of employment, can bring a person to seek spiritual direction to face the disruption and their vulnerability. Mark, an executive officer of a large government body, speaks about his experience of beginning spiritual direction in a time of crisis:

> I was the director of personnel of a government department and there was major restructuring... my job was made redundant and so I left and then I fell apart. I didn't recognize it at the time, but

---

14. Scharmer and Kaufer, *Leading from the Emerging Future*, 127.
15. Barrett, "Seven Levels of Leadership Consciousness," 4.

it had been building for years because I had just pushed myself into my career. I was working 60–70 hours a week. I was doing my Master's degree part-time . . . we had young kids, mortgage all of that stuff and I was just basically burnt out but didn't recognize this until this happened and it tapped a whole lot of things for me about failure. . . .

I had started to go to therapy. . . . I came across this Jungian analyst and . . . she said to me . . . "have you thought of going back to your faith?" Well I hadn't been inside a church for 15 years. . . . She gave me the card of [a spiritual director] so I rang [him] up a few months later . . . I remember sitting down and saying to him "I don't even know why I am here, and I am not really sure what I am supposed to do." And he said, "Oh well just sit down and have a chat." And that was what he did, and I didn't even know it was spiritual direction. But he gradually . . . drew me around to talk a bit more about God.

This went on for about six months . . . it was very important because he listened in a different way to what the analyst had. . . . I would go to this analyst and he'd sit behind a big desk . . . if I was two minutes late, we would have a big analysis about why I was late. . . . You always felt like you were on the spot with him and . . . [spiritual direction] wasn't like that. . . . There was a gentleness and we just kind of meandered. . . . It was the listening. . . . I don't know that he understood things in great depth psychologically. You know he was an experienced man . . . to have somebody, another man listen to me deeply, that was very profound for me it was very significant. . . . My experience is that that can be quite transformative in itself without having to do much else. . . . Hence my growing belief . . . that there is more common ground between the therapist and the spiritual director than differences. . . . If you trained to be an analyst back in the late eighties or early nineties, or even today from what I have heard recently, religion was never part of their training, never part of their conversation and for two generations of analysts after Freud, religion was diagnosed as part of the problem that needed to be cured. . . . my experience of that first retreat is that God took over.

. . . I came out of that retreat knowing that my life would not be the same and yet I had no idea . . .what that was going to look like, all I knew is that I wanted to get to know Jesus more and I wasn't sure where that was going to take me but I knew that I didn't have any choice. This is where I was drawn.

Though Mark was not actively practicing his faith when commencing spiritual direction, the restoration of his relationship with God facilitated the beginning of his journey back into life and beginning a new career. Mark moved from being driven in his leadership style to being drawn towards a new future.

Indifference in Ignatian Spirituality

Indifference is a central characteristic of Ignatian spirituality. Indifference in the Exercises is not regarded as an attitude of apathy or lack of concern, but a disposition of freedom from attachments. In the *Spiritual Exercises* Ignatius invites the exercitant to be indifferent to all created things in order to be free to choose the path that will lead us more closely to God and towards freedom from disordered attachments that distort our decision-making:

> We must make ourselves indifferent to all created things, as far as we are allowed free choice and are not under any prohibition. Consequently, as far as we are concerned, we should not prefer health to sickness, riches to poverty, honor to dishonor, a long life to a short life. The same holds for all other things [23].

As the spiritual director listens to the directee share their experiences, they are listening to what might impede freedom. James Martin describes disordered attachments,

> those things we are so attached to that they keep us from God. It could be a desire for popularity or a love of money or an obsession with perfect health. Or maybe it's something even darker, like an unhealthy relationship that keeps you from freedom.
>
> Another way of looking at this is as an entanglement. When Jesus first calls the disciples by the Sea of Galilee, the Gospels say the fishermen "dropped their nets," to follow him. Those nets are a great emblem for all that keeps us entangled in life.[16]

Anne has a leadership role in a large network of educational facilities. She describes the movement she experienced in spiritual direction during the Week One of the Exercises. Accepting herself as being flawed, freed her from her attachment of a self-serving ego. She had to *get things right* in order to be seen by others as getting things right, stopping her from

---

16. Martin, "Millennial."

speaking what was her actual truth. Anne describes the freedom that she received in coming to this new disposition:

> What I love is that when I can recognize the tendencies creeping in, that I know will lead me astray, it is less ego driven, and then I am far less likely to speak self-serving truth. And far more likely to speak a truth that is actual truth even if it's going to cost me.

Spiritual formation begins with being open to noticing what might be keeping me trapped in disordered patterns of behavior. When Anne describes what spiritual direction and making the Exercises has done for her, she describes becoming grounded in acceptance of the self she is, rather than being attached to a self-image of who she thinks she ought to be in order to be liked by others:

> So much more operating out of the heart space, which is not to the neglect of the head... it is not that I am a different person; it is just that it [spiritual direction] has unlocked potential.... I think I had pigeonholed myself to be: I am like this because this is what I am good at. I am a logical, reasonable, rational, practical person who gets things done and takes care of details and all of those sorts of things. And so that's who I became... which is not to say that it was false, but it was sort of limited... I think there is just so much more. I don't feel trapped by that anymore, so...
>
> I knew that I was unhappy in my work... I just didn't know how to escape that.... I understand now what my hooks are, what brings me down... what leads to that sort of negative... spiritual battle inside, that I will always take things personally,... and I think that that is a real challenge in work like mine. If someone doesn't like what you are offering, then I will think, "Oh I am not doing it right" or "there is something wrong with what I am doing."

Spiritual direction supported Anne to differentiate herself from her colleagues, while building a sense of self-worth and increased self-esteem (level three of the SLLC). Pam, a spiritual director, speaks of a major restructure in her workplace where she had been supporting some of the staff using spiritual direction and short forms of the Spiritual Exercises. I asked her whether this had an influence on her workplace.

> There's been some impact... I can definitely see that in some immediate colleagues because we have had this big transition and restructure and so most of the old guard are leaving. But some of them are leaving to embrace a call—you know, something they

have long wanted to do, and they are even beginning to name it like that.

I ask whether they are leaving in freedom?

> Yes, I think they are. There is that slight shift, you know kicking and screaming for a while and railing against the way it has all been done and then movement to . . . what is really stirring in them and their deep desire.

So, what about the ones who are staying?

> Fear, trapped, can't see how they will get something anywhere else or trying to appease, violation.

Indifference in this case means letting go and trusting the unknown, even in the face of redundancy. Fear keeps people trapped in old patterns and stuck places. The desire to move towards the freedom of indifference was evident in all interviews conducted. The disposition of indifference is a central characteristic of leadership for participants in this book.

Disordered Tendencies and Vulnerability

Having clarified images of God operating at the beginning of the spiritual formation journey, the directee will then start to become aware of his or her own patterns of disorder. For spiritual direction to support leadership development, the directee must be willing to be vulnerable and look at the way in which he or she might limit his or her own capacity for leadership. Sarah is a leader in the education field where she works with young adults. She speaks about what "going off track" looks like for her and how spiritual direction is more than positive thinking:

> Its disorder . . . what my disorder will look like will be quite different from somebody else's. . . . Potentially for me, my disorder could be going down negative pathways and maybe falling into depression or deep resentment and bitterness. I know that is one of my weaknesses . . . but having another voice in there . . . saying: "What do you think God wants in this situation?" or speaking the truth. . . . Some of it is unpacking lies, but some of it is also just opening me up to what opportunities are there . . . other options that could be possible.

I asked Sarah whether this could just be positive thinking?

> No. Positive thinking . . . can only go so far. . . . It engages the head, but I am not so sure how far it goes in engaging the heart and the soul, which has lasting impact. Whereas positive thinking might get somebody through a day or two days, or if they are really vigilant maybe six months, but I don't think it has the lasting impact. . . . I don't know what you would call it, the shaping of the soul or the heart and the mind . . .
>
> It helps me travel more and more on the journey of who God calls me to be . . . the gifts and skills and the desires that he has placed there. . . . God created me and everybody else for this freedom and it helps me be more of who I am and not be afraid to use the skills and call the skills for what they are that God has given me.

Sarah goes on to explain that spiritual direction is empowering her to be her unique herself.

> I've got all these skills so maybe I should be doing this type of role, but it's also the freedom to say no . . . where exactly are you calling me to be?" And the freedom to say . . . you are choosing to be in this space because you feel as though that is where you are called to be and there is greater peace in that . . . [and] confidence as well.

When a directee comes to spiritual direction with an awareness of their own brokenness and a trust and confidence that God is a benevolent God, they begin to ask: how can my own skills and gifts be released for the service of others? This question opens them for further exploration within the dynamic of Week Two, Three and Four of the Exercises, which parallel levels 4–7 of Barrett's levels of leadership consciousness. The focus shifts from self-awareness towards supporting the directee in naming their identity, vocation and mission, and clarifying their unique vocation and leadership style.

Called to Service

In the Week Two dynamic of spiritual formation the focus is on transformation, integration and interconnection. When the directee transitions from the dynamic of Week One to Week Two of spiritual formation, the directee begins to move beyond unhealthy aspects of their own behavior, becoming more conscious of what inhibits their freedom to make decisions. Spiritual direction in the dynamic of Week Two of spiritual formation illuminates a sense of call and develops a clearer understanding of leadership capacity and style, paralleling the development levels four and five of leadership consciousness.

Participants in this research rarely spoke about religion; rather they consistently spoke about relationship with Source (generally Jesus and/or God) and how this relationship affects their engagement in the world. The word "religion" was used *thirty-two* times in contrast to "relationship" which was mentioned *three hundred and eight* times. Fiona, a spiritual director and psychotherapist explains that she is speaking about spirituality rather than religion: "we are spiritual beings on a human journey . . . We all have the spiritual . . . I think it is when we engage with . . . a sense of purpose of something greater than ourselves or when life is not just about us, about me."

In the TEF, connectedness with Source is understood to be present in all domains of experience (person, system, context and role) and is present at all times whether conscious or not.

> Connectedness with Source is present in any action that is taken both as person and on behalf of the system. . . . Every action I take expresses a level of commitment and motivation to some form of truth. . . . The overlap area of role also includes the word "vocation". It is a word that indicates that through behavior in role is perceived the amalgam of the beliefs, faith, and spirituality of those on whose behalf action is taken.[17]

Connectedness with God in the Week Two dynamic is primarily facilitated via a relationship with Jesus.

Relationship with Jesus, with Self and with God

A personal relationship with Jesus was identified by participants in this research as being important to them and to the spiritual direction relationship. Anne identifies her relationship with Jesus as being at "the foundation of everything . . . and . . . is the foundation of all others. Therefore, if your foundation is perfect that is what you are operating from."

Intersubjective theory suggests, "selfhood is found through recognizing, or "mutual", relations with the other." [18] For Christian leaders,

---

17. Bazalgette, "Connectedness With Source," 255.
18. Harding, "Intersubjectivity and Large Groups," 35.

engaging in spiritual direction can facilitate mutual recognition via personal relationship with Jesus, releasing the potential that lies within the self. Harding, building on the work of Jessica Benjamin, explains,

> These are reciprocal relations of assertion and recognition through which the subjectivity of the self and the other is affirmed. Mutuality implies the subjectivity of the other is required for one's own self to be recognized. This means it is in our own interest for the other to be real, not solely a projection of our inner world. Mutual relations facilitate agency and creativity.[19]

The *Spiritual Exercises* intentionally invite the exercitant into situations of imaginal dialogue with God, Jesus, Mary and other characters in the scriptures.[20] Spiritual direction explores the intersubjective encounter of engaging in dialogue with biblical characters.

> From a theological perspective, the interaction of the retreatant in the Gospel Contemplation is one in which, through faith, there can be a transformative encounter with an other or others, who though not physically present are nevertheless not merely a construct of the imagination but exist also beyond the imagination of the retreatant. Even if one were to deny this theological perspective, from a psychological view the retreatant is shaped and changed through the encounters with those people and situations which constitute the narratives which are entered into via the imagination.[21]

Dialogical Self Theory (DST) developed by Hermans considers the multi-voiced self in which our mind takes up multiple "I-positions" representing minds of other people and various points of view typical for other nations, cultures or social backgrounds.[22] Experienced spiritual director Martin explains: "the relationship with Jesus is much more than another "I-position" or a relationship with the self. There is something distinctly different. Prayer is not simply self-talk. It is a relationship with a transcendental Other." Participants in the research are clear that encounter with

---

19. Harding, "Intersubjectivity and Large Groups," 36; Benjamin, *Bonds of Love*; Benjamin, *Like Subjects, Love Objects*.

20. Paulin-Campbell, "Impact of the Imaginal and Dialogical," 19.

21. Paulin-Campbell, "Impact of the Imaginal and Dialogical," 79.

22. Hermans, "International Institute for the Dialogical Self." The foundations of DST come from American Philosopher William James (1842–1910) and Russian philosopher, literary critic and semiotician Mikhail Bakhtin (1895–1975).

Strengthening Spirit–Releasing Potential

Jesus was more than another "I-position" and that a relationship with Jesus facilitates agency and creativity.

Jennifer, a religious leader, recognizes that hearing God speak to her is different to other voices in her head because it is always fresh:

> All those "I-positions" are stored in your filing system, you have got them there. It's all part of your history but with God it's often new or it's . . . different, it's something fresh and beyond you that you didn't dream up yourself and you recognize that—Oh that's got to be God.

Experienced spiritual director Veronica describes how she relates to Jesus and how in her understanding it is possible that Jesus is real in the here and now:

> Can I have a relationship with him *[Jesus]*? Yes. And is it a helpful relationship? Yes. Because I see in him something I would want to model my life upon and somehow or another, when I spend time with him, I become more like him. . . . I become that truth, that person who can stand up for what I believe in and dare to be wrong. Which I think Jesus probably did too, dare to be wrong, and dare to be right.

I asked Veronica how could she spend time with him?

> How can I spend time with anybody who has died? . . . I have conversations with him . . . it is all about anamnesis which is the experience of bringing to life the one whom you remember . . . he becomes present in the conversation.

Pam explains why having a relationship with Jesus is important to her. She begins by sharing her experience of seeing the face of the child Jesus in the face of a young boy traveling on the train with his grandfather and how this (experiential) relationship had an impact on her identity and capacity for creativity:

> It's through that relationship *[with Jesus]*, that's the core relationship. . . . the transforming relationship. . . . It was about meeting Jesus in his humanity . . . I remember my director saying, "When you are travelling around have a little look at other people with children at that age." . . . I was on the train and I saw a grandfather and a little lad, and . . . that was a turning point. . . . It sounds so simple, but it really was a turning point.

Was it something about the humanity?

> Yeah and the nearness . . . I loved that. Since then, the more that I can think of him and imagine him as . . . not knowing what's coming to him and allowing him to be like that, the better. I find that so attractive and helpful . . . what he says and does and how he has relationships, his relationship with God, his anointing. That whole parallel journey of his life and my life, our life, I really love all that.

I check with Pam: But what I am hearing . . . is something about coming to know that humanity of Jesus as that little vulnerable person with someone who loves him to bits and the reality of that . . . and your life parallels that too, you can be just as remarkable, you're anointed, you're called.

Yes, absolutely! It is utterly central.

The data is clear insofar as interviewees experience their relationship with Jesus as transformative and real, and that this has a positive effect on the way they take up their identity in the world. What emerges next is that this relationship with Jesus is about allowing vulnerability to be present, and through vulnerability creativity is enabled.

Vulnerability, Personal Power and Creativity

In the Week One dynamic of spiritual formation, vulnerability is described as a willingness to be broken open to look at our own patterns of disorder. Here in the Week Two dynamic vulnerability takes on a different aspect, drawing the directee to take up personal power and creativity.

Through the support of spiritual direction, Pam notices that her relationship with Jesus takes her to a place of vulnerability. Once she has been freed from being stuck in old patterns, Pam becomes open to new opportunities and moves into a new and creative space. I check with Pam whether she is saying that moving into relationship with Jesus requires vulnerability?

> Yes . . . vulnerability. When I think of the little child on the train the vulnerability . . . feels delightful really . . . it's tender . . . and the child is vulnerable; it can't manage being on the train by itself . . . it's a different vulnerability than adult relationships.

Relationship with Jesus, relationship with others, relationship with self?

> Yes, with self. And that's a more recent understanding and recognition . . . standing up . . . I only recently learnt that humility can mean . . . that. But relationship with others is no good without the

> relationship with Jesus . . . and that's a frustration of my workplace, it feels like it is all about us, and we are the resource, and it's not the creative friendship and intimacy of God.

When you bring that relationship with Jesus or God, is that when the creative stuff flows?

> Yes, yes, yeah absolutely . . . Oh, God is always new . . . and . . . the bad spirit is the contrary of that: being stuck in a pattern or whatever. That was a real aha! It's always going to be new and the new things that we are engaged in and new understandings.

The movement described by Pam of being freed from old patterns and being open to new opportunities to move into a new and creative space aligns with Barrett's level five of leadership consciousness in which self-actualization becomes the core of leadership identity:

> Level 5: The inspirational leader is a self-actualized individual who builds a vision and mission for the organisation that inspires employees, customers, and society. They promote a shared set of values and demonstrate congruent behaviours that guide decision-making throughout the organisation. They demonstrate integrity and are living examples of values-based leadership. They walk their talk. . . . By creating an environment of openness, fairness, and transparency, they build trust and commitment among their people. The culture they create unleashes enthusiasm, passion, and creativity at all levels of the organisation. They are more concerned about getting the best result for everyone rather than their own self- interest. They are focused on the common good. They are creative problem solvers.[23]

Speaking from her experience as a spiritual director, Veronica names a loving relationship with the self as central to the possibility of potential and creativity being released in spiritual direction.

> Well it's even about relationship with self . . . it's about loving that self you are created to be. . . . In Ignatian spirituality that's probably what we are doing [releasing] apostolic zeal, apostolic endeavor. If I love God so much, I will do anything . . . for that relationship. . . . I will walk through fire . . . I will go to the cross for that relationship because it is just the only life that really matters. . . . I think God wants you to be who you are and if that involves walking through fire, well then that's what it does. I think you walk through fire for

---

23. Barrett, "Seven Levels of Leadership Consciousness," 6.

love. And you know, people like Ghandi, he walked through fire for the sake of the people and for the sake of a principle and for the sake of peace, and so he was being who he had to be, and he got shot. . . . I mean they're extreme things. It would be quite easy for me to justify not doing that: to say, "God doesn't want you to do that Ghandi, or God doesn't want you to put yourself in difficult positions Veronica." But I, you know God just wants you to be loving, but what is love? Love is quite a—it's got a lot of faces.

In my own experience as a spiritual director, when the directee becomes aware of their potential through the eyes of God or Jesus, the limitations they place on themselves can begin to dissipate. Author Joseph Jaworski, who began his career as an attorney and has devoted most of his life to exploring the deeper dimensions of transformational leadership, echoes the hypothesis that connection to God releases potential:

> There is a creative Source of infinite potential enfolded in the universe. Connection to this Source leads to the emergence of new realities—discovery, creation, renewal and transformation. We are partners in the unfolding of the universe . . . Humans can learn to draw from the infinite potential of the Source by choosing to follow a disciplined path toward self-realization and love, the more powerful energy in the universe.[24]

Spiritual direction helps a person to tap into and explore the creative potential enfolded in the universe and to discover new possibilities by supporting directees in exploring their connectedness to Source. "Everyone has access to Source. The capacity to connect to Source is "an enduring truth." There is no one religion or specific belief system that grants access to this realm."[25] For participants in this research, relationship with Jesus is one way in which they experience connectedness to Source and discover potential within themselves. The data also reveals an invitation to become more like Jesus and be willing to become Christ as an emerging concept.

Becoming Christ

In a conversation with eight experienced spiritual directors, we grappled with themes emerging themes from the data around the concept of relationship with Jesus, and the differences between: (i) becoming Christ-like,

24. Jaworski, *Source*, 136–37.
25. Jaworski, *Source*, 197.

(ii) becoming Christ, and (iii) taking on the role of Christ. When interviewees talk about their relationship with Jesus, they are speaking about an historical figure upon whom they can model their lives by remembering his way of being and bringing his story alive through memory and imaginative contemplation. As I was curious about the power of a personal relationship with Jesus, I presented the following idea to the discussion group:

> Bruce Irvine from the Grubb Institute, invites leaders to understand that followership of Jesus enables one to find, make and take the role in today's world of a Messiah or Christ by following the example Jesus gave us.
>
> Bazalgette explains: "Jesus was not actually baptized 'Jesus Christ' rather Christ was the role that he took, and just as Siddhārtha Gautama took the role of Buddha, Ghandi took the role of Mahatma, and ancient Sanskrit writings talk about Braham. These are roles which as we take them in the world in which we find ourselves, we begin to find the way in which we connect with Ultimate Reality, and the domain in the TEF which we call connectedness with Source."[26]
>
> So, are we saying we are forming leaders in the image of Christ or to take up the role of Christ?

The reflection group responds first by grappling with the theological implications of the proposal and second considering whether we are baptized Christ, born Christ, or called to become Christ, or Christlike:

> Veronica: That is a huge theological question.
>
> Fiona: It is really important though . . . who is Jesus if he is not Christ? . . . I am doing a theological unit this semester and just that idea of . . . who gave him that title? He didn't give it to himself. . . . As I understand in Baptism we are baptized as Christ aren't we? Prophet, priest and king. What else does Messiah mean? These are all really important questions I am also . . . wondering around the juxtaposition in that guy's quote. What is he saying about . . . about Christ, Buddha, Ghandi . . . I feel quite disturbed by this. What would Jesus say about this? Would he say this is what he took up?

---

26. John Bazalgette speaking about the philosophy of Bruce Irvine at the book launch (April 14, 2016) for *The Transforming Experience Framework*.

> Veronica: . . . I've got that question too are these characters all equal? . . . Was Jesus born Christ or did Jesus become Christ? . . . It is like us thinking about ourselves as spiritual directors. Are we born spiritual directors or do we become spiritual directors? So, my question is: I have a sense, I feel this rather deeply, that we are called not to be like Christ but we are called to be Christ. And I think there is a massive difference between those two things.

Veronica raises an interesting question about role and vocation and whether to take up a vocational role is something we are born with or it is an emergent reality that is brought into fruition when person, system and context intersect. Jesuit priest and spiritual director Herbert Alphonso notes,

> [spiritual formation] of a person is not "input" from the outside, but the releasing of liberating or drawing out of the rich inner resources that reside within that person. . . . To help a person discover or discern these inmost resources of "personal vocation" is then to radically and fundamentally to form or educate him/her in the deepest sense.[27]

In this sense vocation and role differ. In spiritual direction it is understood that vocation lies within a person and the task of the spiritual direction session is to help release the vocational potential, and in releasing potential, leadership capacity is enabled. To become Christ is perhaps a disposition in the world that would influence any role a person might take, particularly in leadership. The word "Christ" comes from *Christos*, a Greek word meaning "anointed." It is the equivalent of the word *mashiach*, or Messiah, in Hebrew. To be the Christ, or Messiah, is to have sacred oil poured on one's head, because God has chosen the person for a special task. The act of anointing with sacred oil emphasizes that it is *God* who ordains a person and gives authority to act as God's representative. Saint Paul describes *Christ*,

> The Son is the image of the invisible God, the firstborn over all creation. For in him all things were created: things in heaven and on earth, visible and invisible, whether thrones or powers or rulers or authorities; all things have been created through him and for him. He is before all things, and in him all things hold together. And he is the head of the body, the church; he is the beginning and the firstborn from among the dead, so that in everything he

---

27. Alphonso, *Personal Vocation*, 65.

might have the supremacy. For God was pleased to have all his fullness dwell in him, and through him to reconcile to himself all things, whether things on earth or things in heaven, by making peace through his blood, shed on the cross. (Col 1:15–20 NIV).

The discussion group of spiritual directors considered the concept of forming people to become Christ for others—rather than Christ-like:

> Alison: Christlike?
>
> Veronica: No, I am saying we are called to be Christ, which means we are to be salvific for other people. We are called to be a source of redemption for other people. It is a massive call. If I try to be like Christ, I will fail, but if I allow Christ to be Christ within me, I can be Christ to others.

The idea of becoming Christ is challenging to the spiritual directors in the reflection group, although this is not new thinking in the Catholic Church. Rohr says: "at the core of human personhood, we discover that *what it means to be human is to also be divine*, the same journey I believe Jesus made on this earth."[28] The spiritual direction discussion group explores the consequences of what it would mean to become Christ:

> Alison: That's a big idea.
>
> Pam: Yes. What does being like Christ mean conversely for you [Veronica]?
>
> Veronica: Conversely it means that we are to model ourselves on Christ, which puts Christ out there as something that we can choose to take up or not choose to take up. Whereas if we are to become Christ, means that we become identified and unified with Christ. . . . It is not "like" God; we actually communicate God to other people or communicate Christ to others. . . . Perhaps it could be said that we are born to be the human manifestation of the divine in the world. So just as Mystery already exists in the organization, this divine Mystery already exists within each one of us. It is the central animating principle without which there is no role and no person. My being emerges from the initiative of God's primary movements within me, and the call is to say "yes" to God's movements, say "yes" to my humanity and divinity.

---

28. Rohr, *Action and Contemplation Week 2*, para. 1.

I add: . . . because we model ourselves on Jesus, so that we too can become Christ.

> Veronica: Modeling is a problem as far as I am concerned. I think modelling is I am looking at you and I want to become like you, whereas becoming Christ is—I am communicating with you, I am entering into a relationship with you and I am becoming like you through that relationship, so like you that I am becoming you.

To become Christ or to take on the role *Christ* is to place everything I do, everything I think within that framework of connectedness to Source.

Who is God?—Connectedness with Source

When I began the research, although I carried the hypothesis that the method of listening in spiritual direction can be transformative for leaders, I had not anticipated the importance of God to interviewees in the spiritual direction relationship. I was surprised and curious in relation to the frequency and importance of God to interviewees as this emerged from the data. Speaking about God, Jesus, relationship and love was a recurring theme for all participants.

Interview	God	Jesus	Love	Relationship
A	91	0	41	13
B	43	4	7	13
C	45	0	9	5
D	33	1	20	2
E	47	2	8	4
F	62	9	9	10
G	19	9	14	32
H	41	4	10	11
I	50	3	7	11
J	46	7	4	21
K	103	17	36	43
L	6	5	2	6
M	40	21	14	50

Strengthening Spirit–Releasing Potential

N	62	16	6	9
O	48	24	5	13
P	36	10	5	25
Q	22	2	18	16
S	123	12	19	22
T	20	2	13	2
	937	148	247	308

Table 9—Word frequency for interviewees and their relationship with God, Jesus and love.

I conclude that when spiritual direction is not centered on a person's relationship with God or connectedness with Source, it is not spiritual direction; rather it might be some form of therapy, counseling or life coaching. In the TEF John Bazalgette describes the experience of connectedness to Source as "the sense of a call from something greater than themselves."[29]

The formative dynamic of the Week Two of the Exercises draws the exercitant to work with God. Interviewees attempt to describe how this is possible. I asked John "How do you know when it is God?"

> Well I am consciously directing my thoughts and my thinking to God . . . I am sitting in God's presence, and to consciously think that, changes something. To recognize that God wants my utter freedom changes something so I enter into prayer, not so much with a list of things that I am worried about or things that I want to happen. There is a different dimension, I think.
>
> Physically, I feel different in myself. When I was in [hospital] after the operation . . . I was surrounded by noise . . . and I could not sleep . . . because I was right next to the nurses' station, and two people in the ward needed constant hourly attention and I would be woken up and I was really feeling ill about it. I knew I needed to talk to God about it and I said "God I am that sozzled at the moment I don't know what to pray and I am not quite certain . . . if I ask you for something you will give it to me straight away. There seems to be times when that happens other times, I seem to ask for something and it doesn't happen, but at the moment I just need a room by myself." And I suppose within half an hour the ward sister said, "We are going to move you down to a private

---

29. Bazalgette, "Connectedness With Source," 204.

ward, a private room". And I can never ever deny the reality of what happened at that moment and I said, "Thank you."

I ask John what he made of that?

Well, God's care is personal . . .

So, if God can get you a private room when you need one, why can't God find that aircraft that has gone missing?

Yes, I don't know. . . . The important thing is to be able to ask and say this is what confuses me. And my response is that I feel it is ok to ask that question, and although I don't get an answer it doesn't cause another reaction having asked the question. I feel that I am heard and I am amazed. But then I am not amazed because we are very limited people. . . . I thought we could do anything as a race that we wanted to, but we can't. . . . The movement of ISIS and all that is happening there, I am appalled. . . . How long can this continue? . . . And that is exactly what the Psalmists asked—"How come?" It is still the same problem we are dealing with here.

For John synchronicity is part of God's personal care when he surrenders his struggles to God. Jaworski in his book "Synchronicity" claims the occurrence of synchronicity increases for leaders who work from a state of commitment and surrender in which there is a realization that we are part of the unfolding of creation. Jaworski contends,

> Leadership exists when people are no longer victims of circumstances but participate in creating new circumstances . . . Leadership is about creating a domain in which human beings continually deepen their understanding of reality and become more capable of participating in the unfolding of the world. Ultimately, leadership is about creating new realities.[30]

Mark tries to explain his relationship with God:

> I can't explain that to people . . . I have had people ask me: "Why are you a person of faith?" . . . I say to them "I have had this encounter with Jesus that changed my life." And they kind of look at you and I can't explain it much more. For me it's something that there is a knowing in my heart and in my soul but in my body as well . . . I grew up with a theological image of God . . . it was God out there and up high in heaven and . . . I was down here and if I wasn't careful, I would end up further down in Hell. So, God was

---

30. Jaworski, *Synchronicity*, 2

awesome and fearsome to me but very much at a distance. It was a long, long time before I discovered that there is this person of Jesus that is intimate, but also mystical and transformative . . . But I can't explain that intellectually to people . . . The best we have are the mystics . . . the poets who write as best they can about it, the artists who shape the sculptures . . . they get a bit closer to it I think, but it's an intangible thing. . . . It is quite real; I have no doubt about that.

The individual's relationship with God has a significant influence on each interviewee's sense of self and how each takes up the role of leader. Across the data it is evident spiritual direction enables interviewees to move from a sense of inadequacy and self-doubt, supported by a limited image of God waiting to judge, to eventually trusting that I am enough, I have what I need and God will enable me. Through the support of spiritual direction, a person's leadership style can become more compassionate, more empathetic, and less controlled by external projections or perceived projections.

Sarah works as a leader with young volunteers who visit the indigenous homeless and speaks about how her work changes when she relies on God in her leadership role:

> It softens my heart sometimes, or also provides courage and strength, but also . . . I take the pulse of the room, what people really need in the room . . . If I relied purely on myself, I don't think I would be able to truly know what it is people need . . . because we actually didn't know what type of environment we were going out to on some of the nights. . . . If I just tried to do it with purely my cerebral knowledge of leadership . . . I think I would have stifled. . . . Stepping into that environment where there is a danger there, I am going to trust that God is there with me and that God is going to give me the ability to see if this situation is too dangerous, to get us out of there in time. . . . But more so than that, I am going to trust that this *[is]* going to be an experience that is helpful and life-giving for myself and these young people but also the volunteers that I have with them; that this is going to be life-giving to them. . . .
>
> When I am really honest with myself, I know that God has never let me down. I might have let myself down. Other people might have let me down, but God has never really let me down. So, it is good, when I reflect back on Africa which was effectively a war zone . . . or other work environments and other social environments . . . it is through that reflection and also through spiritual direction, through speaking it out and really seeing this is where

> God was in the midst of all this . . . mess. This is where God was, and spiritual direction does provide some of that clarity.

Sarah's experience of confidence in her leadership through her dependence on God is consistent with Level five leadership consciousness:

> They view problems from a systems' perspective, seeing beyond the narrow boundaries of cause and effect. They are honest and truthful and display integrity in all they do. They feel confident in handling any situation. This confidence and openness allows them to reclassify problems as opportunities. They clarify priorities by referring to the vision and mission. They display emotional intelligence, social intelligence and intellectual intelligence. Integrator-inspirers are good at bringing the best out of people.[31]

Connectedness to Source (in this case, God) is central to the way Sarah takes up her leadership role. Jaworski claims "[a]nyone can participate with Source . . . if they are willing to do the work to remove the filters and barriers that have been inculcated into us."[32] Spiritual direction supports leaders in removing filters and barriers and to connect with Source as they develop their leadership potential. I ask Sarah how she knows she is connected to God:

> There is a certain peace that comes about and also; I wouldn't be able . . . to achieve it in my own right. . . . . . It is just like systems' leadership . . . everybody knew what they should be doing . . . and there were beautiful connections happening . . . just that level of detail that every individual felt connected and felt purposeful. I don't have the capacity to do that . . . to really impact hearts to that level.

What happens if you do?

> . . . it becomes too much about me and . . . about the rules and the guidelines and things.

So, the focus moves from the personal, the spiritual and the relational, to the regulations.

> Yes, and it just becomes more of a utilitarian approach.

So how did you get to be so confident in this realm?

---

31. Barrett, "Seven Levels of Leadership Consciousness," 6.
32. Jaworski, *Synchronicity*, 198.

> Well I had good spiritual directors. . . . I am still very much on this journey of letting go of the things that haven't worked, and relationships that haven't worked . . . I don't think I would be able to move with the freedom that I have . . . I could have moved from this State Government job to that State Government job, not necessarily taking a risk and trusting that actually I feel in the spirit I should be studying full time. And . . . the world would probably say: Well that is a really foolish thing to do, you are probably cutting off your career and do you really have enough finances to do that? . . . That is going to impact whether or not you get married . . . and all those sort of things. But just that trust, no I can step out in faith . . . and I can spend a while in discernment and walk into it with my eyes open knowing that this might be difficult . . . but there . . . is a greater good in this. And just trusting in that and seeing that there will be hard times that it won't all be super rosy.

Sarah is speaking here about how discernment becomes a natural part of decision-making for a person who engages in spiritual direction, which is a common theme among research participants.

Discernment and Spiritual Direction

Discernment is a core element of the spiritual direction process. Ignatius offers Rules for Discernment to help the director to "understand to some extent the different movements produced in the soul and for recognizing those that are good to admit them, and those that are bad, to reject them." [313] During the spiritual direction session, the director, in collaboration with the directee, listens for movements of the Spirit. The key questions the director holds in mind are the following:

- is this person experiencing an increase in peace, hope, love, freedom and joy? or
- is this person moving towards fear, isolation, disintegration, with a lack of hope and a lack of love?

The spiritual director helps the directee to listen to "voices" within and recognize what might be drawing them into life and what draws them away from life. Ignatius advises that "it is characteristic of the evil one to fight against . . . happiness and consolation by proposing fallacious reasonings, subtleties, and continual deceptions." [329]

In a similar way to Ignatius, Bion suggests that every human person has a place within the "ineffable, inscrutable, and constantly evolving domain that intimates an aesthetic completeness and coherence."[33] In the place of "Absolute Truth" for Bion, there are no more words and the mind is stilled. The opposite of "Absolute truth" is "the lie" which has to keep on arguing and talking and "rattling on".

> Bion believed that truth is as necessary for mental growth as food is for physical growth, and the lie is the negative validation of the truth that needs to be disavowed. Bion believed that the truth spoke for itself and therefore required no thinker, whereas the liar did require a thinker . . . The ego, in seeking to disguise, repress, or alter the unconscious, becomes disingenuous and dissembles the truth.[34]

Pam describes leadership as "standing up, being oneself but not in a way that takes space from others, just to be fully present and the truth of oneself, and the core of oneself in that. And spiritual direction is such an enabling way of stepping into that and holding there and discovering 'the more' of God."

In what follows, I present three examples of interviewees speaking about different aspects of discernment and how this has supported their leadership development.

- Sally describes noticing the inner critic and how this changed her perspective.
- Anne explores the experience of being driven or drawn and being in a culture of excessive busyness.
- Jan speaks about following her call.

Noticing the Inner Critic and a Change in Perspective

In the first weekend of a two-part workshop on spirituality and leadership, Sally's inner critic dominated her capacity to participate in group discussions during the course:

---

33. Grotstein, "Bion's Transformation in 'O,'" 1.
34. Grotstein, "Bion's Transformation in 'O,'" 6.

> I never express myself well even in the small group . . . I wanted to participate more but I couldn't . . . I kept on saying to myself "You are not good, you couldn't hear well, you couldn't express yourself, you are very slow." . . . I drive myself hard to participate in the group but . . . the more I drive myself I just find that the more nervous . . . and actually I was exhausted after the first weekend because I use a lot of energy on the negative voices . . . I just kept on criticizing myself.

Her disposition changed for the second weekend where she was able to silence the inner critic and be more compassionate with herself:

> And for the second weekend . . . the feeling was different. I had downloaded the PowerPoint before the weekend and I . . . had some idea what will be happening in the weekend. I hoped that I could participate more in the group. But . . . I still find [it] not easy to participate in the group. [There was an] issue of my family that distracted me and I was a little bit emotionally distracted. . . . But I can be more compassionate with myself . . . in the half hour before we started, I got that message [of family illness] so it is understandable that I was not there.

Although, in her opinion, Sally's participation in the workshop did not really improve, the inner critic, leading her to exhaustion, no longer took control. Ignatius suggests that the voice of the one who moves us towards God "is delicate, gentle, delightful. It may be compared to a drop of water penetrating a sponge", whereas the voice of the one who leads us away from God "is violent, noisy, and disturbing. It may be compared to a drop of water falling upon a stone." [335] For Sally, learning to listen to the gentle voice changed her leadership style which, when she began spiritual direction, was dominated by fear. Sally speaks of the work that she did in her spiritual direction sessions during the spiritual leadership course:

> I remember in the first session I just talked to [my spiritual director] "Actually I am afraid of you". . . and then he asked me "so why are you afraid of me? Because I am the boss?" I said: "might be! I think just like . . . the person who is the authority. I don't know why." I just couldn't sort it out, why I am afraid of him. . . . Maybe [he is] some kind of authority figure.

Sally identifies that some of the senior members of her parish held religious authority or seniority over her in her leadership role. Spiritual direction helped her to see that she seemed to be handing power over to them even though they had no formal authority over her work:

> During the weeks with *[my spiritual director]*, ... we *[were]* always on that point. So, he asked: "So why are you afraid of the people like that?" ... They have power over me ... *[My spiritual director]* said "Oh I don't need that power, you don't need to give that power to me." ... I give them the power, but they may not need that power.... For me it is the church authority.... It is important ... I can relate to this kind of person with less fear. Also, I can relate to ... the people ... I am leading and I can be more compassionate and ... understand where they are, and who they are, and to lead them to work with them where they are.... It is not easy but at least I have that awareness.

Sally was able to experience how she let fear dominate her disposition both in the way she participated in the course and in the way she had been taking up her leadership role in her ministry. Sally created a role drawing during the leadership course, which she brought to the book interview (Figure 16). She was asked to draw herself in role using symbols within her work system.

- Sally is the yellow circle;
- the green and pink circles are her parishioners;
- the orange circles are her ministry team;
- purple represents God; and
- the two blue circles are the senior pastors to whom she refers in her interview.

Figure 16: Sally role drawing

When Sally drew this image, she saw the senior pastors as overshadowing her work, leaving her fearful. At this stage, prior to her spiritual direction sessions, the gaps in the external circle represented leaching energy and spirit from the parish. At the end of her spiritual direction sessions, when she had come to the realization that she was handing over her power without checking whether the senior pastors wanted this, her perspective changed. Sally saw two things: first, that the two blue circles were actually supporting her in holding the difficult leadership role she had, and second, that the gaps around the edges all opened her parish to the world allowing God to fill her parish. From these perspectives she felt confident and supported and took up her leadership role from a more compassionate perspective, leading to compassion for herself, the senior pastors, her ministry team and her parishioners.

Driven or Drawn and a Culture of Excessive Busyness

Discernment rests on listening to movements of the Spirit. One method of identifying whether the movement is life giving is to observe whether the directee is being drawn or driven[35] in what they bring to the direction session. Anne talks about how spiritual direction helped her to stop and clear away all the noise in order to be able to notice whether she is being driven or drawn:

> I can remember having a conversation with *[my spiritual director]* last year: "Where are you driven and where are you drawn?" . . . That was really helpful for me . . . particularly in a school where there are so many calls on your time. To be able to say: "I don't feel that we are meeting our purpose or what I see as being the important aspects of my role, and so I am going to get rid of that so that I can focus on this."
>
> I would say for me that is probably the biggest change . . . to be able to know. . . . You have to stop. You have to clear away all the noise and just be able to listen and that's listening deep down. . . . This is what I was reading in that chapter last night. She *[Ruth Haley-Barton[36]]* talked about the loneliness of leadership; of when you are the only person who will hold onto that vision. You can see things that other people can't see. I don't know how that's different from just being pig-headed and arrogantly sticking to a course because you refuse to listen to anybody else's viewpoint, but somehow, it's not. . . . Because I think you can listen as well and you can be able to sift what other people are saying to you.

Anne's experience aligns with level four leadership consciousness where leaders:

35. Silf, *Inner Compass*, 89.

36. Jan is referring to the book by Ruth Haley Barton, *Strengthening the Soul of Your Leadership*.

promote participation, equality and diversity. They ignore or remove hierarchy. They are adaptable and flexible. They embrace continuous learning. They actively engage in their own personal development and encourage their staff to participate in programs that promote personal growth.[37]

Following Your Call

Jan, an experienced spiritual director, recalls her experience of supporting a young man, who held a significant leadership position in his workplace, to make a career change through the process of spiritual direction. She supported her directee in making a big decision, trusting in his movement towards freedom and believing that things would open up for him if this was an authentic discernment.

> I witnessed a man . . . who had been journeying for quite some time . . . in discovering who he was and what he was called to do and be in the world and wake up to that. . . . He made a radical choice to give up his huge income and place the poor at the center of his life . . . he was going to change ministries and work with severely disabled children instead of the wealthiest of the wealthy. So, it involved giving up income, centering his life totally on Christ. [He] had . . . this awareness for some time, and he . . . made the concrete decisions . . . at one stage during this time he had nowhere to go—he had given it up but was trusting.

I clarify with Jan: Given up his previous role?

> Made his decision, given it up and was just waiting. And then, out of the blue, the next thing presented itself. God didn't leave him too long.

And how were you feeling in this in-between stage?

> Confident. I was just waiting, very confident . . . and then when it did unfold it was just more than he could have imagined.

So how do you make sense of that, leaving a responsible position where he was making a massive impact and then choosing to work with just a few people?

> There is no sense.

37. Barrett, "Seven Levels of Leadership Consciousness," 4.

What was the cause of the decision?

> God wants nothing less than all of us. It's about . . . God's crazy love. . . . How can I have all of you without limits without anything in between; wholeheartedly and whatever that looks like. And it always ends up being for the greater glory of God and service of others.

How did you know he was making a good decision?

> The peace and the fruits of the spirit were there, joy mainly.

What was the benefit of having regular spiritual direction do you think?

> To witness what was happening . . . as he was articulating it was helping him, and encounter enabled the joy. . . . And support, he did say a few times that his friends didn't understand what he was doing. And I totally did understand.

Is it because he was going to work with the poor? Or is it because it was life giving to him? What was your understanding—could it have been equally of God to take on *[a senior leadership position in his current work]* instead?

> Yes, totally. It was the joy he was given, and peace and love.

Jan is describing leadership at level five of leadership consciousness where leaders "demonstrate integrity and are living examples of values-based leadership. They walk their talk. They build cohesion and focus by bringing values alignment and mission alignment to the whole company. . . . They are focused on the common good."[38]

Supporting leaders to practice discernment is a key feature of spiritual direction. In the Week Three dynamic of spiritual direction, the spiritual director accompanies directees through experiences of suffering.

Committed, Confirmation in Suffering, Anointed

In the Week Three dynamic of spiritual direction the directee deepens her commitment to the call to leadership through confirmation in suffering, aligning with a deepening commitment to make a difference in the community and level six of leadership consciousness.

In Week Three of the Spiritual Exercises the exercitant meditates on the passion and death of Jesus. The challenge is to be able to enter the

---

38. Barrett, "Seven Levels of Leadership Consciousness," 6.

experience of suffering and remain committed to following Christ, finding the strength to carry out one's mission. Willing to be vulnerable and stay true to purpose, even in the face of death, becomes a core leadership value, correlating with level six leadership consciousness where leaders work as mentor/partners and are motivated by their need to make a difference in the world.

At level six, leaders display empathy and utilize intuition in making decisions and the leader's own ego and agenda become secondary. When supported with spiritual direction the experience of vulnerability through suffering can strengthen leadership identity.

*Vulnerability as a Basis for Leadership—
Strengthened by/and in the Face of Suffering*

Fiona speaks from her experience as a spiritual director, and of her personal experiences of wounding, suffering and great losses in her life. She suggests that strength comes from the memory and scarring of "woundedness". As I listened, I wondered about different models of leadership. One model of leadership is to be ego strong, "I am OK, I am together, I can manage," but what Fiona seemed to be suggesting is that the strength comes from the reminder of our wounds:

> There is something that happens . . . a complete change in the psyche . . . and the person begins to live and work out of that. But it doesn't mean that the scar is not there and that it can touch into that occasionally. I mean I have a great scar from [an operation] and that's probably twelve years ago . . . but I can still feel the tenderness of that and I think that is the same with our own woundedness. The scar is still there but the slough is not there, the woundedness itself is not there.

I wonder with Fiona: I am thinking as you are speaking that one model of leadership is to be ego strong, you know, I am OK, I am together, I can manage. But what you are suggesting is that the strength comes from the reminder of the woundedness.

> Because I think the first can come out of power. . . . There is a difference between power and confidence. Confidence comes from that deep knowing that . . . I am a human being and I am open to making mistakes. . . . I am not on my own and I can keep listening and . . . learning and working towards . . . leadership. But it doesn't

mean I become a leader that is powerful and the . . . ego leading forward. . . . Jesus was just that; the leader who could be vulnerable; the leader who could care for himself; the leader who could take time out for himself when he needed to; the leader who could be with others in their greatest pain.

And is that what happens to the people you work with?

Once they're transformed.

It is important to note that all directees will have had an experience of the transformative processes in the Week One and Week Two dynamics of spiritual formation prior to entering the Week Three. Without this prior experience the graces of Week Three are difficult to comprehend.

Anne had been talking about the importance of being willing to be vulnerable in her leadership position. She identifies that if she is able to trust it is appropriate to be vulnerable in positions of responsibility and under pressure. Being free to be vulnerable is life changing.

> Life changing! And . . . that is what has changed my life. . . . Week Three for me was the most important even though it was awful and I couldn't wait [for it to be ended]. . . . The intimacy . . . was extraordinary, but the image that I keep having over and over again is this: I'm on a cliff top and there is a wind just coming at me, it is [like] Jesus before Herod and they are . . . hurling insults at him and he just stands there, and what I keep thinking is that he doesn't get angry. He just says: this is who I am, all of me, as I am. There is no more I can be.

> And . . . that was so powerful, and I . . . keep coming back to that all the time because . . . I pray now . . . [for] growth in that area . . . to stand there fully as I am but without pride or defiance or anger or defensiveness, just to speak the truth. But then not to get angry about it and . . . not . . . churned up about it afterwards. . . . It's a big ask! . . . When you ask does it have to be about God, to me, it does because, . . . that relationship is at the core of everything.

In the Week Three of the Spiritual Exercises, the exercitant prays through the experience of Jesus letting go of his life, which in turn opens the possibility of resurrection. The experience of death and resurrection cannot in reality be separated in the spiritual journey. When we allow a part of ourselves to die, space is opened for new possibilities to be born.

The spiritual director who can accompany leaders through suffering can support them to enter level six leadership consciousness.

Living the Call to Leadership

The Week Four is the final stage in the spiritual formation process. When spiritual directors work with directees who are in the dynamic of the fourth week of the Spiritual Exercises, they expect to see clarity around their sense of call and their identity, vocation and mission. A disposition of freedom, generativity, abundance and joy is evidence that a directee is moving within the dynamic of the fourth week. During Week Four the exercitant will come to the point where they, William Barry states,

> now know more intimately the Mystery we call God and, in the process, know themselves and their world more intimately. They are well on the way to being contemplatives in action, people who find God regularly in their actual lives of prayer and action. Indeed, for such people, prayer and action are not two different activities, but in some mysterious fashion one.[39]

Week Four aligns with level seven in Barrett's SLOC, which is to be visionary and a wisdom figure and to have a global vision with a holistic perspective on life. Level seven leaders focus on ethics, social responsibility, sustainability, and future generations, and display wisdom, compassion and humility.[40] Spiritual direction in the dynamic of Week Four is about being on the continuing spiritual journey, surrendering and trusting that it is God who enables and supports the leader.

Being on the Spiritual Journey and Making Meaning

Fiona identifies her experience of spiritual direction as supporting her growing sense of herself as a leader. She is a trained therapist and spiritual director and in recent times has developed her own formation course, is writing a book and doing public speaking. I asked her what helped her to step into these leadership roles.

> It is . . . my spirituality that helps me make meaning because I think from a very early age, I knew God was in everything. In the

---

39. Barry, *Letting God Come Close*, 190.
40. Barrett, "Seven Levels of Leadership Consciousness," 7.

pain, in the suffering, in seeing my dad so sick as a seven-year-old.... Somehow right throughout my life I've known that God is with me in whatever I am doing.

... I know, there have been many times in my life when humanly I could not have done what I have done. It's like something greater than myself that enables me, supports me, ... it has be Grace, it has to be God ... it is in the moments [when] ... I have experienced something; in the absolute silence of being with—experiencing ... myself with God and nothing else.... In those moments, a confirmation comes that I feel in my body.... It is not just the head knowing. I know it in every part of me. Something shifts in me. Something opens up in me.

[In] ...today's session it was like I came into this large room and it had been closed up for so long and I opened up the doors ... I could feel that it was stuff that had been closed up and ... I opened the doors, opened the windows and the breeze came in and then the light; the light just absolutely poured in this place and something happened in me and I just knew. I was experiencing God in that moment.... I am invited into something that I could never have thought possible; that is way beyond me ... yet I am enabled somehow to do something that is beyond.

When directees experience the grace of Week Four, transformation enables leaders to work with God in ways they may never have thought possible.

Has Spiritual Direction Supported Your Leadership Development?

Participants in this research without exception agree that spiritual direction has supported them and the people they have directed in developing leadership potential. Interviewees identify that spiritual direction helps to bring into consciousness the ways in which leaders can undermine themselves, clarify their unique sense of purpose and call, and keep leaders on track. I asked Fiona whether she thought spiritual direction has supported her development as a leader.

Spiritual direction is so important for working on that part of my spiritual self that can undermine everything I do ... this is a leadership role I have undertaken ... and I think my spiritual journey along the way has been so pivotal in enabling me to begin to take up that role.

Sally identifies spiritual direction as having clarified understanding of her purpose in life:

> I think it helped me to have a deeper understanding of what is the purpose of my life, and what God is calling me to do.

Anne speaks about how making the Exercises and being in spiritual direction changed her leadership style:

> It was a lifeline to a deeper knowing, an understanding, to a connection, to the realization that I am not an isolated little nothing . . . I am part of the air that's out there, I am part of the clouds. . . and they are part of me. . . It's way beyond the human interconnection. . . . The air that I breathe . . . Jesus breathed these same molecules. But so do the animals, so do the trees . . . everything is alive and connected. . . . I can't thrive without that, I can survive. There is so much more to life than just the physical of what I am doing or who I am.

I asked Sarah if she thought spiritual direction could support people in leadership.

> I have seen good examples of leadership and I have seen a lot of bad examples in leadership. Or leadership that just goes off track because it just becomes more about . . . the ego . . . the structures and the rule book, and then they lose the myth of what they are really about. . . . People seem to lose that sense that there should be some joy in your life in this role and you should be seeing . . . how Christ or the spirit is moving in this organization. And I think it goes back to what . . . how important reflection is.

Sally speaks of the transformative experience she received through spiritual direction in making the full Spiritual Exercises and then spiritual formation as a spiritual director and in spiritual leadership programs. Though she had been a religious minister for more than thirty years, she had not experienced spiritual formation in the way that Ignatian spirituality and spiritual direction had offered her. Sally sums up her experience of receiving spiritual direction during this time:

> I think . . . spiritual direction . . . has helped me to experience deeper the love of God so that I can love myself and I can have a greater capacity to love others in my leadership role.

Spiritual direction can make a positive contribution to leadership development. In the Week Four dynamic, spiritual direction supports leaders in living their call to leadership and service to humanity and the planet. Leadership is performed with compassion and humility with a focus on future generations, an expression of level seven leadership consciousness.

Chapter 5

Spiritual Direction and Organizational Development

As mentioned earlier, organizational consciousness is "the organization's capacity for reflection; a centering point for the organization to "think" and find the degree of unity across systems; and a link to the organization's identity and self-referencing attributes. It operates at three stages: reflective, social, and collective consciousness."[1] When an organization has the capacity to reflect on the past and simultaneously look forward to the future it wants to create, the organization can become conscious of patterns of life, death and resurrection that lie within, and thereby raise awareness of what might be holding back any potential for flourishing. Spiritual direction provides a process for exploring organizational life that is simultaneously reflective and anticipatory.

I re-introduce Barrett's three stages of organizational consciousness as a framework for exploring benefits of spiritual direction in organizational development:

Stage one—personal mastery:

- level one: survival—pursuit of profit and shareholder value
- level two: relationship—relationships that support the organization
- level three: self-esteem—high performance systems and processes

---

1. Pees et al., *Organizational Consciousness*. Para. 3.

Stage two—internal cohesion:

- level four: transformation—adaptability, continuous renewal and learning
- level five: internal cohesion—shared vision, values building community

Stage three—external cohesion:

- level six: making a difference—strategic alliances and partnerships
- level seven: service—service to humanity and planet; social responsibility[2]

Stage one personal mastery: survival, relationship, self-esteem

Spiritual direction contributes to organizational development by supporting the group in identifying any fears and limitations the group holds collectively. When working within early stages spiritual formation, the director will explore the group's relationship with God/Source and each other, identifying the patterns of behavior that keep the group locked in fear and shame.

From Corporate Shame to Shared Identity

An essential first step for individuals and groups in spiritual direction is to identify and own patterns of grace and disgrace in light of their relationship with God/Source. Spiritual direction creates an environment that can enable the group to risk becoming vulnerable and let go of control, in order for the group to move from being caught in shame as members try to maintain an illusion that all is well.

An executive leadership team (ELT) participated in this study. By sharing the truth of their history with all members of their organization, they were able to see that events of the past, which they believed were too dark to be spoken about, were actually important turning points in the formation of the identity of their institution. Members of the ELT; Vera, John, Jackie, James and Bill share their experience.

Vera first experienced the transformative power of exploring the history of her group when she attended a spiritual leadership course where she

---

2. Barrett, "Seven Levels of Organisational Consciousness," 1.

publicly explored the history of her organization in a group session. Vera recounts how, through her own experience of vulnerability in the course and by working through personal shame in spiritual direction, she was able to risk inviting her organization to look at their corporate shame together.

> I found it really hard because it brought up all my issues. . . . There is no way I would put our history out there in front, especially to the new members, because I had the whole sense of shame about our history. It is such a mess and you don't want them to know everything. . . . I had to work through that myself in spiritual direction.
>
> Then a year later I actually gave [a corporate retreat in which we explored our history] and it was such a good thing to do together. I went from thinking this was really bad and our history is a mess, to realizing there is so much grace in everything. . . . The main thing we got out of doing the history line together, is that all the things that have happened to us, like good and bad and messy, have shaped us and formed us, and God's grace has been through all of that.

The history line is a group spiritual direction process developed by ISECP to help a group tell their story in light of their relationship with God. The history line presupposes that in exploring the communal graced history, the group will become aware of God's self-revelation to community.[3] Working through the history line enabled the group to see that group identity is shaped in their vulnerability, and moments of struggle are turning points.

> Vera: You can just see that the vulnerable messy part was really important because [in it] . . . were turning points that . . . shape us and send us to where we really needed to go. I think before we did it . . . I just thought of them as mistakes . . . bad things had happened and we didn't do that very well. . . . But then looking at God's grace all the way through, it made you see and accept our history as a grace-filled thing which makes us see hugely differently, . . . which is a really helpful thing.
>
> John: . . . it was pretty eye opening and gave me a deeper sense of unity with all [the group] but also with what we all held in our heritage.

---

3. Borbely et al., *Leadership, Spirituality and Organisational Practice,* Mod 5, 2.

Strengthening Spirit–Releasing Potential

Jackie: . . . For me, and from hearing [what] others say, gave us a deeper appreciation . . .[of] our beginnings; . . . a sense of a deeper appreciation and . . . really knowing where we came from.

James: . . . [what] Jackie is touching on is taking the shame away from some things. . . . When I was in formation . . . certain things happened and you weren't allowed to talk about them . . . and that creates a sense of, not even shame so much, but it is held within you.

Bill: . . . God's grace in the middle of it all. . . . That's what came out of it. It was like whatever the story . . . it was really, really clear that God is just remarkably amazing, and big, and doing all this stuff, that is so much more than us.

Groups carry a collective history and when this history is unexamined, it can undermine the group's capacity to move forward, keeping it locked in early levels of organizational consciousness. Facing shame requires a willingness to become vulnerable. As the ELT recollected their history in light of their relationship with God, group members were enabled to see how their identity as a group had been shaped by what they identified as positive and negative events. When organizational consciousness includes an awareness of the possibility of transformation, the group can move beyond the fear of being exposed. Jackie noticed the change in her disposition through the communal exercise of exploring their graced history. She now recognizes that: "The potential for transformation is always there . . . rather than: I am going to be crushed by this . . . I don't like it, and I am feeling bad and not necessarily reacting well in the middle of it."

Spiritual direction differs from coaching, therapy, consulting or counseling insofar as the main purpose of spiritual direction is to support the group in recognizing the presence and effect of God/Source on organizational life. When the ELT's organization put their communal focus on God, they were able to release their collective shame and become conscious of the potential for transformation. In the case of the ELT, the leader was initially impacted personally through her experience of spiritual direction and was then freed to enable the rest of the leadership team to engage in the spiritual formation process and move beyond levels one to three of organizational consciousness.

Spiritual Direction and Organizational Development

Relationship Consciousness

Though there is evidence in Vera's case that the process of raising organizational consciousness can begin with just one person entering into spiritual direction before engaging the rest of the leadership team in spiritual formation, it is not always that simple. In the case of Pam, (although a spiritual director with considerable experience in Ignatian spirituality and engaged in spiritual leadership courses), she was not able to make any significant impact on organizational development in her workplace within a male religious order. Pam notes "there's been some impact . . . in the life of some people. . . . Nominally but I think, not structurally."

Despite her efforts in trying to engage the group in spiritual formation, the group have been resistant to entering any group spiritual direction process. I wondered if the organization was working from a scarcity model, hypothesizing that they might be working within level one, survival consciousness:

> Yes, absolutely it is! Cut, cut, cut, slash, slash, slash. . . . That is so superficial at one level. It is not what everything is about. . . . How do you speak into that? We are speaking different languages. . . . How far can you go? And how do you have relationships, professional relationships and a depth of trust, and sharing, and vulnerability? And how you speak truth to power?

Pam highlights the fact that when a group is stuck in level one consciousness, it is not possible to communicate on issues active in higher levels of consciousness such as relationships and building an internal community where vulnerability is able to be shared. The current context of a rapidly changing environment within the Catholic Church is creating pressure on this organization to evolve, but the risk for the group is that the change could be so big it might actually look like death for the current organization. Pam suggests that members of the group need to enter relationships centered on their relationship with God in order to be in touch with what is missing.

> I think what's missing is the relationship. It's allowing God to take the initiative. . . . I would like to think we might consider what God's dream for our parish might be. But . . . you can't speak in that kind of language. . . . What's missing? Vulnerability, Jesus, God dealing directly . . . that's missing.

Though this group identifies itself as being Ignatian and therefore at least theoretically holding the values of Ignatian spirituality, this was not enough to create openness to spiritual formation or a desire for a change in organizational consciousness. Openness to spiritual formation does not seem to be present at level one of the SLOC. At level one, focus is on financial stability and control, and when the organization's consciousness is limited to this level, it will be caught in survival mode.

When the group understands the importance of healthy relationships, it becomes possible for it to enter a communal spiritual formation process. One starting point of the spiritual formation within ISECP is to have each member of the group tell their personal story during a group spiritual direction session of how and why they joined this particular organization. This initiates a process of moving from being individuals within an organization to recognizing how relationships create a shared corporate story. Consciousness is raised to the importance of relationships and to what each individual brings to the group. Again, we see relationship with God at the center of spiritual formation for individuals and for the group. Pam compared her experience of working with a female Ignatian religious order where there seems to be a more relational approach:

> [There is] ... a much greater sense of understanding that we are all in this, you know, yes to the mission. A common yes to the work at depth ... to this way of being in leadership. But it's pushing boundaries and it is frontier work.... I did a retreat with ... six in that leadership team from a school, three participants were men. Two of them were speaking to me and saying that for them there was a significant difference teaching in an all girls' school having taught in an all boys' school.... It is the relationship. This makes all the difference...
>
> ... Relationships are critical ... particularly relationship with God ... and Jesus in his humanity.... About standing up being oneself but not in a way that takes space from others, just to be fully present and the truth of oneself and the core of oneself in that.... Spiritual direction is such an enabling way of stepping into that and holding there and discovering "the more" of God.

Spiritual direction helps to raise consciousness as to how a group manages interpersonal relationships and internal communications. This is an important element of organizational development. Barrett notes that "without good relationships with employees, customers and suppliers, company survival is compromised."⁴ Group spiritual direction facilitates the building of healthy organizational relationships.

Pam identifies a difference between the male and female Ignatian religious groups in the way they understand the importance of healthy relationships. I attribute this to the fact that it is generally (but not exclusively) understood that "women are better qualified in terms of people skills (sensitivity toward others, being kind, having good listening skills, and developing efficient relationships with their team and their superiors)" than men.⁵ Women tend to "be better evaluated in terms of empathy (showing good people management skills and their needs by establishing a strong connection with their team) and communication . . . when compared to men."⁶ What is interesting to note here is that the gender balance of participants in this research was eighty-five percent female and fifteen percent male. This reflects the gender balance of the community of spiritual directors in Australia. At the time of writing this book membership of Spiritual Directors International is ten percent male and ninety percent female.⁷ Perhaps this suggests that spiritual direction can help integrate the feminine aspects of organizational development. I address the question of the feminine nature of spiritual direction in more detail in the final chapter.

Group Spiritual Direction for Leadership Teams

Anne's workplace has been providing monthly group spiritual direction for the leadership team. The company directors and executive staff meet as a group with a spiritual director to explore how they can become more conscious of their shared connectedness to God and how this impacts the way they make decisions on behalf of the organization. I asked Anne if she thought these meetings had any influence on the way they worked together as a team.

> I think so, a lot, on a number of different levels. One most superficial level is that we are making a declarative statement that this is important and we are saying it to the rest of the organization

---

4. Barrett, *New Leadership Paradigm*, 323.
5. Radu et al., "Leadership and Gender Differences," ch. 4 para. 3.
6. Appelbaum et al., "Gender and Leadership," 43–51.
7. Statistics given by Anil Singh-Molares, Executive Director SDI private communication June 17, 2017.

in the office, but we are also saying it to everybody else out there, that our team formation . . . is fundamental.

The group spiritual direction sessions offer a place where members of the leadership team can allow themselves to be vulnerable and share what is happening for them personally in the workplace. This seemed to enable a deeper sense of trust across the organization.

> That sort of relationship that we can form with each other because we are working in a confidential space. We all get to know each other in a different way . . . I think it's important actually to have a space where people can . . . just be accepted for who they are and where they are at in their lives.

I asked whether they were they different in that space to other spaces they meet in.

> We don't meet as a group like that otherwise . . . for me personally, because my work can be a bit isolating . . . to have a group where I am so completely supported and we are all so on the same page . . . has helped me enormously. . . . I think having that establishment of trust; it couldn't happen if people didn't think that they could speak freely. . . . I would love for the principals to have it, love it, but it can't be forced.

What do you think it would do for them?

> Give them a space where they can actually dig into what's really going on there for them, and so if there is a level of mistrust in their relationship with us, then that can come out. . . . We bring so much negativity and so much stuff that is not of God to our work, and even when we are working with the best intentions, we bring our own insecurities and that sort of stuff. I mean they have ridiculous jobs . . . they have also got this sort of corporate overlay, billions of dollars that they have to look after and huge responsibilities. They would be out most nights of the week. Awful job.

Group spiritual direction provides a place in which healthy relationships can be developed that support the organization in developing a sense of belonging and loyalty among employees, reducing internal competition, manipulation, blame, internal politics, and discrimination. Belonging is an important aspect of the human experience:

> A deep sense of love and belonging is an irreducible need of all people. We are biologically, cognitively, physically, and spiritually

wired to love, to be loved, and to belong. When those needs are not met, we don't function as we were meant to. We break. We fall apart. We numb. We ache. We hurt others. We get sick.[8]

Stage One: Towards Transformation via Vulnerability

Moving beyond the three lower levels of SLOC requires a "shift from fear-based, rigid, authoritarian hierarchies to more open, inclusive, adaptive systems of governance that empower employees to operate with responsible freedom (accountability)"[9] Group spiritual direction creates an environment where vulnerability is possible, and difficult issues within the group can be raised in a safe and positive environment. In level three SLOC we see a focus on self-esteem which begins by accepting that I am enough as I am.

When the ELT participated in the spiritual leadership course they were invited to read and reflect on different aspects of spiritual leadership using Ruth Haley Barton's book *Strengthening the Soul of Your Leadership* as a guide. Each team member attended individual weekly spiritual direction sessions in which they explored how individual leadership styles were either enabled or disenabled, and also sessions in which they shared their own insights and the impact this had on them as a group. The ELT found by accepting what they perceived as their imperfections, first individually and then as a group, they were helped to recognize the creative tension of working at the edge of chaos. This requires a willingness to be vulnerable and to recognize the group is not required to have to have it all together:

> Vera: You know we feel like we are often on the edge of chaos and we're just holding it together but . . . that's where the creative tension is and that's where corporations and groups and leadership are, it's not because we haven't got it together, and we are new, and we don't know what we are doing, it is just normal, and that is where God works to, . . . there is so much encouragement and hope in that.

Sarah also confirmed that incorporating the practice of spiritual direction into her workplace allowed the group to raise difficult issues in a positive way:

---

8. Brown, *Daring Greatly,* 6.
9. Barrett, "Seven Levels of Organisational Consciousness," 3.

It allowed us to raise a whole lot of issues that have been going on for years . . . in a positive way and a safe way, and therefore that led on and opened it up to other discussions. OK what else do we need to improve? And also, I think it helped people's sense of ownership.

Once a capacity for vulnerability has been enabled in an organization, trust can be established among the group and it becomes possible to raise difficult issues, helping the group to establish a shared identity. It is essential that the group remain conscious of the way they deal with issues of survival, relationship and self-esteem as a continuous process of self-reflection. Issues residing at levels one to three of SLOC are always present within organizational dynamics and when they become apparent it is possible to work from the healthy rather than unhealthy aspects of organizational consciousness (Table 10).

Level of Organizational Consciousness	Healthy/Positive focus	Unhealthy/Excessive Focus
Level Three—Self Esteem	High performance: systems, processes, quality, best practices, pride in performance.	Bureaucracy, complacency.
Level Two—Relationship	Harmonious relationships: loyalty, open communication, customer satisfaction, friendship.	Manipulation, blame.
Level One—Survival	Financial stability: shareholder value, organizational growth, employee health, safety.	Control, corruption, greed.

Table 10—Positive focus and negative focus aspects of levels one to three of SLOC.[10]

10. Adapted from Barrett, "Seven Levels of Organisational Consciousness," 2.

Stage Two: Internal Cohesion: Transformation, Adaptability, Continuous Learning

The dynamic of spiritual formation in Week Two of the Spiritual Exercises aligns with levels four and five of organizational consciousness (Table 11). The focus here is on transformation and continuous learning, adaptability and discernment.

Level of Organizational Consciousness	Spiritual Formation	Focus
Level Five	Week Two: Illumination, the call of Christ, corporate identity.	Building internal community: shared vision and values, commitment, integrity, trust, passion, creativity, openness, transparency.
Level Four		Continuous renewal and learning: accountability, adaptability, empowerment, teamwork, goals orientation, personal growth.

Table 11—*Dynamic of Week Two of the Spiritual Exercises and levels four and five SLOC.*[11]

Spiritual Formation as Different to Teaching Skills

As discussed previously, spiritual direction facilitates the process of spiritual formation in which the focus is on the person and how they manage themselves in role. The process has a flow-on effect within the organization. Lynda applied her learning from her experience of formation as a spiritual director to the way she runs training programs for nursing staff dealing with grief and loss in their daily work. Lynda recognizes that the shift from simply providing information and teaching skills to facilitating a formative experience had a significant impact on her work:

> I was doing training for . . . staff on grief and communication skills . . . it reached a point that I didn't want to do it anymore because often the staff were sent by their managers . . . they don't sign up by themselves. . . . I felt that I just taught them the skills. They were

11. Adapted from Barrett, "Seven Levels of Organisational Consciousness," 2.

> so busy... [and] short of staff that they can't use the skills.... I came to a very dry place that I thought it is not worth doing and then I had input on spiritual formation... [where] the training is to focus on forming the students, not teaching the skills... after that I... incorporated what I learned in the spiritual formation.

The change for Lynda emerged when she began helping the staff to touch what was going on inside themselves as they dealt with grief and loss every day in their work. Prior to this Lynda was trying to teach them skills to manage themselves in the role. Barrett explains,

> The focus of the fourth level of organizational consciousness is on adaptability, employee empowerment, and continuous learning. The critical issue at this level of consciousness is how to stimulate innovation so that new products and services can be developed to respond to market opportunities. This requires the organization to be agile, flexible and take risks.[12]

When spiritual formation is integrated into staff training, it impacts the way staff conduct themselves in role. Lynda notes that when staff are helped to touch their own anger and helplessness, they can be more present to the patients and families of patients:

> When I would teach about grief and loss, I would ask the students to think about... an experience of loss; losing their purse, or losing some money, or losing some relationship.... I would ask them to recall what they experienced.... When I had spiritual direction formation training, I put more emphasis on how they feel as a carer when they care for dying patients and relatives, what are their feelings.... Many in the group feel helpless; many feel angry.... So, we went to a deeper place then I could work with them... not just to help patients' relatives grieve, but how to deal with their own grief, where does that anger come from? It usually comes from... the patients who are angry because they are dying; relatives are angry because of their loss.... Very often it is placed on them. And how can they be more objective and not... take it personally.
>
> And also, a huge part is about helplessness and I help them to examine where this comes from. Is it because they expect so much from the patients and relatives? They expect them to die well; they expect them to make a will; they expect them to accept their dying; they expect them not to complain; and they expect

---

12. Barrett, "Seven Levels of Organisational Consciousness," 6.

them to communicate well between all of them; all the ideologies, which seldom happen in life. . . . I try to put them in the patients' relatives place, . . . imagine that their most loved person is dying. Would they be able to accept this? I try to help them to see their expectation was good from their yearning, but it is too high, very unrealistic. . . . If they can have just one encounter the person will feel accepted, being listened to . . . and they feel a bit safe because their nurse or doctor can listen without judgement. So, that is already a huge thing that you have done for them. . . . When I have changed that focus, I feel that the work is much more satisfying and I can see that the students . . . are much more into the training. . . . Before some of them are keen to learn but now they are much more involved. Because it is not about them, it is about them doing it for somebody else.

. . . I enjoyed it more because I can see that somehow they are touched, they are touching their true self, their genuine feeling. And I think what I have got from the spiritual training is to learn to value myself.

Lynda notices the flow-on effect of formation. As she learned to value herself, so she was able to help others to value themselves. What she encountered in spiritual formation was a safe holding environment in which she could reveal her most vulnerable self and in turn she was able to do the same for hospital staff:

Spiritual formation training helped me to really to value the students to appreciate them and to help them see their goodness. To help them to accept who they are, where they are, and appreciate how much effort they have put into their work. . . . They put every effort into it but they don't always get positive feedback. But can they really appreciate themselves?

Lynda is helping the organization with her spiritual direction skills by providing spiritual formation for staff and by helping the organization to move towards levels four and five of organizational consciousness through continuous renewal and learning. This process is building commitment, integrity, trust, passion, creativity, openness and transparency.

Organizational Development and Communal Discernment

Seventy-five percent of participants in this research described discernment as central to their experience of spiritual direction. Though communal discernment can be understood as a method for decision-making, it is also an ongoing disposition that the group takes on in attempting to notice what conscious or unconscious forces are moving the group:

- towards God and a willingness to be adaptable, open, transformative, building internal cohesion and a clear sense of purpose; or
- away from God which can be recognized as a movement back into some of the unhealthy aspects of lower levels of consciousness such as the presence of excessive control, internal competition, manipulation, blame, an increase in bureaucracy, hierarchical power and status seeking, "silo" mentality,[13] confusion, complacency, and/or arrogance.

For the ELT a key change in organizational development for their group since engaging in spiritual direction is the inclusion of spiritual discernment within their meeting procedures. When the process of discernment is integrated with organizational decision-making processes, shared purpose and core values become more important than individual ambition. The ELT discuss how becoming more conscious of communal discernment changed the way they work together:

> Vera: The whole leadership thing has changed in the way that we operate together.... We started looking at corporate discernment... and how we make decisions.... It is not just the ends that matter. We can't have really ugly meetings as long as we get to the finish and make good decisions.... Meetings have to express [who we are—name removed] as well as the end.... I thought meetings are just terrible and you suffer it for a good cause...
>
> ... How do we discern not just in a meeting, but also in our life? What's going on here? And spiritually where are we at? Are we in a good place to make a decision?... How do you evaluate what happened and how do you improve on that?...
>
> All of those things have helped us a lot... we operate differently. We consciously try and bring those factors into our meetings so we are consciously discerning a whole lot better than we used to.

Vera noticed that meetings became "a lot less personal" and rather than attempting to win arguments or defending their individual personal

---

13. "Silo mentality is an attitude that is found in some organizations; it occurs when several departments or groups within an organization do not want to share information or knowledge with other individuals in the same organization." "Investopedia: Silo Mentality."

investment in issues, discernment helped them to maintain a focus on their shared purpose. Prior to incorporating practices within spiritual direction the ELT seemed to be unaware of how to detach from the emotional content of meetings particularly when individuals felt that the core identity of the group was being threatened.

> Bill: Meetings have been the worst . . . when it hits into what I consider a core value. If we do that then we are changing something about what I think is essential to our identity . . . That is why we all have conflicts . . . I am probably still attached to those things . . . there is a bigger corporate value. . . . One of our strengths is that even if we get into chaos or we get into conflict . . . there is a general commitment towards moving back into unity . . . and so there is a confidence, it will be painful, but, given time space . . . move back . . . into the core of who we are.

> Jackie: . . . the crucial question is "is this leading us closer to God or is this leading us further away from him?"

By introducing discernment into meeting processes and through their ways of working together as a leadership team, the ELT are becoming more conscious of the direction in which the spirit of the group is moving, towards God or away from God. The group also became aware of the importance of remaining focused on their core values rather than the personal agenda of individual members. The ELT recognizes that maintaining focus enabled a process of continuous learning, which is in line with level four of SLOC of transformation:

> Adaptability and continuous learning: Giving employees a voice in decision-making and making them accountable and responsible for their own futures in an environment that supports innovation, continuous improvement, knowledge sharing, and the personal growth and development of all employees.[14]

As with the ELT, for Anne's organization listening to spiritual movements enabled her group to move away from conflicts at the personal level and to listen more deeply to what might be going on within the group as a whole. A key aspect of the change for Anne was in knowing how to listen to the movements deep within her, noticing disturbances and discovering the truth of what was actually going on in the dynamics of the group rather than reacting to projections she was picking up from the rest of the team:

14. Barrett, "Seven Levels of Organisational Consciousness," 2.

> I think . . . the conflict is less personal. . . . It took me a long time to realize that the resistance is not about me and what I am offering, it is about the relationship with Head Office and . . . a shifting dynamic which is way bigger than me but I am the one at the table.
>
> . . . [My spiritual director] said to me "go and listen to what is going on for you and think about where you are feeling uncomfortable and why you are feeling uncomfortable."
>
> I had this meeting . . . [where] one of the principals was getting all worked up about stuff getting imposed upon them. . . . I came away and . . . I was very worked up at the end of that whole thing . . . by the time I was on the plane on the way home I had such insight into what was in play. . . . Not long after that, a meeting was called with all the principals . . . for them to air all their grievances. It was not about me, it was about governance and money and all sorts of things. These were absolutely nothing to do with me. But I think for me the big shift was that I was able to recognize that.
>
> . . . This is where . . . ongoing spiritual direction is so important for me . . . my ongoing challenge . . . is not . . . getting heated and getting sucked into this sort of defensive conversation about things.

When individuals in an organization have the support of spiritual direction it can help the rest of the group bring into consciousness underlying issues that bring disturbances into the group.

Internal Cohesion and Interconnectedness

A strong cohesive organizational identity is founded on a shared mission and clear sense of purpose—which can be understood as the group's identity, vocation and mission. Irvine proposes that vocation is "a call from a context which is imbued with interconnected energy to take part in a system with a clear purpose and offers you an opportunity of becoming more of what you want to be."[15] Participants in this research identified this interconnected energy as coming from God.

Jan describes spiritual direction as central to leadership and organizational development. From her own experience Jan recognizes that spiritual direction can tap into an enabling life force within the organization that is love, the power of God:

---

15. Irvine, "Background to the TEF," 29.

> I think it is central for a number of reasons . . . it's tapping into this spring of life, this power of God that will energize that person and the organization. . . . It enables community, which is essential for an organization to connect with each other in all ways. . . . And particularly also for discernment as a leader to be able to listen to the Spirit, so to keep listening to where that energy is; that life force is that love.

Spiritual direction helps a group to become aware of interconnected energy, and draw on that energy to "unleash enthusiasm, creativity, and passion."[16] Sarah integrates skills taught through her experience of spiritual direction and through group leadership and discernment courses into her work with young people in preparing them for an encounter with homelessness. In her leadership role, Sarah provides young people with an opportunity to work with indigenous homeless. Many of the youth come from privileged backgrounds and have not encountered poverty or violence firsthand. At times they find themselves face-to-face with potentially dangerous and violent situations. She speaks about the value of helping the young people to discern and to connect with God in silence before they enter immersion with the homeless. The benefit this brought to their experience enabled the youth to recognize the importance of interconnection with each other and with homeless people:

> I think it really allayed some of the fears, or it allowed people to verbalize "actually I am feeling really quite anxious." And . . . "that's OK . . . this is what you do in this . . . or this situation if you are feeling anxious." But also . . . allowed for those issues to rise up and then to give voice to that [and] . . . to mitigate any possible risk. Risk mitigation was important in that environment. . . . I loved doing debriefs afterwards, particularly with those ones who were quite fearful or reticent about going out. And then for them to see . . . that we are not looking down on these people . . . this could actually be any of us. . . . . And then . . . to come back and then say, "oh I made a connection with this person and they liked the same music as I do." And for . . . the homeless and other patrons . . . asking the students "how are you going with the study? Is everything going OK?"
>
> And for [the students] to come back and say, "do you know what—we went there but they were actually really concerned how my study really was." . . . Not one of them didn't ever have some kind of like really positive beautiful sharing about the connection

---

16. Barrett, "Seven Levels of Organisational Consciousness," 2.

that effectively they made with the homeless . . . really changing their perspective.

What Sarah alludes to is that when their relationships are created, mindsets change:

> Mindsets change . . . these young people will . . . probably be future leaders. To have that kind of knowledge at that age, hopefully will shape some of their perspective. . . . There was a lot of racism that still exists [here]. . . . They saw indigenous but also non-indigenous people; and also people who did have an education but still . . . ended up losing a job, missing a payment in their rent and then it just becomes a bit of a downward spiral that effectively, this could be any of us.

In the TEF Irvine notes that when looking at the domain of contextual experiences, we "need to look beyond current experience whether this is toward an awareness of multiple cultures, political dynamics, or possibilities into the future."[17] Through her experience of spiritual direction Sarah has been supported to see beyond surface issues in the context of her work and potentially to impact future leaders' perspectives by helping them to recognize the importance of interconnectedness.

Stage Three: External Cohesion, Making a Difference

Spiritual direction can support an organization to face the difficult task of finding meaning in suffering and in any dying aspects of group life. Dying aspects of group life might be a program that they run that is no longer working, or a service they provide that has become irrelevant, or perhaps committees that have lost their purpose. Borbely et al. recognize,

> In the wide experience of the ISECP staff in our own apostolic groups and in working with hundreds of other leadership groups, it is our conviction that many leadership groups get to the "Second Week," but very few indeed progress to the "Third Week" and beyond. Groups find it easier to dissolve and start all over again rather than work through the demanding challenges, conscious and unconscious, necessary to be a well-honed instrument in the hands of God.[18]

---

17. Irvine, "Background to the TEF," 12–13.
18. Borbely et al., *Focussing Group Energies*, 1:xv.

Spiritual direction supports the development of group identity, and commitment to service is confirmed and strengthened by facing the possibility of death and/or suffering for their shared purpose. When a group has been able to shift its focus from ego development and self-satisfaction towards a commitment to a life of service, even when the cost to group might be high, Level six of organizational consciousness is present. Level six SLOC has a focus on "making a difference in the world, either through its products and services, its involvement in the local community or its willingness to fight for causes that improve the well-being of humanity."[19]

Life-Death-Resurrection Cycle

Fifty percent of interviewees spoke about the life-death-resurrection cycle (LDR)[20] as a tool for diagnosing the life cycle of an organization and the influence this has on the way they work either as a spiritual director or within their organization. The LDR as developed by ISECP is "a sociological model for the life-cycle of a collaborative team which names the important dimensions of group life, indicates where those dimensions may cause intra-group conflict to occur, and signals how to address those conflicts when they occur."[21] Drawing on earlier work by John Sherwood on cycles and levels of organizational life, ISECP use the life of Christ as their paradigm to describe the rise and fall of the morale, feeling and energy of a team as a social reality. If the *Life-Death-Resurrection Cycle* (LDR as explored in chapter 3) is not understood or consciously attended to by the team and the leader, various unconscious forces may contribute to destructive interpersonal conflict within the group and lead to its dissolution.[22] The LDR cycle is a tool that spiritual directors can use when working with groups, to help the team notice blind spots in organizational consciousness.

Melinda is an organizational consultant and a spiritual director. She uses the LDR as a tool to help groups look honestly at where the group is located in their life cycle. She argues that if a group is going to continue work together as a group, they must first recognize their shared story (Figure 17):

19. Barrett, "Seven Levels of Organisational Consciousness," 6.

20. Borbely et al., *Leadership, Spirituality and Organisational Practice*, Mod 3, Borbely et al. develop earlier work on the life-death-resurrection cycle by Sherwood, *Leadership: The Responsible Exercise of Power* and Dalmau and Dick, *Diagnostic Model for Selecting*.

21. Borbely et al., *Leadership, Spirituality and Organisational Practice*, Mod 3, 5.

22. Borbely et al., *Leadership, Spirituality and Organisational Practice*, Mod 3, 5.

The other thing that I have used with not-for-profits mostly . . . is to go through the life-death-resurrection cycle. It is a very useful tool I find, to help them look at why they are falling apart now. I've used it with groups from the National Australia Bank, the Army, Career Counsellors to the Australian Futures Foundation and the participants in the advocacy groups. . . . It was really important to give them the capacity to look at how can we continue to live if this is the story that we share.

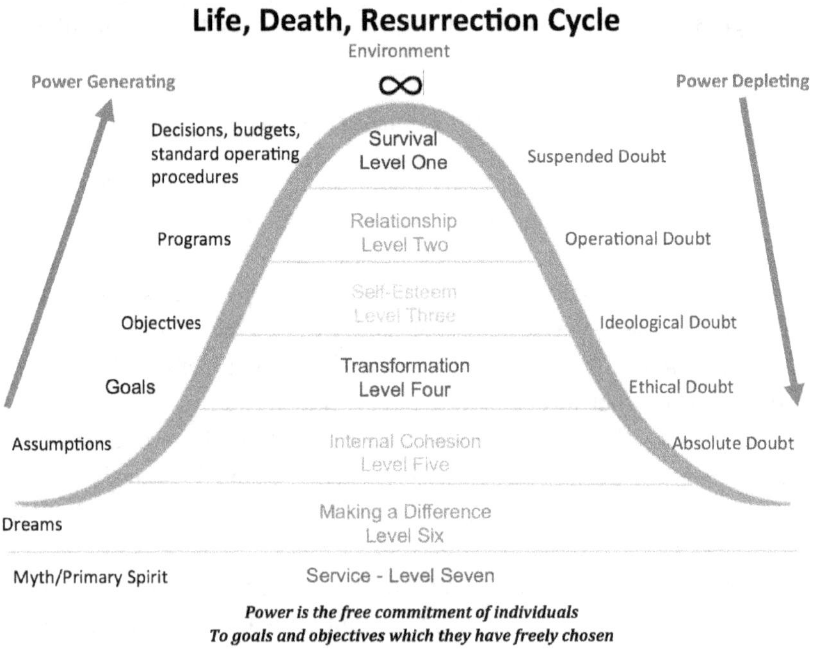

Life, Death, Resurrection Cycle

Environment

Power Generating ∞ Power Depleting

Power Generating side	Center	Power Depleting side
Decisions, budgets, standard operating procedures	Survival — Level One	Suspended Doubt
Programs	Relationship — Level Two	Operational Doubt
Objectives	Self-Esteem — Level Three	Ideological Doubt
Goals	Transformation — Level Four	Ethical Doubt
Assumptions	Internal Cohesion — Level Five	Absolute Doubt
Dreams	Making a Difference — Level Six	
Myth/Primary Spirit	Service — Level Seven	

Power is the free commitment of individuals
To goals and objectives which they have freely chosen

Figure 17: Life, death and resurrection cycle and the Seven Levels of Consciousness [23]

The central hypothesize of the LDR is that the group needs to keep the primary spirit/myth in mind, checking regularly to see whether goals, objectives, programs and decision-making remain congruent with the primary spirit/myth of the group. This will enable the group to be more conscious of what stage the life of the group is experiencing. Primary spirit is that which breathes life into an organization. It is the animating principle

---

23. Adapted from Barrett, "Seven Levels of Organisational Consciousness," 1–7.

Spiritual Direction and Organizational Development

and is absolutely fundamental to organizational existence, giving meaning for connecting around a particular primary task.[24]

Anne explains how losing sight of the primary spirit/myth can leave an organization rudderless. She explains also the importance of all members of the organization, even volunteers, being invited to participate in spiritual formation, again placing connectedness with God (which is at the core of primary spirit/myth of her organization) at the core of organizational life:

> An organization has to know what it is about otherwise it is just rudderless. And it's not about giving it rules . . . it is about giving it clarity about purpose. . . . There will be mission drift if you are not aware of who you are and what you are on about. Then all of a sudden you find yourself delving into stuff that is not actually who you are. For the volunteers I think . . . it is actually . . . really important. . . . What became really clear for the Executive Officer was that she said "It's two-fold; half of it is . . . to go and to serve the projects and to help [the group], but also half of it is about the ongoing life journey for these volunteers. I don't think that we have ever really clearly identified that before . . . we have to continue to accompany them if that's what they want.
>
> . . . I think what we're saying is: "this is what drives the work of [the group]." . . . I don't mean about religion it's about something far bigger than that . . . a relationship with Jesus, which is how they understand their relationship [with] the people that they are working with. That's the foundation . . . the platform . . . we are functioning from. So, we are inviting you to be part of that and if you don't have a relationship with Jesus but you feel some connection to a spiritual world, then that's how you understand that. It's not about saying that everybody has to look the same, but it's about saying that this is the domain, I guess.

I ask Anne whether keeping it in that domain, makes a difference to the work.

> I think it does because . . . what's been demonstrated is that losing sight of that has led to a huge mess. Because of that lack of understanding of who we are and what we're about. I don't think it is about giving it a rigidity, I think it's about giving . . . clarity of understanding of who we are. I think it is then much easier to say well then that doesn't work for us, that project is actually in contradiction to our values.

24. Bain and Bain, "Note on Primary Spirit," 2.

Group spiritual direction can support an organization to remain clear about their shared identity and shared purpose. Anne goes on to explain that her experience of having a relationship with God is much bigger than her relationship with the church or just another ideology and is her compass for decision-making. Rather than creating a rigid environment, spiritual direction supports intuition and freedom. This enables her to stay focused even at times when she feels at risk, or that death might be imminent:

> Your relationship with God ... forms your values.... The biggest gift ... for me is forming a relationship with Jesus. That was way bigger than church. And so, knowing what that's about, and having that as a foundation and strengthening that gives me a compass. It's not about an ideology; it's way, way bigger than that. It's sort of all-pervading ... a case-by-case decision that I can come back to that [relationship] and say ... what feels right for me here because of that relationship. Well I guess that's discernment isn't it? ... I have grown up in a family that is fairly conservative ... Liberal voters and belong to a certain football team and I think church can be like that as well. I feel far less constrained by that. So I guess that is what I mean when I say: having that relationship at the core ... doesn't give you rigidity, it actually gives you more openness to be able to respond to situations and the work and whatever it is, knowing that is at the core.
>
> ... I would say for me the greatest gift of the spiritual direction, is [discern] the ... decision that brings me the most peace ... to think what brings me freedom.

Anne recognizes that spiritual direction supports group movement towards peace and freedom, though it is not just about positive thinking or feeling happy. Spiritual direction enables a group to find freedom in all aspects of life, death and resurrection, helping the group to endure suffering long enough to find freedom and new life.

> So, my sense is then with the spiritual direction, it is not about everything being happy and easy all the time. That's not freedom, it's ... all encompassing, every aspect of the human existence which sometimes is really crappy and sometimes is lonely and despairing and ... understanding who I am and what my gifts are and that my work is pioneering work and it is sometimes really lonely.

It is difficult to separate the formative dynamic of Week Three as the experience of facing suffering and death, and Week Four which is the experience of resurrection. As Anne has mentioned, "you can't have

Spiritual Direction and Organizational Development

resurrection without death." Spiritual direction supports individuals and groups to face aspects of organizational life that need to be allowed to come to completion and at the same time acts as midwife for new elements as they emerge.

Maintaining Consciousness of Original Purpose and Primary Spirit

Although altruistic organizations may begin with level six and seven organizational consciousness with the purpose of making a difference and acting with social responsibility, remaining conscious of the original purpose can be difficult. Lynda describes her experience of being part of a group who developed a team of doctors, nurses and oncologists purposefully selected for their desire to work with dying patients and given training to support them in taking up this work. In recent years the organization was given funding by the government and they lost control over how staff was selected. As a consequence, induction training was withdrawn. It would seem that, although the organization had been operating in the higher levels of organizational consciousness, the decision to accept government funding came at the cost of alignment of primary spirit where level one consciousness—survival, seems to have become the dominant focus and spiritual formation was no longer available to staff:

> It is so very different because at the time when I worked there, we interviewed every nurse to find out if they are really interested and that they know what they are doing, so there is a selection process, and . . . one month full-time training before we take in patients to make sure that you know the special ideology. . . . But now it goes to the government [and] they just send any nurse . . . they just say, "we are sent there and I am just newly graduated and I don't know what to do." And some are . . . really afraid of caring for the dying. . . . So, you can imagine. . . . That is a terrible thing to send a nurse who does not want to do "care of the dying" . . . but that is the way it is when you go to this huge government machine. Like people are not really treated as people.

It seems that once an organization loses sight of and alignment with their primary spirit, their animating principle and altruistic consciousness, openness to spiritual direction and spiritual formation is also lost. I asked Lynda if there was a spiritual component in the way that management made the decisions, whether she thought that would make a difference?

> No, it wouldn't help if it is part of this big machine.... When I worked there, I was trained in hospice care, the consultant was trained ... the medical director was trained and we selected oncologists and trained them, so you know we can work as a team. But now after we left, they sent ... one of the big hospital's chief executive to oversee this one ... they are not trained, they have no idea what hospice is.... So even with a spiritual component I don't think it will work unless you have a new set of people that you select carefully, when you select them you will make sure that they have this spiritual component.

I check with Lynda to see if people have to align with the purpose or it doesn't work

> It doesn't work in the existing system.... I think apart from the training there are also some hierarchical issues too ... the style of management ... would be more collaborative.... So, I think even if we had ... style of the management [that] would make a big difference.... Especially for this type of work that we are doing ... we [are] expected to care for the patients and be very compassionate to them, but if we are [not compassionate] among our team and among ... management to the staff ... that is a lie.... So, that is why the staff are very stress[ed] and they cannot perform well.... The problem ... is the formation of the managers, I think.... Society really gives another kind of forming, like valuing achievement, getting high positions, ... it is not like a more compassionate collaborative style ... powerful people, ... the perfectionist, the compulsive people, the people that strive for achievement, they go to the top.... They become managers because they strive and strive.
>
> ... Money is a question too ... because we don't have money to run it on our own so we have to go into this big system.... It is hard to solve ... the big picture, but I think now my goal is to ... reach the people that we can get in touch with, we can do our only bit that we can.... It is important to form and to give input to the managers.... When I teach these courses, it is always the front-line clinical staff who come and very often they would say that they want their managers to come because they need to hear what we hear.

Again, we see that when an organization becomes stuck in level one of organizational consciousness, the organization seems to be no longer open to spiritual direction and spiritual formation, with the cost being a misalignment in primary spirit and high stress on front line staff. Lynda identifies the difficulties an altruistic organization can experience once management lose sight of the core purpose for which the organization was founded and cease to be inspired by the shared primary spirit or animating principle that breathed life into the organization. Instead the group can become enmeshed in hierarchical and bureaucratic issues within the earlier levels of consciousness. If these earlier levels of consciousness are not attended to as they begin to emerge, they will disintegrate interconnectedness and shared primary spirit. Individual and/or group spiritual direction intentionally designed for managers will help them to stay in touch with the spiritual health of their organization and recognize changes in organizational consciousness before they undermine the primary spirit of the group.

Stage Four: Working in the Spirit—Lasting Change

Spiritual direction can support an organization to align spiritually with core values by working with the spirit of an organization to build vitality and innovation. Sarah explains:

> In organizations it will be the Spirit that moves and sustains things, whereas law hopefully will keep things on from getting way off track or going way off track, but that's actually not going to give it the vitality or . . . innovation. If organizations are really moving in the Spirit, innovation will come.

Spiritual direction helps individuals to trust their initial and confirmed call and recognize when they are working in an organization that enables them to use their gifts. This in turn enables them to have a much greater impact on the system they are working in. I asked Sarah whether there is a difference for her when working in an organization that allows her to be herself and use her gifts, compared to working in an organization where she is trying to fit into a role.

> Definitely . . . it can really be quite stifling and if it is just fitting into a role and somebody is micromanaging then you actually can't work as well as you want to. And you can't use all the gifts that you've got.

And the impact on the organization?

> They lose out. I think things like that also lead to a higher rate of absenteeism and also presenteeism, so a person is present but not really.

So, when you are fully alive and living out of your full gifted self, do you actually impact the organization?

> Undoubtedly, particularly in a role of communications. I think that is a really special place to be.

Sarah recalls her experience of working as a communications officer, a role in which she was able to create lasting change by supporting the community to change their perspective of the State School system in Australia. Sarah uses the language of "povo schools" to describe disadvantaged schools that might be understood by the community to only serve people experiencing poverty.

> In the past people would say, "don't engage the media because they only do negative things." And state schools, well it was just . . . "they're really just povo schools . . . people aren't really teaching, it is kind of second rate." When I started getting a whole lot of positive news stories consistently into the newspaper . . . the radio was more interested; and then the TV were more interested; and they ended up coming to us on a number of occasions. . . . I think it really changed some of the perspectives about state schools and the pride in the organization; that actually we are doing things and helping our students, our young people to grow up with more confidence. But also, I think some of the teaching staff and some of the principals as well too; they were still in the mindset that this was just an institutional approach and just a means to an end. When actually working in the Spirit, your school has its own identity and its own special place in the community and your students do have every opportunity to achieve and succeed rather than just going to a povo school, and I will probably end up either not working or with a povo job, in a povo household.

So, you have created and promoted permanent change.

> I hope so . . . I always get goose bumps thinking about it, because the state schools . . . 33 percent of our students were indigenous. Whereas the Catholics and privates only had 7–11 percent of their students were indigenous. . . . The state school system was embracing a lot more of . . . the forgotten people and the people who were seen as a drain on the system. And that will be an ongoing thing

in that area particularly [where I am working] and for a couple of generations I think. It also helps me sit back when I was disappointed at some people's attitudes that I could say well "OK, Holy Spirit this is your work I can only do this much but it is not up to me." And also letting go of that Savior complex too which I think some people fall into the trap too and they can go really down—this is far bigger than any individual.

Sarah recognizes that by taking up her role in leadership as an individual from level seven organizational consciousness, she has the capacity to make a difference to society and create permanent change within organizational systems.

Spiritual direction can influence organizational development by raising organizational consciousness. In the early phases of spiritual formation and organizational consciousness, spiritual direction supports organizational development by developing relationship and self-esteem consciousness through:

- releasing corporate shame to develop shared identity;
- raising relationship consciousness; and
- moving towards transformation via vulnerability.

In stage two development of organizational consciousness, spiritual formation supports groups as they move towards transformation, adaptability and continuous learning. Key elements of the spiritual direction process include stimulating communal discernment that develops internal cohesion and awareness of interconnectedness. In stage three of organizational consciousness, spiritual direction helps the group to come to recognize and embrace the depth of its primary spirit and become conscious of patterns of life, death and resurrection within the group. When the group works in the Spirit, it enables lasting change.

Spiritual direction can influence organizational development by raising organizational consciousness. Organizational consciousness can be defined as "the organization's capacity for reflection; a centring point for the organization to "think" and find the elements of unity across systems that link to the organization's identity and self-referencing attributes. It operates at three stages: reflective, social, and collective consciousness."[25] Spiritual direction provides a process for simultaneous reflective and anticipatory

---

25. Pees et al., "Organizational Consciousness," 505.

exploration of organizational life. When an organization has the capacity to reflect on the past and simultaneously look toward the future it wants to create, the organization can become conscious of patterns of life, death and resurrection that lie within, and thereby raise awareness to what might be holding back any potential for flourishing.

The data revealed that for participants in the study, a strong cohesive identity of the organization is founded on a shared mission and clear sense of purpose—properly understood as the group's identity, vocation and mission. Spiritual direction can support groups as they move towards transformation, adaptability and continuous learning. Key elements of the spiritual direction and organizational development include communal discernment, developing internal cohesion, and awareness of interconnectedness. When the group is aware of and connected by a shared primary spirit, lasting change becomes possible.

Chapter 6:

The Role of the Spiritual Director in Leadership and Organizational Development

THE SPIRITUAL DIRECTOR CAN become a resource for leadership and organizational development by creating a place of safety and holding where there is freedom to explore the interior dynamics of leadership and organizational life from a spiritual perspective. In order to create an effective container for the work of spiritual direction, the director must have the capacity to hold the leader/group with compassion and love, without judgement, and to be able to listen in-depth to experiences of life, death and resurrection.

Although it is helpful for the spiritual director to have some experience in leadership and organizational development, it is not essential. What is essential to the role is that he or she has undertaken his or her own in-depth spiritual formation journey. Appropriate formal and informal spiritual formation would include: a deep exploration of the director's own experience; knowledge of discernment of spirits; a well-developed trust in God (Source) as an active experience of interconnectedness; and the capacity to recede when the leader or group is working directly with God. The spiritual director must understand and respect the importance of confidentiality and clear boundaries around the spiritual direction system. Careful attention to boundaries is essential for creating an effective working environment for spiritual direction. I will explore the *role* of the spiritual director in the setting of leadership and organizational development by drawing on the Transforming Experience Framework.

The Transforming Experience Framework (Figure 18) separates the five domains of experience for the purpose of working with a person as they explore how they can take up authentic action through role, though in reality all domains of experience are interconnected and influence each other at all times. In this chapter, I take each domain of experience individually to explore how the role of spiritual director is shaped:

i. being a person (psychological, physical);

ii. being in a system (organizations and institutions);

iii. being in a context (social, economic, global, political);

iv. connectedness with Source (spiritual domain and the domain of deeply held values); and

v. role (the intersection of the four aforementioned domains of experience).[1]

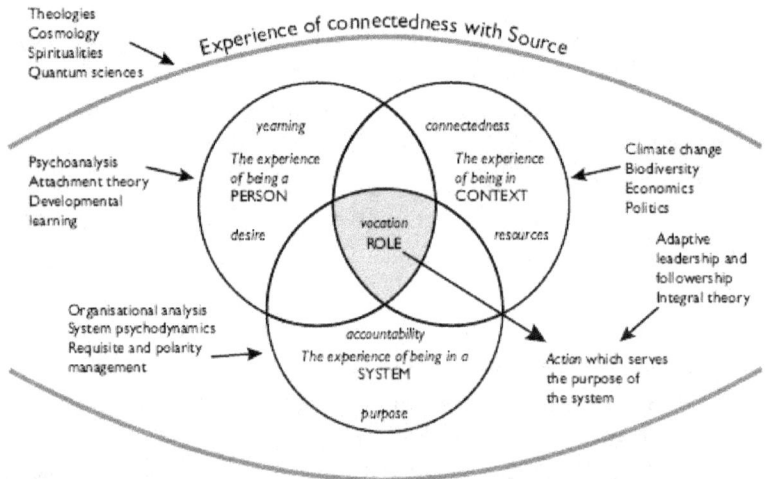

Figure 18: Transforming experience into authentic action through role (TEF)[2]

What follows is an exploration of the role of the spiritual director drawn from the experience of experienced spiritual directors. To protect their identities, I have used pseudonyms.

---

1. Long, *Transforming Experience in Organisations*, 5.
2. Long, *Transforming Experience in Organisations*, 5.

Role of the Spiritual Director in the Domain of Person

The experience of being a person is described as being "profoundly related to others: "a nexus or network of relationships that center in the person . . . [within whom] are carried one's personal images of parents, siblings, colleagues, aspirations and fears.'[3] This includes:

- developing and transforming an identity through the different ages and contexts of life;
- developing intellect, skills, and what Bion[4] calls the apparatus for thinking the thoughts that exist in the social context around us; and
- the construction of a personality, the adoption of values, purposes, spirituality and the creation of personal strategies for managing emotional and relational life.[5]

Both spiritual direction and the TEF recognize that desire and yearning are at the core of personhood. Desire is a function that rests within a person, drawing them towards some object or person and it is accompanied by a positive affect. Bazalgette names desire as "one of the primary sources of energy to act in the world, connecting with other human beings to make a difference."[6] Gillies Cusson posits: "The dynamism of desire is a divine grace, the gift of God's love."[7] The spiritual director's role is to support the directee in following their deepest desires in order that they may connect to "the vivifying action of the Holy Spirit within. . . . Likewise, the interior dynamism of the Spiritual Exercises is a movement that ceaselessly invites individuals "to grow as persons on a journey towards a divine presence through an ever-closer union with the whole of creation."[8]

Yearning is deep desire and expresses the experience of intense longing, consciously and unconsciously, for something. "In spiritual terms, yearning is the link between person and source. It is the longing of the

---

3. Roberts and Bazalgette, "Daring to Desire," 143.

4. Bion, *Attention and Interpretation*, in Long, *Transforming Experience in Organisations*, 66.

5. Long, *Transforming Experience in Organisations*, 6–7.

6. Roberts and Bazalgette, "Daring to Desire," 143.

7. Cusson, *Biblical Theology and the Spiritual Exercises*, 118, in Lonergan, *Dynamism of Desire*, 37.

8. Cusson, *Biblical Theology and the Spiritual Exercises*, in Lonergan, *Dynamism of Desire*, 37.

spirit or soul that impels the person towards finding meaning and identity within a purpose beyond the self."[9] Fourth century Christian theologian and philosopher Augustine of Hippo, names yearning as our deep desire for connection with God, and God's desire for connection with creation: "because you have made us for yourself, our heart is restless until it rests in you."[10]

The role of spiritual director is influenced significantly by each person's unique experience of personhood. The depth of self-awareness and spiritual formation the spiritual director has undertaken themselves will determine and influence the effectiveness of the spiritual direction session. All spiritual directors in this study were formed or have worked at Sentir Graduate College of Spiritual Formation and base their practice on the principle "that students will gain the greatest benefit from their study when the head and the heart come together to know deeply the content being taught from within their own experience."[11] of personhood.

When a person takes up the role of spiritual director, personhood is their primary resource. The director applies his or her knowledge, personal experience and relationship with God to guide them in accompanying the directee. Veronica explains the importance of understanding the relational nature of spiritual direction and, in particular *who* the *person* is in the role of spiritual director. The director sets the tone from which the directee will instinctively know what is allowed in the room. Veronica explains,

> It's really important that the spiritual director . . . is committed to that ongoing growth in knowledge and in self-awareness, and in prayer in relationship with God. I think if you don't have that then your directee can't do the work of spiritual direction. . . . We are not just talking about companioning here. A companion is a person who just sort of says "yes, yes, three bags full" and accepts it. We are talking about somebody who will go to the dark places, who will go to the joys, and can go there because they know them in their own personal life and know[s] . . . life can be found in dark and light. And it is all for that ongoing relationship with God . . . relationship with self, and with other, and how that can be creative.

It is critical that the director makes time for self-reflection or self-supervision after each spiritual direction session, honoring all that has been

---

9. Long, "Transforming Experience Framework," 7.
10. Augustine of Hippo, *Saint Augustine Confessions*, 3.
11. Miles, "Ignatian Spirituality, Apostolic Creativity and Leadership," 41.

shared and becoming aware of what has happened to her as the director as part of her ongoing formation. The collective knowledge and wisdom gathered over years of listening to directees and being touched by their stories, deepens the director's understanding of how the Spirit moves in the lives of people and contributes to their ongoing formation. Leanne describes spiritual direction as a two-way process and highlighted the importance of openness on the part of the director and the directee:

> [Spiritual Direction] is a two-way process. I have to be in that space of openness in order to accept fully whatever may come out of there. I have got to be vulnerable in order to allow that to happen. If I am defended it's not going to happen. So, I've got to be in a space where I can be open myself. Otherwise, I'm going to put the limitations on what is going to happen. And I'll do that subliminally or it might be quite overt . . . Can you honor my experience? . . . Can they be in touch with their own stuff? . . . Can I allow the other to explore anything? Can I be in there?

The director's personal experience in all aspects of their life history has a direct influence on the spiritual direction relationship. Leanne spoke of being with directees who have experienced some form of childhood abuse. She postulates that as she has worked through her own experiences of childhood abuse, her experience has become a resource in accompanying others. Where there is shared experience, even though it is not named overtly in the spiritual direction session, the relationship between director and directee can develop deep trust. Leanne explains,

> There is a different . . . level of understanding. There is a connection. . . . It's an innate awareness that I know that you understand. And I have found this when people come . . . who have been sexually abused. It's amazing how often people will say to me "you understand what I am saying." I haven't told them anything of my history, but they know that I understand in a way that somebody who hasn't been through a similar process, cannot understand, can be present, but can't be present with that subliminal connection of similar experience of knowing.

So, is the connection at the level of experience?

> Yes, but it's a subliminal connection . . .

You know if the person you are speaking to has actually touched into something close to what you are talking about, and when you have been heard at that level, what happens?

> It's wonderful. It is just a sense of . . . I can relax into who I am, because I know that you are connecting. . . . Not at an intellectual level. We are connecting at a very deep subliminal spiritual level. . . . When I leave, I am different. . . . And [as a spiritual director] the time that I spend [reflecting] after somebody's gone, is vital. To honor the reality of not only what has been entrusted to me, but where I am in it. . . . I am different, because of that touching at that level. We are both different.

The depth of spiritual formation that the spiritual director has undertaken directly influences the role. Rohr is clear: "When you are transformed others will be transformed through you."[12] Pettit describes spiritual formation as "the holistic work of God in a believer's life whereby systematic change renders the individual continually closer to the image and actions of Jesus Christ."[13] The spiritual director will be limited by his or her own experience and by the image of God they carry for themselves. If the director's image of God is more restricted and limited than the image of God the directee carries, the work of spiritual direction is thwarted. Pam describes four different experiences of spiritual direction in which she articulates how spiritual direction in her experience has been: enabling and encouraging; disabling and damaging; dissatisfying and pointless; and finally challenging and enabling.

Pam's first experience of spiritual direction came in her early twenties where her spiritual director provided an enabling environment for her:

> It was after a turning point in my own life post university where I thought I was launching into one career, which was so obviously not me, and then I was going towards teaching which was really me at that time. . . . I saw her in direction . . . it was . . . an easy conversation in which I felt totally at ease, trusted and valued, honored. . . . I trusted her experience and her wisdom. She was a good bit older than me, maybe 15 years or so . . . it also led into the time of meeting my husband . . . I remember speaking to her "I am sure he is going to ask me to marry him" so some sort of discerning but always very enabling and encouraging. . . . She gave me myself . . . that sense of who I am is good. . . . It was helpful and

---

12. Rohr, *What the Mystics Know*, 121.
13. Pettit, *Foundations of Spiritual Formation*, 19.

> it really nurtured my relationship with God and others. There was a lot of freedom about it and depth, but a light touch . . . her faith was very strong and she loved scripture and had a great sense of humor and you know just good company. . . . So, I think of her as really important in my life . . . and big horizon, that's what I feel with her, that sense of the reach of God and not laborious.

Pam's first spiritual director created a place of safety and holding where she felt totally at ease, trusted, valued and honored which enabled her to trust her director's experience and wisdom. She describes her director's disposition as: encouraging, enabling, having a wide horizon; strong faith; great sense of humor and great company; the way she lived her own faith and her own relationship with God echoed throughout the spiritual direction relationship.

Pam's second experience of spiritual direction came at a time in her life when she was vulnerable, recently married, a new migrant to Australia and having her first child. Her spiritual director was patronizing and did not respect confidentiality, evidenced by the breaking of boundaries of the spiritual direction session and assuming the role of "expert". During the spiritual direction session, the directee hands over authority to the director, and when the director abuses that authority, the spiritual direction session will become damaging for the directee:

> I had a really bad experience then moving to . . . Australia . . . I sought out someone and I met another religious sister. . . . It was a very vulnerable time. . . . She was very patronizing, and she would say things out of the session. . . . She was the expert and I knew nothing. And I felt there were things wrong with me and she advised me to seek psychotherapy, which I did. But the person she recommended was totally not right; didn't have the right skill set or background experience. So, that was a damaging thing. I felt very vulnerable because I was in her hands, I had given authority to this spiritual director and she took advantage. . . . We'd finish the session and she accompanies me to the front door and then . . . she would say something that pulled the rug from under me. I don't know why I kept going to see her really. That was not a healthy or good choice.
>
> . . . There was a lot of power going on there. . . . It wasn't good. . . . She just made me feel that there was something wrong with me, and that I was lonely. Well, I probably was. But the way I heard it was . . . "I was weak" or "other people aren't lonely like you."

> I don't think her experience of life was helpful. It was like there was something missing whereas my first [spiritual director] was fully alive. . . . She trusted me, and she had really lived, you know big discernments in her religious life, in love, in health and . . . at lots of levels integrated and not afraid. . . . Whereas this [spiritual director] was sort of reduced or . . . not really fully alive. There was a lack of joy and a lack of love and freedom.

Pam speaks of a third experience of spiritual direction in which she felt dissatisfied and spiritual direction was unhelpful. The spiritual director does not seem to have the skills to work with the directee's experience or to challenge her to grow in her relationship with God:

> I did see a spiritual director . . . who was another religious sister. I made some retreats in daily life through the parish and then kept going with her but . . . that was not satisfying. She offered for me to see her but she would just twitter on for 45 minutes of the hour . . . I remember saying to her "are you going to ask me about my prayer?" . . . She was just going on about, asking me questions, circling around and not really going anywhere, really very frustrating. She was encouraging and affirming but she didn't really challenge me. [I was] looking to go deeper and to really be stimulated and challenged and discover things about myself and God.

Pam's fourth spiritual director was formed in Australia in the Ignatian tradition and it seems a new dimension is now added. Her director challenged her to consider "What difference does your relationship with God make in the world?" The director explores her desires, longing, sense of call and of being drawn into life and she becomes stronger, bolder and more aware of her own giftedness:

> Her way of accompanying was always "where is this leading?" A realization, and affirmation . . . that I might have a call. So exciting . . . that same thing of my desire . . . I had never had direction like that . . . and it just blew me away and I really felt so alive . . . questions that take you deeper . . . that very active style. That has been my big turning point, to the extent that I really want others to know that and to have that experience. . . . It wasn't a feel-good experience because it enabled me to go into the lion's den of where I work and to grow stronger in my call in who I am, in my identity to really keep circling around these dynamics of the Exercises and to see how I am being drawn to life.

The Role of the Spiritual Director

> . . . [I grew] bolder and more overt I suppose or more courageous or more able to speak my desire or to advocate for others and to say yes to things that might seem a bit crazy. . . . I could see that she really wanted to nurture the gifts and it's always about the relationship with Jesus.

Pam's varied experiences demonstrate that not all forms of spiritual direction will necessarily support leadership and organizational development, in fact, some experiences were damaging to her and her leadership potential. The depth of experience, the disposition of the spiritual director and the quality of the director's formation will have a significant influence on the spiritual direction experience. When the spiritual director is trained in the Ignatian tradition there is a deliberate focus on apostolic outcome and a desire to strengthen a person's spiritual self so that potential might be released. It can be expected that a spiritual director trained in the Ignatian tradition will: have a deep understanding of discernment; have worked through their own experience of pain, suffering and joy; know that being on the spiritual journey is a journey towards freedom. Sally also had two different experiences of spiritual direction: one in Australia through Sentir and the other in an overseas Ignatian retreat center. She notices the difference:

> I think the biggest difference between the direction here and the direction during my 30-day [retreat] is more on my personal identity. . . . Spiritual direction here is much deeper on who am I and what am I doing . . . I have a better integration of my identity, my vocation and my mission. . . . I think it helped me to . . . have a deeper understanding of what is the purpose of my life, and what God is calling me to do.

If spiritual direction is to offer genuine and lasting support in leadership development, the director needs to be skilled at supporting the directee in discerning their call so that this can then become the compass point for future discernment. Discernment of call involves discovering and exploring the "true self."

A Compassionate Gaze as a Disposition in the Role of Spiritual Director

A central aspect of the spiritual director's role is to support the directee in discovering their *true self*. Donald Winnicott clarifies this goal:

- *True self*—a sense of self based on spontaneous authentic experience, and a feeling of being alive, having a real self.
- *False self-defensive façade*—one which in extreme cases could leave its holders lacking spontaneity and feeling dead and empty, behind a mere appearance of being real.[14]

In her experience of spiritual direction Pam asserts that the director: "gave me myself, you know that sense of who I am is good." Melinda identified a similar experience when her director created a space where she knew she would not be judged. As a consequence she was able to let go of her negative self-image or false-self, and begin to see the goodness in herself, or "true self". At the time Melinda had just completed a significant leadership role. She describes her experience of two spiritual directors: the first an abbess from an enclosed monastery, the second an Ignatian-trained laywoman. Melinda recounts her experience of spiritual direction with the abbess:

> I remember coming out having spoken to her the first time . . . Though there were no clear directions, talking to somebody who actually understood and who didn't say much, but at one point, pointed out the dangers of trying to help others, too much, or from the wrong reason. . . . [It was] definitely not her worldly knowledge; I wasn't looking for worldly knowledge at that point. I did not trust my own judgement at all by that stage because I have been so wildly trusting of people who weren't worthy of it and . . . that early stage when I was busy turning on myself and believing everything nasty said about me.

I asked Melinda what she thought her spiritual director saw in her.

> I have no idea. As far as I was concerned the most important thing was to feel accepted. I was full of self-blame and confusion, desolation. . . . It was a really, really difficult time, so to just be able to go there and say that I feel terrible, grief and lack of certainty. . . . She [was] a pair of ears, it was more than that . . . the idea that you form . . . a Christ-like relationship, it was like that to me. It was somewhere I could explain something and wouldn't get judged or told I was wrong.

Melinda reiterates the importance of the spiritual direction space as a place where she felt she would not be judged. She describes her experience

---

14. Winnicott, "Ego Distortion in Terms of True and False Self," 140–57.

of her second spiritual director and highlights the importance of the spiritual director being able to help the directee to be free to lower their defenses and enter the session with vulnerability:

> [She] was another one who sat and listened and said very little really, but asked questions that made me consider my position . . . so she was not a threat to the ego which was going in fairly guarded. I think we made quite a connection . . . I was still highly agitated. She was a very calm presence . . . I would say that is awfully important because if someone had tried a different approach, . . . I would have come . . . with natural and ingrained oppositional defense.

The capacity to create a working environment that enables the directee to lower defenses is an important aspect of the role of the spiritual director. When the director has confidence and trust that every part of the directee's story has the potential for redemption, she will be able to journey to the most difficult and dark places with her directee, confident that God will support them both.

Lynda explains how her experience of being in spiritual direction was one where her director saw her at her "lowest, darkest self, at her most vulnerable and still her director could see the goodness in her." This not only affected the way she saw herself but also how she interacted with others and her disposition as a counsellor.

> I saw my counseling client yesterday. . . . During the process, I invited her to look at herself with the compassionate gaze of Christ, and she experienced his gaze of unconditional acceptance, firmly affirming her goodness despite her uncertainty about it. It was such a grace-filled and healing experience. I experienced what you had been telling me many times, that my experience could be my asset of helping others to heal. . . .
>
> In the three-day course that I [ran]. . . I offered the [participants] what I have experienced from [Sentir, which is] . . . to value their goodness while understanding the pain and stress they experience in witnessing human suffering . . . raising their awareness, and validating for the need of self-care and compassion. I felt I had never taught in that depth before, and never felt such profound connection with participants. They gave very positive and grateful feedback and wanted to have another course as follow up.[15]

---

15. Lynda, email received March 31, used with permission.

Lynda shared with me an image that she drew (Figure 19), which depicts her experience of the compassionate gaze of Christ.

Figure 19: "The Compassionate Gaze of Christ" Illustration by Lynda

> You have seen me at my lowest, my darkest self, at my most vulnerable and still you can see the goodness in me. If there is one thing that I am most grateful for it's that you see this in me.

I suggest that the image above symbolically reflects the disposition of the *person* in the role of spiritual director as he or she takes up the role of Christ in listening and simultaneously sees Christ within the directee. When working in the area of leadership and organizational development, the capacity to hold the leader and the organization with compassion and love, without judgement, and to listen in-depth to experiences of life, death and resurrection are central to the role of the spiritual director.

Role of the Spiritual Director and the Domain of System

> "System" refers to a set of activities with a boundary... that differentiates systems from their environment and from other systems.

The Role of the Spiritual Director

This enables managed connection, collaboration and engagement through transactions across the boundary.[16] . . . Each system has a purpose to which every activity within it contributes (or not!) . . . Purpose is about why; why the system exists, why the context demands that the system exist, and, therefore, it relates fundamentally to context.[17]

The spiritual direction relationship is a closed system where the shared purpose between the director and the directee is to engage in a spiritual direction relationship (Figure 20). Maintaining the boundaries and confidentiality of this relationship is essential to enabling a successful spiritual direction system. Spiritual direction is primarily conducted in a private room with the door closed and any possibility of interruption minimized. Ideally, multiple relationships are avoided wherever possible and contact between spiritual direction sessions is none or minimal.

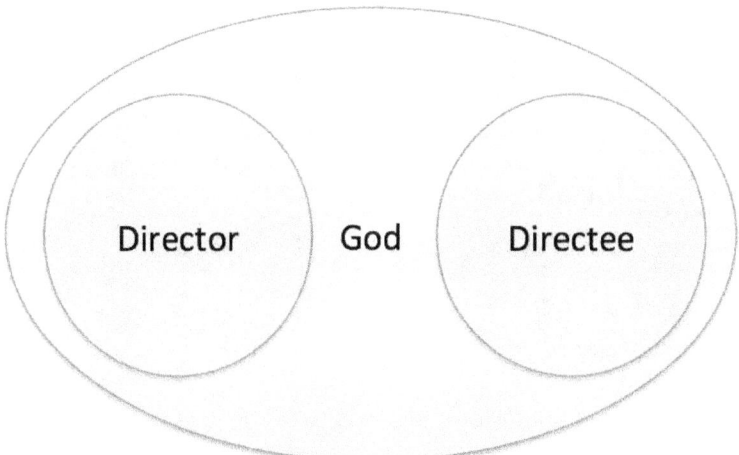

Figure 20: Spiritual direction system

Both the director and the directee will bring other systems with them into the relationship. Systems that support the spiritual director may include:

- a particular spiritual tradition and genre of spiritual direction in which he or she has been trained and formed;
- a workgroup or organization they participate in or are employed by;

---

16. Roberts and Bazalgette, "Daring to Desire," 144 cite Miller and Rice, *Systems of Organisation*.

17. Roberts and Bazalgette, "Daring to Desire," 144.

- professional spiritual direction bodies they belong to such as Spiritual Directors International and the Australian Ecumenical Council for Spiritual Direction; and
- a support system, which includes supervision and their own personal spiritual direction.

Though these systems support the spiritual director in role, they are external to the spiritual direction relationship (Figure 21). According to the interviewees, other systems the director belongs to such as family, recreational, political and others, should not enter overtly into the spiritual direction system.

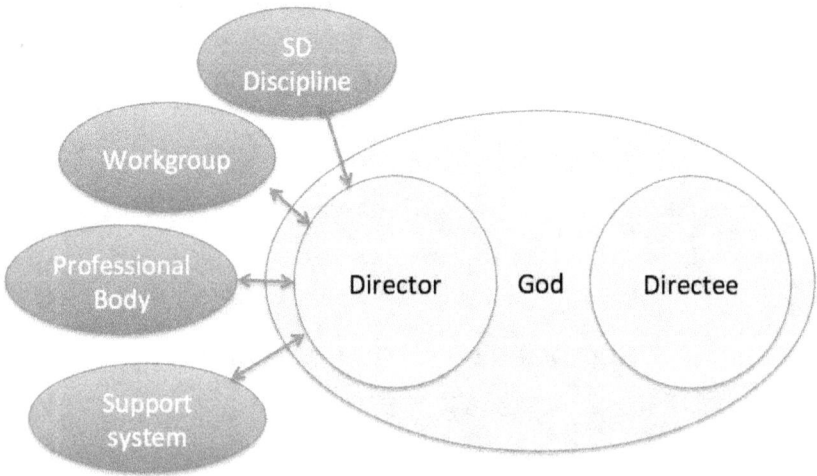

Figure 21: The spiritual direction system for the director

A traditional understanding of the spiritual direction system for the directee is that he or she will bring themselves and their relationship with God to the spiritual direction session. Though other relationships will come into the session from time to time, these are not the traditional focus of spiritual direction. This book, however, expands the idea of spiritual direction to consider how spiritual direction can support leadership and organizational development and therefore the directee will be encouraged to bring multiple relationships into the spiritual direction system, in particular, their workplace systems (see Figure 22).

The Role of the Spiritual Director

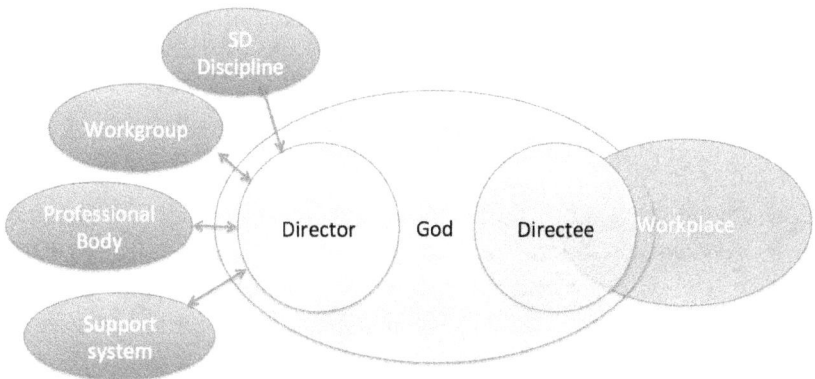

Figure 22: Spiritual direction system incorporating leadership and organizational development

All participants in the research identified the importance of confidentiality and clear, effective boundaries in the spiritual direction relationship. Leanne explains how for her, knowing that the spiritual direction space was a place where she could feel safe because confidentiality was maintained, enabled her to face challenging and difficult personal work in spiritual direction:

> It was through her ability to hold a space that was safe. It was confidential. . . . I knew that I was being honored irrespective of whatever I might have been grappling with, trying to get in touch with, talking about. . . . It was challenging. It was frightening. It was and all of that, but there was a very intimate relationship, not only with the director, but encouraged to be with God. . . . That's what changed the whole process of who I am now.

Pam shared a similar experience where she describes how the professional boundaries maintained in the relationship enabled a depth of trust that encouraged her to be vulnerable:

> How far can you go and how do you have relationships, professional relationships and a depth of trust and sharing and vulnerability and how you speak truth to power. . . . I think . . . the ability to name stuff in direction and knowing that it's confidential.

Maintaining confidentiality and healthy boundaries are essential to the work of spiritual direction. This is particularly true when leaders bring their working relationships and company issues into the spiritual direction session. If confidentiality is broken, trust is undermined and the work of spiritual direction is no longer effective.

Centrality of God/Source in the Spiritual Direction System

The unique character of the spiritual direction system rests on the conscious inclusion of God/Source as a living and active presence, a dynamic in which the director and the directee both depend on God/Source for guidance and support. The directee might experience dependency on the director at times, in which case the director returns the focus and dependency back onto God wherever possible.

Three participants in this research are trained spiritual directors and practicing psychotherapists. We spoke about cultural differences between the spiritual direction relationship and the therapy relationship. Fiona notes that in her experience as a therapist, the client might become dependent on her in the therapy relationship, making weekly visits and having access to the therapist after hours in case of an emergency. I asked Fiona whether in her experience as a spiritual director a similar culture of dependency exists:

> No! Spiritual direction is diametrically opposed to that. Yes, I am a companion on the journey, but this is about you and God. This is about your spirituality and if I can help you . . . to deepen that, to touch into that to enhance that in any way, that's what I am here for. But I am not here to take that away from you. I am not here to create dependence; I am here to create independence.

That is not to say that therapy does not encourage independence as well, rather it highlights that dependency in the spiritual direction relationship is on God/Source, not the director. Mark notices how different he found the experience of receiving spiritual direction after having been in therapy for some time:

> He listened in a different way to the analyst that I had gone to when I was in the public service. I would go to this analyst, he'd sit behind a big desk you know, he'd talk about all sorts of things. . . . If I was two minutes late, we would have a big analysis about why I was late and that sort of thing. You always felt like you were on the spot with him. Well [my spiritual director] wasn't like that. Somehow or another there was a gentleness and we just kind of meandered. And I did feel that he listened. I think that was the thing.

The Role of the Spiritual Director

For Mark the spiritual direction relationship is encouraging and supportive and when trust has been established it can become challenging. Mark is a practicing psychotherapist and spiritual director. He explains that the content of spiritual direction and therapy can be exactly the same, but the focus is different.

> One of the pieces of book I came across when I was doing my research was a study, which identified that the actual content of what people brought to spiritual direction, was exactly the same as what they brought to therapy. . . . The difference is the focus . . . what's quite open and up-front in spiritual direction is that the focus is on the person's relationship with God. Well, that is not necessarily the case in therapy; it can be. . . . I have some people who come to me who want to explore whatever they need to explore psychologically but in the context of their relationship with God and so the two of them are talked about together. When it's like that, it's not much different to spiritual direction in my mind, except for the fact that I have knowledge and skills and experiences to unpack it in a psychological form that helps them to listen more deeply psychologically. . . . But I also want to link that to their journey with God and that relationship. . . . When I do spiritual direction; I don't stop being a therapist.

God/Source is central to the spiritual direction system and when this focus is maintained, other skills within therapy, counseling or even leadership development can enter the system and support the work of spiritual direction.

Role of the Spiritual Director and the Domain of Context

The domain of *context* is the environment in which the social system occurs and includes aspects of what might influence the role holder's experience of the "physical, political, economic, social, historical, international, and emotional context for the system."[18] The rapidly evolving world of the twenty-first century has changed the setting for spiritual direction considerably. The dawning of a new Axial Age[19] where interconnectedness supersedes individualism, calls for a wider understanding of how spiritual direction can support an evolving world.

18. Long, "Transforming Experience Framework," 9.
19. See ch. 2 for a discussion on the new Axial Age.

The role of spiritual director has traditionally been held by religious men and women, often with minimal or no training, intrinsically connected to a religious setting and supported by a religious community. Now women and men from many walks of life, religious and spiritual traditions, and with a variety of professional backgrounds, are being trained as spiritual directors. Formation programs for spiritual directors are readily accessible throughout the world and many are aligned and accredited with post-graduate university awards. The Australian Ecumenical Council for Spiritual Direction lists eighteen formation programs for spiritual directors in Australia, all of which have emerged within the last thirty (or so) years. Spiritual direction is moving out of the confines of religious settings and emerging in new places and as a professional practice.

I introduce one example of how spiritual direction can be introduced into a workplace as an integral part of the work system and describe the influence spiritual direction can have on the organization.

Spiritual Direction in the Workplace

The context of spiritual direction as a professional role within an organization is an emergent one. Joy has considerable professional experience in the field of residential care and has a Master of Arts in Spiritual Direction. She was recently employed by a not-for-profit care facility in the role of spiritual director for the organization. Her role is to facilitate spirituality and spiritual direction across the organization by being available for consultation to management, staff and residents. At the beginning of each work-shift, she is given a formal handover by staff and updated on what is going on in the facility, and which residents or staff might need individual care.

Because she is embedded in the organizational system in a formal way this gives her access to information and resources as well as the capacity to speak into formal management processes within the workplace. As with the current approach to professional chaplains and pastoral/spiritual carers being appointed as allied health practitioners in healthcare settings this is a considerable change from the system of volunteer pastoral carers who generally came from a church setting outside the system and had minimal training.

> Pastoral carers were not seen to have any real role or authority in an organization and so I think the title is important because it gives you some impetus in the organization and some

The Role of the Spiritual Director

> acknowledgment. I think it is important for the residents and family members to realize I am not from the local church because that's their understanding that I must be. "What denomination are you? . . . What church do you come from?" I say that I am here as the spiritual director. I am here to look after your emotional wellbeing and spiritual wellbeing and I don't represent any church.

One of the outcomes of her role is that communication between the residents and staff is improving. Residents feel they can speak openly to Joy during spiritual direction sessions:

> It helps them because they know that (a) it is confidential and (b) that I will listen to them and (c) there will be some outcome. . . . I can bring issues up . . . and they get some sort of resolution in that.

I asked Joy if she had noticed any changes in the organization since she started in this role:

> Yes, the manager has become very dependent on me. [Particularly] in asking me to talk to the family members. . . . She is identifying that I am better to sit with the family member than another staff member [is], and not that they have articulated the reason why, but it is about how I approach them.

So, your skills of listening and speaking make a difference?

> Very much so and it is also about making the family members feel as though they are being listened to and that they are cared about.

Joy's spiritual direction conversations with the most vulnerable part of the organization, the residents, are having a significant impact on management decisions. Because of Joy's expertise in residential care, she can combine her knowledge of the systemic issues with the needs of vulnerable residents. Joy described to me how one of the residents, John (not his real name) had been refusing care. When staff came to wash him or change his linen, he refused them entry to his room. Joy over time gained the trust of the resident and slowly he revealed his deep story to her. She heard about his pain, his family, his career, his loneliness and his erratic relationship with God. Having gained his trust, she was then able to speak to management about how to resolve the issue of his room. She pointed out that they had a responsibility to act and if they didn't clean his room and remove all the soiled linen and clothing, they would be closed down immediately if they were inspected. The combination of listening to the most vulnerable part of the institution and then speaking with authority from her role to management allowed both the resident to live more comfortably and management to act appropriately.

Joy shared many stories like John's with me. Joy explains:

> What you get is . . . a resident who is less aggressive; who might have a better meal that night; who might sleep better; who hopefully . . . [can] reduce their medication. So, you know the spin-offs are enormous. . . . You have your clinical care and you have your spiritual care and combine those two together. You can feed them and give them all the medications and bomb them out as much as you want to but really, you are not nurturing them.
>
> Trust is very important. They have to trust me, if they don't trust me then they are not going to tell me what is on their mind or their story, or what do they feel in their heart.
>
> They are just not bodies that are sit in a chair . . . when you talk to them, they . . . become animated. . . . One man . . . he is a very big man with his head . . . down. He has spinal problems . . . he is a bit of a scary looking person. Anyhow, I sat down with him and talked with him and he is one of the nicest gentlemen. . . . He is in an enormous amount of pain but he talks . . . so openly. He said, "no one has bothered to listen to me." . . . And now, he seeks me out.

As I listened to Joy speak about the encounters she has at the care facility I wondered whether a pastoral carer could do the work she was referring to and what the difference might be. Joy was clear that it was the fact that it was a professional appointment and the depth of formation that made the difference. It is also true that now there are very few volunteers and most pastoral and spiritual carers are professional appointments with very similar roles (and often power/advocacy/influence) as Joy.

> No, volunteers . . . sometimes they go in for a reason like the represent their church. Like they have the Jehovah Witnesses or . . . that come in.

So, it must be deliberately not religious? . . .

> Definitely not. . . . You can't be seen to be a denomination. . . . It is not just a visit. It is more than that. It is the presence and the continuity.

The Role of the Spiritual Director

But also, there is something about being integrated into the staff, and the handovers and what you are hearing feeds back into the system instead of just staying with you.

> Yes, yes, it is a real cycle. . . . I am not just on the outside.

Professionally appointed pastoral and spiritual care practitioners routinely have formal roles in care facilities and as allied health professionals work in a multi-disciplinary way. The distinction is often around volunteer/professional rather than just pastoral carer and the depth of formation that spiritual directors undertake. When spiritual direction is formally integrated into the workplace, it can impact the system as a whole. To appoint a non-religious person into a formal spiritual direction role in a residential care facility has become possible. This is perhaps due to the changing context where 'spiritual but not religious' is a common pathway and the diminishment of formal religious institutions' availability to provide spiritual care to individuals.

Role of the Spiritual Director and the Domain Source

The domain of experience of interconnectedness and Source/God permeates every element of the role of the spiritual director and has already been well defined in exploring the other domains of experience in this chapter. A well-developed relationship with God/Source is essential to the role of spiritual director. I asked Veronica whether she thought a student in formation for spiritual direction who isn't clear about his/her relationship with God or their understanding of Source, could be a spiritual director?

> No. It is quite simple, if they can't be clear . . . and cannot make themselves as vulnerable as a directee, then they can't be a spiritual director really. They can't be effective as a spiritual director.

Fiona worked as a therapist before training as a spiritual director. I asked her if her work had changed because of her relationship with God?

> Yes, definitely . . . even before I knew too much about spiritual direction . . . when I started my [therapy] work I was being supervised by someone who is a deeply spiritual woman and has a great trust in God and relationship with God. I said to her one day, "I don't feel I can do this work on my own." And she gave me this little prayer song that I continue to use today when I go to meet a client. "Holy Spirit come, make my eyes to see, make my ears

to hear, make my mouth to speak, make my heart to seek, make my hands to reach out and touch the world with your love." . . . So right from my early days in my working [as a therapist], I was inviting the Holy Spirit to come into my work. And that is where I feel the Holy Spirit . . . inspires me and often I will go to put something on in the music or a program on, and I feel the movement of the Spirit there, moving me to do something else. And I follow that and it is just so right.

How do you know when it is the Spirit and not you?

> Because I am so clear that it was something else . . . the voice of the spirit. . . . It comes from a deeper place . . . in me . . . that invites me in to do something else . . . a sacred moment. . . . There is risk involved . . . trust is required because my head knowing would say something different.
>
> . . . I'm just blown away at times [in spiritual direction] where someone can go to a major, major life wound can be brought out into the light, and . . . experience healing. And how that then affects their experience of God, their image of God and then how they then go out and . . . be with the people that they're working with because . . . their own experience and image of God has changed and their own experience and image of themselves has changed.

I asked Leanne what she was looking for when she worked as a spiritual director:

> The presence of God and how God is working. . . . I suppose a secular person would say I am looking for my inner truth. . . . It is not just a matter of me seeking my own inner truth, it is much bigger than that. The connection . . . being on that interface with that which is compassion, is respect, is graciousness, is wisdom, it's in the very air that we breathe. But it's also here . . . truth, openness . . . It's beautiful. It's real. It's that essence of being.

The experience of interconnectedness with God/Source and between the directee and director permeates every aspect of the role of spiritual direction. Shared connection at the level of the experience of God takes the spiritual direction session to the place of the essence of being, where compassion, respect, graciousness and wisdom lead both the director and the directee towards freedom and wonder.

In this chapter, I have explored the role of the spiritual director in the context of leadership and organizational development. The director's

The Role of the Spiritual Director

capacity to hold the directee with compassion and love, without judgement, and to listen in-depth to the directee's experiences of life, death and resurrection are central to the role of the spiritual director. Spiritual formation that includes a deep exploration of the director's own experience, knowledge of discernment of spirits, a well-developed trust in God, and the capacity to keep out of the way when the directee is working directly with God, enables and supports the director. Confidentiality and clear boundaries around the spiritual direction system are essential in creating an effective working environment for spiritual direction. Changing contexts for the ministry of spiritual direction in the twenty-first century are opening up new challenges, pathways and workplace opportunities. The experience of interconnectedness with God/Source and between the directee and director permeates every aspect of the role of spiritual direction. Shared connection at the level of the experience of God takes the spiritual direction session to the place of the essence of being, where there is compassion, respect, graciousness and wisdom that leads the director and the directee towards freedom.

Chapter 7

Spiritual Direction for the Twenty-First Century

THE TOPIC FOR THIS book was sparked by an invitation at the 2010 Spiritual Directors International conference to consider how spiritual direction can help transform organizations to meet the challenges of the twenty-first century. As I draw this book to a conclusion in 2020, the challenges presented a decade ago—climate change, political instability, threat of nuclear war, food insecurity, globalization, forced migration—have all escalated, and the world is increasingly unstable and unpredictable. Who could have predicted that the chaos would escalate so dramatically in ten years where in 2020 we have drastic bushfires, unprecedented weather patterns, ongoing drought, floods, the constant threat of terrorist attacks, and now the pandemic COVID 19 which has forced global shut down and social isolation?

Ilio Delio suggests that for humanity to survive this phase of evolution, we must "transcend our world of individual persons in conflict and competition toward a new level of humankind, one that is co-reflective and co-evolving."[1] Additionally, "union with God, Omega or Love, brings us to a new level of consciousness."[2] Spiritual direction is a process of raising consciousness via union with God, and can support leaders and organizations to transcend conflict and competition and move into a new level of consciousness that is co-reflecting and co-evolving.

Spiritual direction can have a positive influence on leadership and organizational development by raising awareness of how organizational dynamics are operating and by using discernment to identify what might

---

1. Delio, *Christian Life in Evolution*, 54:10.
2. Delio, *Christian Life in Evolution*, 54:20.

be blocking or enabling organizational development. In this final chapter, I summarize the benefit of spiritual direction for leadership and organizational development and look at the challenges and opportunities for the work of spiritual direction into the future.

Spiritual Direction and the Experience of Personhood for Leadership and Organizational Development

Spiritual direction has a positive influence on a person's leadership potential through transformation of the inmost dimension of the human being, the *kardia*. Spiritual direction offers a framework for leaders to explore their identity as leader through critical self-reflection and by raising leadership consciousness. Leadership consciousness is the capacity of a person to "understand and master his or her personal dynamics, as well as the cultural dynamics of the organization, business unit or division he or she leads."[3]

Spiritual direction can facilitate a change in perspective by raising a person's consciousness to a deeper understanding of how their personal dynamics operate in light of their relationship with God. There is a direct correlation between a person's image of God and their image of self. If a leader identifies with God as a dictator or demanding taskmaster, it is likely that this will influence their leadership style, both in the way they might drive themselves, and in expectations they might place on others. Through the support of spiritual direction, a person's leadership style can become more compassionate, empathetic and less controlled by external projections or perceived projections.

The practice of discernment is a key element of spiritual direction. Discernment helps the leader to become sensitive to interior movements within themselves and the organization in which they work. Discernment is a process of decision-making based on listening to interior movements, noticing what leads individuals and groups towards freedom, hope, love and life; or what is drawing life away leading towards isolation, disintegration, despair, conflict and fear. Discernment involves addressing maladaptive tendencies and exploring yearning and desires. Spiritual direction helps leaders and groups to move towards full consciousness by "facing their own contradictions and making friends with their own mistakes and failings."[4]

---

3. Barrett, "Seven Levels of Leadership Consciousness," 1.
4. Rohr, *Falling Upward*, 135.

Participants in the study identify spiritual direction as helpful in bringing into consciousness the ways in which leaders can either undermine themselves and to clarify their unique sense of purpose and call. Spiritual direction can support leaders through periods of suffering and difficult experiences of leadership, strengthen commitment to leadership and deepen the desire to make a difference in the world. Accepting ones vulnerability becomes a basis for leadership when leaders are strengthened by/and in the face of suffering.

When a leader allows both their desires and the group's desires to surface, energy and creativity can be released in their leadership role. When inner reality is strengthened and becomes stronger than their outer reality, leaders can choose more freely to create their own life and be less constrained by external pressures. When the leader becomes aware that their leadership context and culture is in conflict with their deep values and desires, spiritual direction can support him/her to become aware of any conflicts and discern a pathway forward. When the leader's deep desires and values are realigned with the organization's renewed purpose and values, energy is generated, increasing capacity within individuals and the organization.

Interconnectedness as an Enabling Dynamic for Leadership and Organizational Development

The experience of interconnectedness and a relationship with God permeate every aspect of spiritual direction and is core to the way participants in the book take up leadership. Participants (all being Christian) identify spiritual direction as a support towards *becoming Christ* as a disposition for leadership. A personal relationship with Jesus can influence a leader's apostolic and creative potential by clarifying their identity and vocation. Vocation lies within a person and the task of spiritual direction is to help release vocational potential, and in releasing potential, leadership capacity is also influenced. Spiritual direction supports leaders to remove barriers that prevent them connecting with God as they develop their leadership potential.

When an organization is imbued with the interconnected energy which participants in the research understood to be the presence of God, the group can experience renewed energy, commitment and clarity of purpose. Organizational development can be positively influenced when leaders engage in spiritual direction. The ability of spiritual direction to support organizational development is limited by the capacity of members of the organization to freely commit to the process of spiritual formation. Confidentiality, good boundaries, and a willingness for the organization and its members to become vulnerable are essential for the work of spiritual direction in organizational development. Because spiritual direction conversations are always confidential, any breach of confidentiality will undermine the process, thwart organizational development and diminish trust. Whether organizations can use spiritual direction formally as a tool for organizational development needs further testing.

Changing context for Spiritual Direction

Changing contexts for the ministry of spiritual direction in the twenty-first century are opening up new challenges, pathways and opportunities for spiritual direction to contribute to leadership and organizational development. The ministry of spiritual direction is becoming professionalized with formal training now widely available and credentialed. Until recently spiritual direction has generally been limited to religious settings and spiritual directors, primarily religious women and men, often with little or no training. Spiritual directors now come from a myriad of backgrounds, often with professional skills in multiple disciplines. The shift for spiritual direction from the limitations of institutional religious settings is opening new possibilities for the ministry, including specializations such as spiritual direction for leadership and organizational development. Spiritual Directors International[5] are currently working towards opening religious boundaries in the ministry, welcoming broader frameworks, and moving spiritual direction beyond current Christian and patriarchal systems.

As religious institutions navigate the transformation into a new Axial Age, spiritual direction can help individuals and institutions integrate their relationship with God into every aspect of their lives, and as this book

---

5. Spiritual Directors International is an inclusive, global learning community of people from many faiths and many nations who share a common passion and commitment to the art and contemplative practice spiritual direction, spiritual companionship. spiritual guidance, anam cara in Gaelic, and mashpiah in Hebrew. https://www.sdicompanions.org

affirms, into leadership and organizational development. Spiritual direction can be offered with or without religious boundaries.

The research demonstrated that spiritual direction has the potential to contribute to leadership and organizational development, but there are some serious obstacles. One major obstacle seems to be the limitations attached to practice within traditional religious settings. In the following section, I explore the challenges and opportunities of the changing context for the ministry of spiritual direction.

Challenges and Opportunities of a Changing Context for Spiritual Direction and Leadership and Organizational Development

I present here some musings and conclusions that have emerged from the research and reflections on my own experience as a spiritual director. I begin by recalling a conversation with an international Ignatian author a few years ago in which I suggested that in my experience the church did not seem to support or even want the ministry of spiritual direction. In fact, it seemed to me that the church through its passivity towards the ministry, actively dis-enables the ministry. Her response was instant: "Oh we have known that in Europe for years!" I have pondered this response and the issue of the church's disinterest in spiritual direction and I identify two key issues.

- Current patriarchal structures of the church do not provide adequate resources to recognize the value of the ministry of spiritual direction, support formation of spiritual directors, or actively promote the ministry.

- There is a strong resistance to freeing the ministry from institutional settings and professionalizing the ministry of spiritual direction, making it difficult to take up spiritual direction as paid employment.

My experience of working within the tension of the enabling and disabling environment of spiritual direction in the church has been a constant aspect of the reflexive process of this research and has echoes within research interviews. Throughout the course of this research, a PhD reflection group supported me in my role as researcher. As I reviewed the transcripts of my work with this group, almost every conversation linked back to the difficulty and stress that I experienced in trying to hold a leadership role in a patriarchal institution. In what follows, I consider some of the disabling factors behind and within the ministry of spiritual direction and what further research might be needed to enable spiritual direction to develop fully into a ministry that can support leadership and organizational development.

Spiritual Direction—a Feminine Ministry in a Patriarchal Container

In 2017 women made up 81 percent of membership of the three major professional bodies for spiritual directors in Australia. Ninety percent of the 6,800 members currently enrolled with Spiritual Directors International (SDI) are female. It is interesting to note that the participants in this book (15 percent male and 85 percent female) give an accurate reflection of the affiliated spiritual direction community in Australia. Table 12 compares the percentage male and female members in the three main spiritual direction bodies in Australia, Spiritual Directors International and participants in this research.

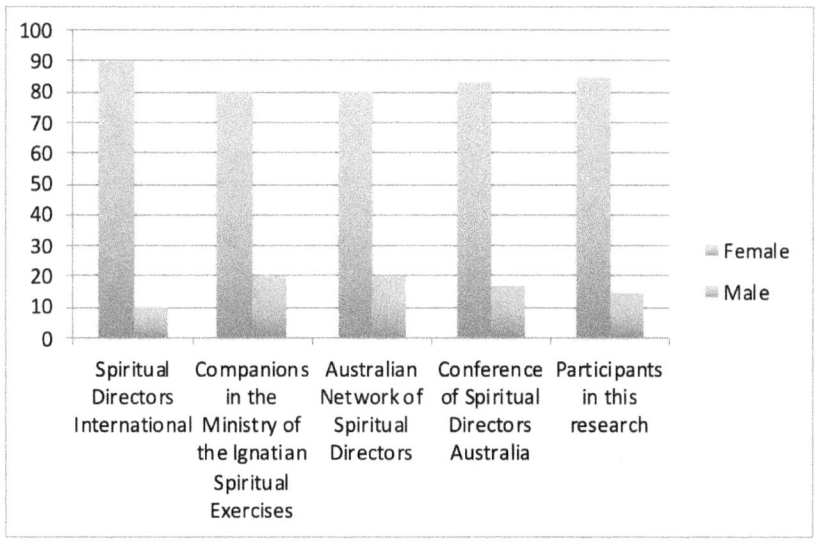

Table 12—Comparison male/female membership spiritual direction community.[6]

---

6. Statistics gathered as follows: SDI—Anil Singh-Molares, Executive Director SDI private communication June 17, 2017, ANSD; Liz-Anne Smith, Secretary ANSD private communication June 21, 2017, Mary McInerney, Secretary CIMISE, private communication July 7, 2017; CSD Australia: *Spiritual Directors near You,* accessed July 7, 2017.

Spiritual direction, an overwhelmingly feminine ministry, has traditionally been located in the system of a patriarchal church.

Anil Singh-Molares, Executive Director of SDI, asserts that historically Ignatian spirituality and the Society of Jesus have been one of the most enabling groups for the spiritual direction ministry internationally.[7] This is certainly true in my experience of working for the Society of Jesus who provided me with the opportunity to be formed and to practice as a spiritual director in Australia. At the same time as being enabled, I have also experienced a resistance on the part of the Jesuits to resource the ministry and to empower women in leadership. Even though 80 percent of staff in the ministry of Ignatian spiritual direction in Australia is female, at the time of writing this book, all five centers of Ignatian spirituality have male directors overseeing the ministry of spiritual direction. I am drawn to conclude that perhaps it is not the ministry of the Jesuits to enable women in the church and that this is historically embedded into their identity.

The PhD reflection group who supported me in holding myself in role as writer and helped me to reflect on my leadership role in the patriarchal institution offered me the image of being "pot bound". I was trying to sustain a flourishing feminine ministry within an aged, masculine container.

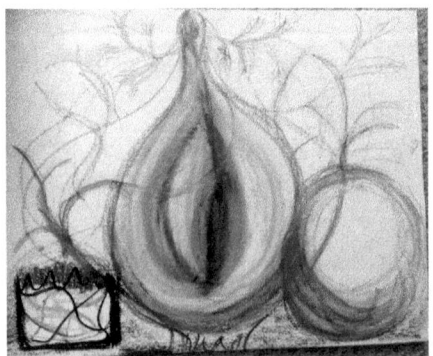

Figure 23 is the image that I drew at the time of my resignation from Sentir of being pot bound. On the left is the closed patriarchal container with limited space for growth. The bulb in the center is my experience of new life emerging for the ministry of spiritual direction in the twenty-first century, with space for other ministries to emerge alongside.

Figure 23: Pot bound

When I arrived at Campion I was planted in rich soil with lots of space, but as the collegial team, the ministry, and I grew, the roots became entangled and there is no soil left in the pot to sustain life let alone support the new growth. In leaving, perhaps I became planted into the earth, spacious and enabling. This image resonated with me, and on reflection I

---

7. Private email conversation with Anil Singh-Molares, Executive Director of SDI June 17, 2017.

believe that for the ministry of spiritual direction to be freed into fullness of life it needs to be replanted into a larger, more balanced container.

I hypothesize that the patriarchal structure of the institutional church is not able to fully embrace a feminine ministry of spiritual direction or the formation of lay vocations, and by default creates a dis-enabling environment for the development of the ministry. Future research is needed to explore the question as to whether the growing feminine ministry of spiritual direction can be properly supported within the current structures of the church.

Difficulties of Clericalism

I have wondered, as the number of professionally trained directors continues to grow, why there is not a spiritual director in every parish. I regularly hear spiritual directors speak about their experience of not feeling the support of their parish. Priests often fail to recognize trained spiritual directors living and working in their parish and rarely encourage parishioners to access the ministry even when is it available to them. At a recent clergy in-service, I gained some insight as to why the clergy might be resistant to the ministry of spiritual direction.

I was working with seventy male clerics and given the task of introducing them to the art of professional listening. I was amazed to discover that for most of the men present, their knowledge of spiritual direction was limited to a few unhelpful experiences of spiritual direction during their formation in the seminary thirty to forty years earlier. Most spiritual directors working with clergy in the mid to late twentieth century would have received little or no training for the ministry. Often, the spiritual director held a position of power over the directee, such as authority to either affirm or refute the capacity of the young men to enter the priesthood, making it unsafe to bring vulnerable material into spiritual direction. It became clear to me: If you have not had a good experience of the ministry of spiritual direction, why would you send people to a spiritual director?

I hypothesize that the lack of awareness by clergy about the value of spiritual direction, and the professional evolution of the ministry in the past thirty years, has limited its propagation within the institutional church. Future research could include an examination on the issue of whether clergy understand the value of the ministry of spiritual direction, and what might be needed to engage the church more fully with the ministry of spiritual direction.

Another reason for the lack of support for the ministry of spiritual direction by parish priests might be attributed to the fact that the priest has traditionally been regarded as *the* spiritual director of a parish, though they have received little or no training in the art of spiritual direction or even active listening. To install a trained spiritual director in a parish might threaten the identity and role of the priest. The role of the cleric is so central to the Catholic Church it can become difficult to recognize the value of any other form of vocation. Pope Francis in dialogue with the Jesuits at their 36th General Congregation warned of the dangers of clericalism:

> Clericalism does not allow growth; it does not allow the power of baptism to grow. The grace and evangelizing power of the missionary expression comes from the grace of baptism. And clericalism controls this grace badly and gives rise to dependencies, which sometimes have whole peoples in a state of very great immaturity. I remember the fights that took place when I was a student of theology or a young priest and the base ecclesial communities appeared. Why? Because the laypeople began to have strong leadership, and the first ones who felt insecure were some of the priests. I am generalizing too much, but I do this on purpose: if I caricature the problem it is because the problem of clericalism is very serious.[8]

Pope Francis suggests that the ministry of spiritual direction is essential to the future of the church and "if we do not convince ourselves that spiritual direction is not a clerical charism, but a lay charism (which the priest can also develop), and if we do not call upon the laity in vocational discernment, it is evident that we will not have vocations."[9]

It is encouraging to hear Pope Francis speak so clearly of the issue.

I hypothesize that the ministry of spiritual direction, though it might continue to trickle through the institutional church, needs to evolve and leave the patriarchal system in order to flourish and find a new professional context to develop the ministry further, especially if the ministry is to become relevant for leadership and organizational development. Future research could explore how the ministry of spiritual direction is evolving outside the institutional church.

---

8. Pope Francis, "To Have Courage and Prophetic Audacity," 8.
9. Pope Francis, "To Have Courage and Prophetic Audacity," 8.

Spiritual Direction for the Twenty-First Century

Moving from a Culture of Dependency to Professionalization

As spiritual direction has historically been embedded in the culture of church, it is generally expected that people can access the ministry for little or no cost. It is difficult for spiritual directors to earn a living without sponsorship. Only those who are not dependent on making an income and have their own resources can afford to undertake formation for the ministry. If spiritual direction is going to flourish and be relevant to leadership and organizational development, this dilemma needs to be addressed. Many spiritual directors have professional qualifications such as a Master's degree and yet they can rarely find full time paid work in the field. Perhaps an analogy can be drawn with the vocation of teaching in Catholic schools and how this has transitioned over the past forty years from unpaid and sometimes untrained religious women and men, to professionally qualified and paid teachers.

It could be argued that spiritual direction cannot be professionalized, as it is a charism, a call, and a gift from God. I agree that spiritual direction is a call, a charism and a gift from God, just as a poet is born with the gift of poetry, or a musician is born with the gift of being musically inclined. But even poets and musicians need training to enhance their giftedness and are encouraged to use their gifted call in professional roles.

For spiritual direction to become accessible to leadership and organizational development, viable, financial and professional structures need to be created to support the ministry.

Impact of Formal Spiritual Direction Training Programs

Formal training programs in spiritual direction began to emerge around the late 1980s. Prior to this, anyone who took up a formal religious vocation might have been understood to be a spiritual director. Formal training programs for the ministry have had a two-fold effect:

- religious women and men can no longer assume the role of spiritual director without undertaking formal training in the ministry of spiritual direction; and
- highly skilled non-religious women and men are taking up the formal role of spiritual director.

Formal training in the ministry of spiritual direction has enhanced and extended the capacity of spiritual directors to offer professional help to women and men who want to take up their lives fully. Complementary skills such as psychotherapy, counseling, art therapy, music, organizational development theory, leadership theory, and much more, can be integrated within practice and thus enlarge the ministry and be of service to professional communities. With an increase in the number of non-religious spiritual directors, spiritual direction has begun to emerge outside of formal religious institutions and is breaking down religious boundaries. The professional body of SDI, founded by Catholic nuns and embedded in the Ignatian tradition of spiritual direction, now respects and recognizes the ministry of spiritual direction within all religious traditions including Buddhism, Islam, Judaism, Christianity, and others who have no affiliation with a religious tradition. "SDI believes spiritual companionship and deepening into the sacred transform individuals, society, and all creation."[10]

For spiritual directors and formation programs of spiritual directors, the challenge is to open the current boundaries of spiritual direction, often limited to church settings, and provide opportunities for leaders to access professional spiritual direction in a secular setting.

The Future

An opportunity exists to develop formation programs that specialize in forming spiritual directors to work in the area of leadership and organizational development. Can spiritual direction enter the workplace by formally appointing spiritual directors to care for the spiritual needs of an organization? When an organization places a spiritual director in a formal professional role, the most vulnerable aspects of the organization are given a voice, which in turn helps the organization to address issues that might otherwise be overlooked. I can imagine experienced teachers offering spiritual direction to school principals, health care professionals offering spiritual direction to hospital executives, business executives offering spiritual direction to Chief Executive Officers. Designing formation programs that support the integration of business disciplines and spiritual direction will reshape the face of spiritual direction and at the same time develop new awareness of the capacity of spiritual direction to support the corporate world.

10. Spiritual Directors International, "History of SDI," 2017.

In order to develop further as a ministry applicable to leadership and organizational development:

- spiritual direction needs to be free to continue to extend beyond existing patriarchal structures and clericalism;
- spiritual direction needs to move from a culture of institutional dependency to models of professional practice;
- formation for spiritual direction needs to include recognition of the existing professional skills spiritual directors bring to the role of spiritual direction by recruiting them into the formation process and formation programs.

Though this book asserts that spiritual direction can have a positive impact on organizational development, there needs to be more research. A long-term study of spiritual direction as a support to organizational development could be undertaken to assess the full benefit and limitations spiritual direction can have. Developing a clearer understanding of what inhibits and what enables the growth of consciousness in organizations might help to clarify and identify the role of a spiritual director in organizational development. Aspects of such a process could include for example:

- Can the growing feminine ministry of spiritual direction be actively supported by male catholic orders?
- By exploring clergy awareness of the value of spiritual direction can we determine whether this has limited its propagation within the institutional church and if so, how do we address this?
- What professional context would best support the ministry of spiritual direction to develop, in particular for leadership and organizational development?

Conclusion

Leaders and organizations willing to be transformed through spiritual direction will progressively raise leadership and organizational consciousness. Raising consciousness clarifies who you are, what you stand for, and focuses energy towards a common purpose. Spiritual direction can help build awareness of the primary spirit of individuals and groups so that they can identify alignment and misalignment in their shared identity and purpose, releasing energy and creativity into leadership and organizational development.

In Christian language, I would say that the most surprising outcome of writing the book for me is to say with conviction and clarity that: Spiritual direction supports leaders and organizations to strengthen their relationship with God and in doing so enhances their work towards becoming *Christ* for the world today. To be *Christ* is to be free from enslavement of fear and limited perceptions of the self, and then to use that freedom at the service of all creation. I have ended this book with the conviction that fostering a relationship with God, Source, Mystery or whatever you name your experience of interconnectedness with all creation, is a rich and vital untapped resource for leadership and organizational development.

Bibliography

Adair, John. *The Inspirational Leader: How to Motivate, Encourage and Achieve Success.* London: Kogan Page, 2009.

Adyashanti. "A Return to the Heart of Christ Consciousness." http://returntotheheartevent.com/offerings/jesus/.

Alphonso, Herbert. *The Personal Vocation: Transformation in Depth through the Spiritual Exercises.* Gujarat, India: Gujarat Sahitya Prakash, 1997.

Anderson, Mike. "The Axial Age—Man Becomes a Philosopher." https://www.mikeanderson.biz/2013/10/the-axial-age-ma,.n-becomes-philosopher.html.

Appelbaum, Steven, et al. "Gender and Leadership? Leadership and Gender? A Journey through the Landscape of Theories." *Leadership and Organization Development Journal* 24 (2003) 43–51.

Armstrong, Karen. *The Case for God.* Toronto: Knopf Canada, 2009.

———. "The Case for God: Karen Armstrong at St Paul's Cathedral." London: St. Pauls, 2012.

———. "A New Axial Age." http://www.adishakti.org/_/a_new_axial_age_by_karen_armstrong.htm.

Aten, Jamie, et al. *The Psychology of Religion and Spirituality for Clinicians: Using Research in Your Practice.* New York: Routledge, 2012.

Augustine of Hippo. *Saint Augustine Confessions (Oxford World's Classics).* Translated by Henry Chadwick. Oxford; New York: Oxford University Press, 2008.

Avramenko, Alex. "Inspiration at Work: Is It an Oxymoron?" *Baltic Journal of Management* 1 (2014) 113–30.

Bain, Alistair, and Joshua Bain. "A Note on Primary Spirit." *Socio-Analysis–Australian Institute of Socio-Analysis Melbourne* 4 (2002) 98–111.

Barrett, Richard. "The Barrett Seven Levels Model." (2020) https://www.valuescentre.com/barrett-model/.

———. "Barrett Values Centre." (2020) https://www.valuescentre.com.

———. *The New Leadership Paradigm.* N.d.: lulu.com, 2011.

———. "The Seven Levels of Leadership Consciousness." https://www.valuescentre.com/wp-content/uploads/PDF_Resources/Barrett_Model_Articles/Seven_Levels_of_Leadership_Consciousness.pdf.

———. "The Seven Levels of Organisational Consciousness." https://www.valuescentre.com/wp-content/uploads/PDF_Resources/Barrett_Model_Articles/Seven_Levels_of_Organisational_Consciousness.pdf.

Bibliography

Barry, William. *Letting God Come Close: An Approach to the Ignatian Spiritual Exercises.* Chicago: Loyola, 2001.

Barry, William A., and William J. Connolly. *The Practice of Spiritual Direction.* Rev. ed. New York: Harper One, 2009.

Barton, Ruth Haley. *Strengthening the Soul of Your Leadership: Seeking God in the Crucible of Ministry.* Downer's Grove, IL: InterVarsity, 2008.

Bass, Bernard M. *Leadership and Performance Beyond Expectation.* New York: Free, 1985.

Bazalgette, John. "Connectedness with Source: Our Collective Reality." In *Transforming Experience in Organisations,* edited by Susan Long, 195–230, London: Karnac, 2016.

Bazalgette, John, et al. "The Absolute in the Present: Role, the Hopeful Road to Transformation." In *Dare to Think the Unthought Known?* edited by Ajeet Mathur, 89–119. Tempere, Finland: Aivoairut, 2006.

Benefiel, Margaret. *Soul at Work: Spiritual Leadership in Organizations.* New York: Seabury, 2005.

Benefiel, Margaret, et al. "Spirituality and Religion in the Workplace: History, Theory, and Research." *Psychology of Religion and Spirituality* 6 (2014) 175–87.

Benjamin, Jessica. *The Bonds of Love: Psychoanalysis, Feminism, and the Problem of Domination.* New York: Pantheon, 1988.

———. *Like Subjects, Love Objects: Essays on Recognition and Sexual Difference.* New York: Yale University Press, 1998.

Bertalanffy, Ludwig Von. *General Systems Theory: Foundations, Development, Applications.* New York: George Brazillier, 1968.

Bion, Wilfred R. *Attention and Interpretation: A Scientific Approach to Insight in Psychoanalysis and Groups.* London: Karnac, 1970.

———. *Learning from Experience.* London: Heinemann, 1962.

Bohm, David. "On Dialogue." In *The Change Handbook: Group Methods for Shaping the Future.* London: Routledge, 1996.

Borbely, James, et al. *Focussing Group Energies: Common Ground for Leadership, Organization, and Spirituality.* 3 vols. Scranton, PA: University of Scranton, 1992.

———. *Leadership, Spirituality and Organisational Practice.* Edited by Bernadette Miles and Michael Smith. Melbourne: Private, 2013.

Brown, Brené. *Daring Greatly: How the Courage to Be Vulnerable Transforms the Way We Live, Love, Parent, and Lead.* 1st ed. New York: Gotham, 2012.

Burns, James McGregor. *Leadership.* 1st ed. New York: Harper Torchbooks, 1978.

Cada, Lawrence, et al. *Shaping the Coming Age of Religious Life.* N.d.: Affirmation, 1985.

Cannato, Judith. *Field of Compassion: How the New Cosmology Is Transforming Spiritual Life.* Notre Dame, IN: Sorin, 2010.

Caputo, John D. *On Religion (Thinking in Action).* London: Routledge, 2001.

Carrington, Damian. "The Anthropocene Epoch: Scientists Declare Dawn of Human-Influenced Age." *The Guardian,* 2016. https://www.theguardian.com/environment/2016/aug/29/declare-anthropocene-epoch-experts-urge-geological-congress-human-impact-earth.

Cashman, Kevin. *Leadership From the Inside Out: Becoming a Leader for Life.* San Francisco: Berrett-Koehler, 2008.

Coghlan, D. "Ignatian Spirituality as Transformational Social Science." *Action Research* 3 (2005) 89–107.

———. "Seeking God in All Things: Ignatian Spirituality as Action Research." *The Way* 43 No 1 (2004) 97–108.

Bibliography

Conroy, Maureen. *The Discerning Heart: Discovering a Personal God.* Chicago: Loyola, 1993.

Cousins, Ewert. *Christ of the 21st Century.* New York: Continuum, 1994.

Covey, Steven. *Principle Centred Leadership,* New York: Fireside, 1992.

———. "The Transformational Leadership Report." (2007). http://www.transformationalleadership.net/products/TransformationalLeadershipReport.pdf.

"CSD: Australia: Spiritual Directors near You." http://www.csdaust.com/home/find-a-director/spiritual-directors-near-you/.

Cusson, Gillies. *Biblical Theology and the Spiritual Exercises: A Method Toward a Personal Experience of God as Accomplishing Within Us His Plan of Salvation.* Translated by George E. Ganss and Mary A. Roduit. Prakash Institute of Jesuit Sources, 1988.

Da Camara, Luis Goncalves. *A Pilgrim's Testament: The Memoirs of St. Ignatius of Loyola.* Translated by Parmananda Divarkar. Chestnut Hill, MA: Institute of Jesuit Sources, 1995.

Dalmau, Tim, and Bob Dick. *A Diagnostic Model for Selecting Interventions for Community and Organisational Change.* Second ed. Chapel Hill: Interchange, 1991.

Darmanin, Alfred. "Ignatian Spirituality and Leadership in Organizations Today." *Review of Ignatian Spirituality* 36 (2005) 1–14.

Delio, Ilia. *The Christian Life in Evolution, A Talk Given to Contemplative Outreach of Washington DC and Maryland.* 2012. https://acireland.ie/the-christian-life-in-evolution-with-sr-ilia-delio-phd/.

———. *The Emergent Christ: Exploring the Meaning of Catholic in an Evolutionary Universe.* New York: Orbis, 2011.

Denning, Stephen. "Forbes–Leadership." http://www.forbes.com/sites/stevedenning/2012/03/29/what-maslow-missed/#4dcde25b455a.

———. *The Secret Language of Leadership: How Leaders Inspire Action Through Narrative.* San Francisco: Jossey-Bass, 2007.

Diaz-Saenz, Hector R. "Transformational Leadership." In *The Sage Handbook of Leadership,* edited by Alan Bryman et al., 299–310. Thousand Oaks, CA: Sage, 2011.

Dibrell, Clay, et al. "Establishing How Natural Environmental Competency, Organizational Social Consciousness, and Innovativeness Relate."*Journal of Business Ethics* 127 (2015) 591–605.

Dyckman, Katherine, et al. *The Spiritual Exercises Reclaimed: Uncovering Liberating Possibilities for Women.* New York: Paulist, 2001.

Edwards, Denis. *How God Acts: Creation, Redemption, and Special Divine Action.* Minneapolis: Fortress, 2010.

Elkins, D. N., et al. "Toward a Humanistic–Phenomenological Spirituality: Definition, Description, and Measurement." *Journal of Humanistic Psychology* 28 (1988) 5–18.

Ellmann, Liz Budd. "SDI World." http://www.sdiworld.org/find-a-spiritual-director/what-is-spiritual-direction.

———. "Seeking God Everywhere and Always: Ten Trends in Global Spiritual Direction." *Presence: An International Journal of Spiritual Direction* 2 (2015) 18–24.

Encyclopedia of the Romantic Era 1760–1850. Edited by Christopher John Murray. Oxford: Routledge, 2003.

Erkeneff, Pegge. "Trust Life, Wake Up." *Listen: A Seeker's Resource for Spiritual Direction* 9 (2015) 2.

Ffytch, Matt. *The Foundation of the Unconscious: Schelling, Freud and the Birth of the Modern Psyche.* Cambridge: Cambridge University Press, 2011.

Bibliography

Fisher, James. "The Emotional Experience of K." In *Bion Today*, edited by Chris Mawson, 43–63. London; New York: Routledge, 2011.

Fowles, John. *The French Lieutenant's Woman*. London: Barnes and Noble, 1998.

Francis, Pope. "Christmas Greetings to the Roman Curia Address of His Holiness Pope Francis." http://www.vatican.va/content/francesco/en/speeches/2019/december/documents/papa-francesco_20191221_curia-romana.html

———. "To Have Courage and Prophetic Audacity: Dialogue of Pope Francis with the Jesuits Gathered in the 36th General Congregation " Paper presented at the GC 36 Rome, 2016.

Freud, Sigmund. "The Unconscious." *S. E.* 14 (1915) 166–204.

Fry, Louis, and J. Slocum. "Maximising the Triple Bottom Line through a Strategic Scorecard Business Model of Spiritual Leadership." *Organizational Dynamics* 37 (2008) 86–96.

Gadamer, Hans-Georg. *Truth and Method*. Translated by G. Barden and J. Cumming. New York: Crossroad, 1988.

Ganns, George. *Jesuits Religious Life Today*. St. Louis: Institute of Jesuit Sources, 1977.

Gardner, Howard. *Frames of Mind: The Theory of Multiple Intelligences*. New York: Basic, 2011.

Gettler, Leon. *Organisations Behaving Badly: A Greek Tragedy of Corporate Pathology*. Queensland: Wiley, 2011.

Ghoshal, Sumantra, et al. *Managing Radical Change: What Indian Companies Must Do to Become World-Class*. New Delhi: Viking, 2000.

Glanz, Karen, et al. "Health, Behaviour and Education: Theory, Research and Practice—Companion Materials." http://www.med.upenn.edu/hbhe4/part4-ch15-organizational-development-theory.shtml.

Grotstein, James S. "Bion's "Transformation in 'O,'" the 'Thing-in-Itself', and the 'Real': Toward the Concept of the 'Transcendent Position.'" *Melanie Klein and Object Relations* 12 (1996) 109–41.

Harding, Wendy. "Intersubjectivity and Large Groups: A Systems Psychodynamic Perspective." Melbourne: Swinburne University of Technology, 2006.

Heifetz, Ronald A., and Donald L. Laurie. "The Work of Leadership." In *H B R's 10 Must Reads on Leadership*, by Bill George et al., 57–78. Boston: Harvard Business School, 2011.

Heifetz, Ronald, et al. *The Practice of Adaptive Leadership: Tools and Tactics for Changing Your Organization and the World*. Boston: Harvard Business, 2009.

Hermans, Hubert. "International Institute for the Dialogical Self." http://www.dialogicalinstitute.com/index.php/approach-methods/19-general/73-what-is-the-dialogical-self-approach.

Heron, John. *Co-Operative Inquiry: Research into the Human Condition*. London: Sage, 1996.

Hoggett, Paul. *Partisans in an Uncertain World: The Psychoanalysis of Engagement*. London: Free Association, 1992.

Hood, Ralph, et al. *The Psychology of Religion, Fourth Edition: An Empirical Approach*. 4th ed. New York: The Guilford, 2009.

"Investopedia: Silo Mentality." www.investopedia.com/terms/s/silo-mentality.asp.

Irvine, Bruce. "Background to the TEF." In *Transforming Experience in Organisations: A Framework for Organisational Research and Consultancy*, edited by Susan Long, 15–30. London: Karnac, 2016.

Bibliography

Jaspers, Karl. *Origin and Goal of History (Original in German: Vom Ursprung Und Ziel Der Geschichte, Piper Verlag, MüNchen 1949)*. New Haven, CT: Yale University Press, 1953.

Jaworski, Joseph. *Synchronicity: The Inner Path of Leadership*. San Francisco: Berrett-Koehler, 2011.

———. *Source*. San Francisco: Berrett-Koehler 2012.

Jupp, Victor. *Self-Report Study, the Sage Dictionary of Social Research Methods*. London: Sage, 2006.

Kinerk, E. Edward. "Eliciting Great Desires: Their Place in the Spirituality of the Society of Jesus." *Studies in the Spirituality of Jesuits* 16 (1984) 34.

Kirk, Alan. "Caracolores: Awakening Our Inner and Inter-Connections." http://caracolores.com/1s-the-individual/what-is-the-spiritual-self/.

"Kurt Lewin." https://en.wikipedia.org/wiki/Kurt_Lewin.

"Leadership-Central.Com: Where Leaders Expand and Share Their Knowledge." http://www.leadership-central.com/leadership-theories.html#axzz47XLGvv01.

Lee, Mei. "Transformational Leadership: Is It Time for a Recall?" *International Journal of Management and Applied Research* 1 (2014) 17–29.

Leech, Kenneth. *Soul Friend: The Practice of Christian Spirituality*. New York: Harper Collins, 1980.

Lewin, Kurt. *Resolving Social Conflicts: Selected Papers on Group Dynamics*. Edited by Gertrude W. Lewin. New York: Harper & Row, 1948.

Lonergan, Bernard J. F. *The Dynamism of Desire: Bernard J. F. Lonergan on the Spiritual Exercises of Saint Ignatius of Loyola*. St Louis, MO: Institute of Jesuit Sources, 2006.

———. *Method in Theology*. Toronto: University of Toronto Press, 1990.

Long, Susan, ed. *The Perverse Organisation and Its Deadly Sins*. London: Karnac, 2008.

———. "The Transforming Experience Framework & Unconscious Processes." In *The Transforming Experience in Organisations: A Framework for Organisational Research and Consultancy*, edited by Susan Long, 31–106, London: Karnac, 2016.

———. *The Transforming Experience in Organisations: A Framework for Organisational Research and Consultancy*. Edited by Susan Long. London: Karnac, 2016.

Lovat, Terrence. "Practical Mysticism, Self Knowing and Moral Motivation." In *Handbook of Moral Motivational Theories, Models, Applications*, edited by F. Oser and T. Lovat, 249–63. Rotterdam: Sense, 2013.

Mant, Alistair. *Leaders We Deserve*. Oxford: Martin Robertson, 1983.

Marburg, Marlene. *Grace Undone: Love*. Vol. 1. Doncaster Australia: Windsor Scroll, 2014.

———. *Grace Undone: Passion*. Vols. 3 and 4. Doncaster: Windsor Scroll, 2015.

———. "Landscapes of Contemporary Spiritual Direction in Australia." *Presence an International Journal of Spiritual Direction* 22 (2016) 28–36.

———. "Poetry and Grace: An Autoethnography Which Explores Writing Poetry as Prayer in the Context of Ignatian Spirituality." MCD University Of Divinity, 2014.

———. *Spiritual Direction: What It Can Be for You*. Carmelite Library Lecture Melbourne Unpublished manuscript used with permission, 2015.

Marburg, Marlene, and Bernadette Miles. "Application to the Australian Ecumenical Council for Spiritual Direction for Recognition of the Heart Wisdom Program." Melbourne: Kardia Formation, 2015.

Martin, James. "Millennial." https://millennialjournal.com/2013/12/05/fr-james-martin-on-disordered-attachments/.

Bibliography

Maslow, Abraham H. "A Theory of Human Motivation." *Psychological Review* 50 (1943) 370–96.
Mawson, Chris. "Introduction: Bion Today—Thinking in the Field." In *Bion Today*, edited by Chris Mawson, 3–32. London and New York: Routledge, 2011.
Mayer, John. "Spiritual Intelligence or Spiritual Consciousness?" *International Journal for the Psychology of Religion* 10 (2009) 47–56.
McArdle, Kate, and Peter Reason. "Action Research and Organizational Development." In *The Sage Handbook of Organization Development*, edited by Thomas Cummings. 123–36. Thousand Oaks, CA: Sage, 2008.
McCleskey, Jim Allen. "Situational, Transformational and Transactional Leadership and Leadership Development." *Journal of Business Studies Quarterly* 5 (2014) 117–30.
McGrath, S. J. *The Dark Ground of the Spirit: Schelling and the Unconscious (Electronic Version)*. London: Routledge, 2012.
Merriam-Webster Dictionary. "Consciousness." https://www.merriam-webster.com/dictionary/consciousness.
Miller, E. J., and A. K. Rice. *Systems of Organisation—Task and Sentient Systems and Their Boundary Controls*. London: Tavistock, 1967.
Merton, Thomas. *Love and Living*. New York: Farrar, Straus, and Giroux, 1979.
Meures, Franz. "The Affective Dimension of Discerning and Deciding." *Review of Ignatian Spirituality* 34 (2008) 60–77.
Miles, Bernadette. "Ignatian Spirituality, Apostolic Creativity and Leadership in Times of Change." *The Way* 50 (2011) 35–41.
———. "Incarnating Our Consolations through Transformative Academic Learning." *The Way* 54 (2015) 37–50.
———. "One Body, One Spirit, One Mission: Uncovering the Essential Elements of Empowering a Collaborative Ministry Team—a Systems Psychodynamics Perspective." MRes diss., Melbourne: RMIT, 2009.
Neumann, Jean E. "Systems Psychodynamics in the Service of Political Organisational Change." In *Group Relations, Management, and Organization*, edited by Robert French and Russ Vince, 54–69. New York: Oxford University Press, 1999.
Newman, John Henry. *An Essay on the Development of Christian Doctrine*. 1845.
O'Murchu, Diarmuid. *Jesus in the Power of Poetry: A New Voice for Gospel Truth*. New York: Crossroad, 2009.
Paulin-Campbell, Annemarie Renée. "The Impact of the Imaginal and Dialogical (Relational) Processes in the Spiritual Exercises, on Image of Self and Image of God in Women Making the Nineteenth Annotation Retreat." PhD diss., Durban, South Africa: University of KwaZuluNatal, 2008.
Pees, R. C., et al. "Organizational Consciousness." *Journal of Health Organizational Management* 23 (2008) 505–21.
Pettit, Paul. *Foundations of Spiritual Formation: A Community Approach to Becoming Like Christ*, edited by Paul Pettit. Grand Rapids: Kregel, 2008.
Pruzan, Peter. "The Question of Organizational Consciousness: Can Organizations Have Values, Virtues and Visions?" *Journal of Business Ethics* 29 (2001) 271–84.
Puhl, Louis J. *The Spiritual Exercises of St Ignatius: Based on Studies in the Language of the Autograph*. Chicago: Loyola, 1951.
Radu, Cătălina, et al. "Leadership and Gender Differences—Are Men and Women Leading in the Same Way?" In *Contemporary Leadership Challenges*, edited by Aida Alvinius Rijeka, 63–83. Croatia: InTech, 2017.

Bibliography

Rahner, Karl. *Foundations of Christian Faith: An Introduction to the Idea of Christian Faith.* Translated by William V. Dych. New York: Seabury, 1978.

Reason, Peter, and William R. Torbert. "The Action Turn; toward a Transformational Social Science." *Concepts and Transformation* 6 (2001) 1–37.

Remen, Rachel Naomi. "On Defining Spirit." http://www.mnwelldir.org/docs/spirit/defining.htm.

Roberts, Vega Zagier, and John Bazalgette. "Daring to Desire: Ambition, Competition, and the Role Transformation in 'Idealistic' Organisations." In *Transforming Experience in Organisations: A Framework for Organisational Research and Consultancy*, edited by Susan Long, 135–52. London: Karnac, 2016.

Roemer, Judith, and George Schemel. *Beyond Individuation to Discipleship: A Directory for Those Who Give the Spiritual Exercises.* Scranton: Institute for Contemporary Spirituality, University of Scranton, 2000.

Rohr, Richard. *Action and Contemplation Week 2: Fully Knowing.* N.d.: Richard Rohr's Daily Meditation, 2016.

———. *Everything Belongs: The Gift of Contemplative Prayer.* Rev. ed. New York: Crossroad, 2003.

———. *Falling Upward: A Spirituality for the Two Halves of Life.* San Francisco: Jossey-Bass, 2011.

———. *What the Mystics Know: Seven Pathways to Your Deeper Self.* New York: Crossroad, 2015.

Rutledge, Pamela. "Social Networks: What Maslow Misses." https://www.psychologytoday.com/blog/positively-media/201111/social-networks-what-maslow-misses-0.

Scharmer, Otto, and Katrin Kaufer. *Leading from the Emerging Future: From Ego-System to Eco-System Economies.* San Francisco: Berret-Koehler, 2013.

Schelling, Friedrich. *The Ages of the World.* Translated by F. de Wolfe Bowman Jr. New York: Columbia University Press, 1942.

Sherwood, John. *Leadership: The Responsible Exercise of Power.* Cincinnati: Management Design, 1997.

Silf, Margaret. *Inner Compass: An Invitation to Ignatian Spirituality.* Chicago: Loyola, 2007.

Siow, Anthony. "Dynamics and Flow in the Second Week Leading to the Election." Unpublished paper, Sentir Graduate College of Spiritual Formation, 2014.

Smith, Mark K. "Infed: Kurt Lewin: Groups, Experiential Learning and Action Research." http://infed.org/mobi/kurt-lewin-groups-experiential-learning-and-action-research/.

Smith, Michael. "Annotations." Unpublished paper, Sentir Graduate College of Spiritual Formation, 2010.

Spiritual Directors International. "History of SDI." https://www.sdicompanions.org/about/history-of-sdi/.

———. Main page. https://www.sdicompanions.org/.

———. "What is Spiritual Companionship?" https://www.sdicompanions.org/what-is-spiritual-companionship/.

Stacey, Ralph D. *Strategic Management and Organisational Dynamics: The Challenge of Complexity.* 5th ed. Harlow: Prentice Hall, 2007.

Steiner, John. *Psychic Retreats: Pathological Organizations in Psychotic, Neurotic and Borderline Patients.* London: Routledge, 1993.

Bibliography

Sternberg, Robert J. "North American Approaches to Intelligence." In *International Handbook of Intelligence*, edited by Robert J. Sternberg, 411–44. Cambridge: Cambridge University Press, 2004.

Teilhard de Chardin, Pierre. *Christianity and Evolution: Reflections on Science and Religion*. Translated by René Hague. New York: Harcourt Brace and Co, 1969.

Thibodeaux, Mark E. *God's Voice Within: The Ignatian Way to Discover God's Will*. Chicago: Loyola, 2010.

Tillich, Paul. *Dynamics of Faith*. New York: HarperOne, 2009.

Troll, Ray. Anthroprocene. https://www.trollart.com/

Urban, Pope, VIII. *Bull of Suppression—Pastoralis Romani Pontificis*. http://marywarddocumentary.com/Bull_of_Suppression.htm.

Varela, Francisco et al. "Autopoiesis: The Organization of Living Systems, Its Characterization and a Model. Biosystems." *Biosystems* 5 (1974) 187–96.

Veltri, John. *Orientations for Spiritual Growth*. Guelph, ON: Loyola, 1979.

Vest, Norvene. *Tending the Holy: Spiritual Direction Across Traditions*. Edited by Norvene Vest. Harrisburg: Morehouse, 2003.

Vigil, José María. "Theology of Axiality and Axial Theology." *VOICES* 35 (2012) 167–78.

Waters, Colin N., et al. "The Anthropocene Is Functionally and Stratigraphically Distinct from the Holocene." *Science* 361 (2016) 137–47.

Williams, Monty. "The Dynamics of Discernment." Hong Kong, 2014. https://xavier.ignatian.net/html/tc/resources/2014ic/review/Monty%20Williams-keynote.pdf.

Winnicott, Donald W. "Ego Distortion in Terms of True and False Self." In *The Maturational Process and the Facilitating Environment: Studies in the Theory of Emotional Development*, 140–57. New York: International Universities, 1965.

Yukl, Gary. "An Evaluation of Conceptual Weaknesses in Transformational and Charismatic Leadership Theories." *Leadership Quarterly* 10 (1999) 285–305.

Zevit, Shawn Israel. "Exploring the God–Field: A Systems Approach to Spiritual Direction/Hashpa'ah in Communal and Organizational Life." In *Seeking and Soaring: Jewish Approaches to Spiritual Direction*, edited by Goldie Milgram and Shohama Wiener, 356–73. New York: Reclaiming Judaism, 2009.

Index

action research, 49–53
    and Ignatian spirituality, 50–53
adaptive leadership, (see leadership)
affections (attachments), 29
    disordered, 21, 24–25, 29, 53, 86,
        96–97, 98–99
annotations for spiritual direction,
    24–27
Anthropocene Epoch, 41-43
Armstrong, Karen, 17–18, 40
attachments (see affections)
Axial Age, 20, 40–43, 171, 181
Barrett, Richard, 10,
    levels of leadership consciousness,
        67–78, 99, 94, 104, 113,
        119–23, 133, 179, 199,
        organizational consciousness,
        78–84, 123, 127–28, 132–38,
        141, 143, 145–46
Barry, William, 28, 123,
Bazalgette, John, 63–64, 100, 106,
    110, 157, 167
Benefiel, Margaret, 6, 8, 39
Bion, Wilfred,18, 33, 66–67, 115, 157,
boundaries, 12, 49, 56, 61, 155, 161,
    181–82, 188
    and the role of the director
        166–70, 177
Call(ed), 11, 16, 22, 26, 74, 77, 85, 89,
    97, 99, 187
    becoming, 105–9
    to service, 99–100
    vocation, 107–9
    following, 119–20
    to leadership, 123
clericalism, 185–87, 189
Coghlan, David, 50–53
collaboration, 45, 56, 68, 74, 76, 167,
empowerment, 34, 44, 75, 83,138,
compassion, 77, 78, 91–92, 112,
    116–18, 123, 126, 150, 155,
    163–66, 168, 176–79
compassionate gaze, 163–66,
confidentiality, 12, 27, 134, 155, 161,
    167, 169–70, 173, 177, 181,
consciousness, 1, 20, 22, 40–43, 63–
    83, 85, 86, 89, 94, 178, 189,
    history of, 64–67
    leadership, 67–78, 100, 104, 113,
        118–26, 179–80
    levels of, 67, 84
    organizational, 78–84, 127–28,
        130–53, 145,
    spiritual, 34–35
    relationship, 131–32
consolation, 25–31, 52, 77, 144,
Covey, Stephen, 44–45,
creativity, 43–47, 66–67, 74–77,
    82–83, 101–5, 143, 180
    tension, 135
    spark, 8–9
    energy, 55–56, 66
    Source, 62, 64
    potential, 74,
desire, 19, 29, 85, 98–99, 157–58,
    162–63, 179

Index

desolation, 26–31, 164
differentiation, 94–99
Discernment, 37, 47–48, 163, 178–79
   the art of, 28–32
   and spiritual direction, 114–29
   communal, 139–42, 155–56
   Rules for, 26–27
   spiritual movements, 29–32
disorder, 94, 98, 103,
disordered affections/tendencies (see affections)
doubt 58-60
   self-doubt, 112
driven or drawn, excessive busyness, 91, 96, 118–19, 162
ego, 5, 29, 37, 44, 63, 75–77, 96–97, 121–22
formation, spiritual (see spiritual formation)
freedom, 17, 20–22, 51, 119, 123, 148, 162–63
   Interior, 35–37, 87
   indifference, 11, 96–99
Freud, Sigmund, 64–67, 95
God/Source, 6–7, 170–71, 175–79
   defining, 15–20
   images, of 19–20, 73, 88–92, 111–12, 160, 176
   and consciousness, 64–67
   as Source in the TEF, 61–63
   relationship with, 92–94, 100–103, 109–14
Grubb Institute, 60, 106
healing, 73, 94–99, 165–66, 176
Heifetz, Ronald et al, 4, 46–48
Ignatian spirituality, 5–8, 47, 65, 131–32, 184
   and organizational development, 49–59
   as action research, 50-53
   and consciousness, 64–67
   and the Spiritual Exercises (see Spiritual Exercises)
Ignatius of Loyola, 7, 20–24
image of God (see God images of)
indifference, (see freedom)
inner critic, 115–18

inspirational leadership (see leadership)
interconnectedness, 41, 69, 78, 142–44, 151, 153–55, 171, 175–80, 190
   with Source, 60
Irvine, Bruce, 63, 106, 142, 144
ISECP (Ignatian Spiritual Exercises for the Corporate Person) 53–60, 79, 129, 132, 144
   life, death, resurrection cycle, 53–60, 78, 127, 145–49, 153–55, 166, 177
Jung, Carl, 65–67, 95
kardia, 70–72, 179
   of leadership, 4–6
leadership, 4–6, 179–81
   theory, 43–45
   adaptive leadership, 9, 43, 46–49
   disposition of, 85
   as a role, 85
   and spiritual direction 85–126
   transformational, 45
   and relationship with God, 88–93
   inspirational, 44–46, 75, 104
   identity, 88–91
   ternary, 92–93
   development, 124–26
life, death, resurrection cycle (see ISECP)
Lonergan, Bernard, 51, 53–54, 157
Long, Susan, 37, 64–67, 156, 158,
magis, 31
Mant, Alistar, 92–93,
Marburg, Marlene, 3–4, 15–16, 22, 32–33, 70, 77–78
Maslow, Abraham, 67–68
mysticism (mystic), 33–35, 112
narcissism, 37
organisational development, 33, 59–63, 179–81
   Ignatian Spirituality, 49–59
   and spiritual direction, 127–54
   and consciousness, 78–83
perspective, change in, 115–17
poverty, 27, 36–37, 96
pride, 27, 36–37, 122, 152

Index

primary spirit, 8, 11, 56–57, 146–54, 189
psychotherapy, 37, 161, 170–71, 188
psychoanalytic, 33, 63, 67
psychological, 24, 37, 49, 67–68, 72, 85, 101
relationship
   with Jesus God and self, 3–5, 16–20, 88–93, 100–103, 190
   consciousness (see consciousness)
religion, 6–7, 16–18, 35, 39–43, 50, 95, 100, 105, 147, 172
Rohr, Richard, 6, 34–35, 108, 160, 179
Scharmer and Kaufer, 1–2, 5, 73–74, 94
Schelling, Friedrick, 64–67
self esteem, 68, 71–73, 79–82, 89, 94–99, 127–36, 153
shame, 128–30, 153
   corporate, 128–33
Source (See God)
spiritual direction, 2–4, 15–39, 64–78
   for leadership, 85–128, 133–35
   corporate, 7–8
   Ignatian, 15–38, 20–34
   for organizational development, 127–54
   as a reflective process for leaders, 88
   role of director, 155–77
   in the workplace, 172–75
   changing contexts, 181–89
   professionalisation of, 187
   training programs, 187–88
Spiritual Exercises, 3–4, 20–31
   Week One, 22, 72–74
   Week Two, 22, 32, 35–38, 74–76, 99, 110, 137
   The Two Standards, 36–37
   for leadership, 85–127
   Week Three, 22, 76–77, 120–22
   Week Four, 22, 77–78, 122–24
   Dynamic of, 22–23
spiritual formation, 34, 63, 85, 97–99
   stages of, 70–78

organizational consciousness, 78–84
   for leadership, 86–87
   for the spiritual director, 158–63
   spiritual direction and consciousness, 64–83
   vulnerability, 103
spiritual movements (see discernment)
spirituality, (also see Ignatian spirituality)
   in the workplace, 39–40
   and organizational development, 127–54
suffering, 11, 26, 76–77, 144–48, 163, 165, 180
   confirmed in, 120–22
survival, 68, 72–73, 92–94, 128–36, 149
synchronicity, 111–13
systems psychodynamics, 49
systems theory, 48–49, 53–54
ternary leadership (see leadership)
transformation, 1–2, 9, 72, 74–76, 127–44, 153
   via vulnerability, 135–35
   leadership, 43–46, 105
transformational leadership (see leadership)
Transforming Experience Framework (TEF) 60–63, 155–56
true self–false self, 139, 163–166,
Two Standards, (see Spiritual Exercises)
unconsciousness processes, 49, 63, 66–67
   in organizations, 53
vocation (also see call), 17, 74–76, 85, 89, 99–100, 107, 142, 163, 180, 185–88
vulnerability, 11, 77, 94–96, 98–99, 121–23, 121–23, 129, 131, 135–37, 165, 180
   personal power and creativity, 103–5

www.ingramcontent.com/pod-product-compliance
Lightning Source LLC
Chambersburg PA
CBHW070256230426
43664CB00014B/2553